ELEMENTARY SCHOOL
GUIDANCE AND COUNSELING

AN INTRODUCTION
THROUGH ESSAYS AND COMMENTARIES

RANDOM HOUSE NEW YORK

Elementary School Guidance and Counseling

An Introduction Through Essays and Commentaries

Edited by

GLEN D. MILLS

To
Rod, Pam, Kim, Phyllis, Keith, Mike, and Sandy;
and may the human spirit
always be free!

Preface

The foremost concern of the elementary school guidance program is to provide counseling services for students, parents, and teachers so that attitudes and emotions may be harmonized for the maximum growth and development of the elementary school child. Indeed, the child is the focus of the elementary school guidance program. Its purpose is to help each child achieve self-direction, self-insight, and maximum development of his abilities. It also attempts to help the child to develop means of coping with anxiety, tension, and frustration. The latter purpose is of great concern, because school adjustment is a difficult problem for each child, especially in our highly industrial, technological, and dynamic society. Yet elementary school guidance must not become totally adjustment oriented. Instead, to achieve our basic purpose of helping the student to attain self-direction and maximum growth, guidance must focus on the growth and development of children. In this endeavor, work with parents and teachers provides much enlightenment. So, developmental counseling in the elementary school with students, parents, and teachers is the most basic guidance service.

Other guidance functions help the counselor understand his population. Collection of data on pupils is probably one of the most important of these, though testing, placement, referral, occupational information, and research contribute much to understanding of and proficiency in working with children. As can be seen, though each guidance service is important in its own right, guidance is a broad field. Consequently, much variation characterizes guidance programs implemented in local schools. Such variation within the elementary school guidance program is healthy, since it allows the counselor to develop a guidance program where each guidance service is weighted so as to reflect the individual counselor's orientation and the needs of the local school.

During the last decade theorists such as Anna Meeks, Don Dinkmeyer, Gerald Kowitz, George Hill, Verne Faust, William Van Hoose, and others have contributed much to the establishment of theoretical foundations for elementary school guidance. A major task, however, lies ahead in the 1970s for all persons in the field of elementary school guidance. That task is to bring guidance services to each elementary school. Presently many elementary school guidance programs exist in more affluent school districts that have more adequate school budgets. Public education can hardly afford to have only the elite enjoy services needed by all elementary school children. In our attempt in the 1970s to bring guidance to each elementary school, it is of the utmost concern that operational programs reflect established theoretical foundations. Communication between theorists and elementary school counselors or practitioners in the field must be facilitated, and the gap between theorists and practitioners that plagues so many professions must be avoided. Already, the *Elementary School Guidance and Counseling* journal, through the conscientious efforts of Don Dinkmeyer, the editor, has done much to bridge that communications gap.

This book is divided into four parts: (1) Introduction, (2) Schooling, (3) Elementary School Guidance and Counseling, and (4) Educational Psychology—A Related Area of Study. This broad comprehensive approach, which departs from the traditional approach of limited readings, is based on research conducted by the editor in the training given to elementary school counselors. The research showed that philosophy, curriculum, and educational psychology comprise the balance of this training. Thus, it is important to introduce the beginning counselor to each of these areas of study.

The purpose of Part I of this book is to introduce some interesting and provocative questions concerning permissiveness, Rogerian psychology, and alienation in society and education, so that the elementary school counselor can evaluate his attitudes, beliefs, and value system along these dimensions. These topics are of critical importance for the counselor, since they are closely aligned with aiding or retarding the growth and development of children.

Part II considers guidance as related to the curriculum. For years children have had difficulty in various areas of the school curriculum. Historically, the reasons for these difficulties have been studied extensively. Achievement discrepancies associated with the sex of the child, for example, have been studied. Studies documented reasons why children fail in reading, mathematics, and science. Because guidance in the elementary school exists for all children, a special function of the counselor is defined when large groups of children experience failures in school that lead to personality problems. It is essential that the counselor be able to help these children. Part of that helping process may be shaping the curriculum to fit the child rather than tailoring the child for the curriculum.

Readings on guidance and counseling in the elementary school presented in Part III constitute the major portion of this book. Here, twenty articles are presented on history of elementary school counseling, cultural influences, definitions of guidance in the elementary school, school and developmental counseling, child-centered techniques, group counseling, identification functions, occupational information, parental counseling, play therapy, guidance organization, and preparation of elementary school counselors. As most will agree, except for the inclusion of articles on history, culture, and play therapy, this is rather a traditional definition of elementary school guidance. Perhaps the influence of history and culture on guidance need not be defended; however, the inclusion of play therapy requires an explanation. In view of the overcrowded conditions at diagnostic and treatment centers for disturbed children, play therapy appears to be an applicable technique for future counselors to employ with children who are not receiving psychiatric help yet who display atypical behaviors in their schools. Play therapy may be utilized extensively in the future elementary school guidance program.

In Part IV, Educational Psychology—A Related Area of Study, readings that consider the development of the child (e.g., "His Struggle for Identity," by Jerome Kagan) are presented. In addition, Walter B. Waetjen's article reviews research from educational psychology related to elementary school guidance. This part ends with an article on a creative mental health program for the elementary school.

A book of readings is made possible through the efforts of many people. First, I would like to thank the contributors for their prompt, courteous, and gracious replies in granting permission for the selected articles to be reprinted. Second, I would like to thank the various publishing houses for their excellent cooperation. Third, thanks are extended to Dr. Funston F. Gaither, Professor Emeritus of Education of the University of Oklahoma, for his help. Fourth, due consideration and appreciation are expressed to Miss Sherry L. Sanchez for typing the seemingly endless correspondence that such a book requires. Finally, I am grateful for the general assistance and typing of Mrs. Margaret Roberts.

Glen D. Mills

Contents

PART I

Introduction

INTRODUCTION

Because man is a rational being it is important to understand his philosophical heritage. Hopefully, this will give him an added insight into why he thinks and acts as he does. Historically, philosophy has been the springboard to the thoughtful, reflective life. General philosophy deals with our beliefs about the origin, nature, and destiny of the universe, man, knowledge, and values. Probably, the philosophical writings of the Greek philosophers Aristotle and Plato best illustrate this. Alfred North Whitehead once said that all of Western philosophy is a series of footnotes to Plato's thought and work.[1] Though an exaggeration, this statement serves well to point out the importance of Plato and general philosophy.

In the field of education, John Dewey departed from formal systems of philosophy. He believed philosophy was a form of thinking from which educational theories and system applications are practical outgrowths.[2] So, to Dewey, philosophy is grounded in earthly problems. Whitehead describes philosophy best when he says: "Philosophy begins in wonder. And at the end, when philosophic thought has done its best, the wonder remains."[3] In the selected essays in this part, philosophy is defined as a way of thinking that is characterized by the wonder it induces.

Guidance personnel have long sought practical, expedient ways of presenting their services. Frequently counseling and psychotherapy are criticized as nebulous processes void of concrete outcomes that can be objectively ascertained. Literature on procedures and techniques in guidance abounds. Perhaps beginning counselors should contemplate and philosophize more about the nature of education and the guidance process.

Three areas of interest for elementary school counselors are: (1) permissiveness in education, (2) Rogerian psychology, and (3) alienation in our society. Permissiveness in education has been a hotly debated topic in intellectual communities. It is discussed by Fred N. Kerlinger in "The Implications of the Permissiveness Doctrine in American Education." In counseling, permissiveness is the gateway to change, openness, and self-understanding, which initiate behavior modifications. Thus,

3

permissiveness is a means to individual and societal change, growth, and development. Ironically, though, much of the blame for the destructive social upheaval in our country is unjustly projected onto permissive child-rearing doctrines and educational theories. It is of the utmost importance that clearly formulated ideas on climates conducive to growth and development in education and counseling be fostered by the counselor.

Idealism is a characteristic frequently identified with youth. Functionally, it is an unattainable level of aspiration that leads to positive change. The work of Carl Rogers is highly idealistic, as Richard W. Deffering shows in "Philosophic Idealism in Rogerian Psychology," and because of his work the field of guidance has been vastly altered. School counselors have had to seek deeper understandings of man and his nature. Among the positive values of Rogerian psychology are the self-actualization and becoming concepts that provide explanations for motivation, social learning, and development. So, the beginning school counselor must objectively evaluate Rogerian psychology and the importance of its concepts to education and guidance.

Among the most talked about topics in scholarly circles are the alienation, detachment, and marginal existence of present-day man. "Varieties of Alienation and Educational Responses" by Louis Goldman delineates the sources of man's alienation in a refreshing manner. Generally speaking, it is a striking tribute to philosophy and to the intellect of man that one who philosophizes can so accurately describe and discuss man's sources of alienation. Another value of this article is that the prospective counselor can formulate a working perspective for dealing with young children who are victims of isolation, alienation, and detachment in our society.

The purpose of this philosophical introduction is to stimulate reflective thought among counselors in the selected areas. Hopefully, the counselor will not limit himself to these topics but will catapult himself to seek the "hows" and "whats" of American education and the guidance process. Perhaps philosophy has much to offer the prospective counselor, since educational development has its genesis in philosophical thought.

Notes

1. Alexander Sesonske (ed.), *Plato's Republic: Interpretation and Criticism* (Belmont, Calif.: Wadsworth Publishing Company, Inc., 1966), p. 1.
2. Hobert W. Burns and Charles J. Branner, *Philosophy of Education: Essays and Commentaries* (New York: The Ronald Press Company, 1962), p. 21.
3. *Ibid.*, p. 3.

The Implications of the Permissiveness Doctrine in American Education

Fred N. Kerlinger

The doctrine of permissiveness in education and its relation to democratic ideology have been tormenting problems to American educators. Most thinkers apparently agree on a rather large measure of permissiveness in the education of children. The idea seems basically to be that children, if they are to mature into democratic individuals and citizens, must not be too restricted in the pursuit of their own interests and needs, since such restrictiveness will somehow have the unfortunate consequence of producing undemocratic citizens. If children are not "permitted" a good deal of freedom—more specifically, decision choice—then they will not mature into autonomous, cooperative, and generally democratic individuals. In short, without permissiveness we run the danger of creating authoritarian individuals and an authoritarian society. Certainly, the argument goes, we now have a generally authoritarian school system which is systematically warping millions of children into undesirable types of human beings, human beings who lack autonomy, maturity, and true democratic potentiality.[1]

That there is much truth in the above argument few educators would deny. The underlying undemocratic and even authoritarian quality of many, perhaps most, American schools and classrooms seems evident, if we are to believe responsible critics.[2] Yet it also seems that a good deal of the older restrictiveness and authoritarianism have been mitigated; improvement, while slow, has occurred.[3] The strong reaction against the older restrictiveness in education which started in the early part of the century has had its effect. Old-line authoritarian educational thinking and methods

"The Implications of the Permissiveness Doctrine in American Education," *Educational Theory*, 10 (April 1960), 120–127, has been reprinted with the permission of the author and of the publisher, *Educational Theory*. Fred N. Kerlinger is Professor of Education at New York University.

are becoming more and more disapproved as the contemporary permissive influence makes itself felt. The superintendent, principal, or teacher who wants to play the boss role must now do it in a more covert and subtle fashion.

The purpose of this paper is to speculate on the possibility of a new authoritarianism springing from a relatively *extreme* and basic emphasis on permissiveness. In a previous paper in which the modern origins of permissiveness in American education were traced, it was claimed that the doctrine of permissiveness in education had its origins in the thinking of Freud and Dewey and that the strong impact of these two great thinkers had laid the foundations for modern ideas and practices of permissiveness in education.[4] It was also suggested that a new authoritarianism might be arising, a phenomenon expressed by two concepts which are becoming influential symbols in American education: permissiveness and group dynamics. It was further suggested that possibly there were manipulatory and authoritarian implications of the doctrines many educators are espousing. Finally, the paper hinted at a covert anti-intellectualism springing from permissivist and group dynamics doctrines. The present essay will be limited to an analysis of the implications of the permissiveness doctrine. Group dynamics doctrine was partially explored in a previous paper.[5] Similarly, the anti-intellectual implications of the permissiveness doctrine will not be directly discussed. It must wait for future treatment.

The argument that follows is based on five main points: (1) that the doctrine of permissiveness is more of a reaction against older restrictive and undemocratic educational ideas than it is a *movement for* democratic ideas; (2) that the espousal and implementation of relatively extreme permissive ideas imply and lead to manipulation of the pupil by the teacher and of the teacher by the pupil; (3) that while extreme permissive practices are claimed to be democratic they may be in effect autocratic; (4) that when permissive ideas dominate a teacher, when they form the mainspring of her educational being, they lead to a basic violation of the integrity of the individual; and (5) that when permissiveness is a fundamental and overriding concern of the teacher it leads to a pervasive conformity of the individual to the will of the teacher and/or the class group.

Before beginning the main discussion, an important point should be clarified. This paper is not meant to be a critique of permissiveness in general. It is assumed that a moderate amount of permissiveness is good and that the older educational restrictiveness is bad. The permissiveness to be discussed is the relatively extreme and unilateral doctrine espoused by a number of educational writers, some of whom will be cited. This unilateral doctrine seems to imply a wholesale sort of permissiveness running from the kindergarten through the graduate school, a permissiveness which labels almost any sort of educational direction from a teacher as a sign of autocracy, which says that to lecture is to impose one's will on students and is therefore bad, authoritarian, and to be eschewed by the democratic educator, which says, furthermore, that group processes in the classroom are in and of themselves good, democratic, to be encouraged since they presumably permit the greatest amount of individual expression through democratic interaction with others. In short, it is the unilateral and extreme doctrine of permissiveness which permits nothing but permissiveness and which threatens to become dogma and religion that is the object of scrutiny.

The first point, that a great deal of permissivist doctrine is a reaction *against* the older authoritarianism and restrictiveness in education rather than a movement *for* permissiveness and democratic ideas is apparent from a study of much education literature. One gets the impression from reading permissivist works that nothing in the older education was much good —except the pupils. This reactivity against traditional education accounts for much of the literature's extreme and rather naive quality, and it leads permissivist authors to be somewhat condescending and patronizing when talking about the older education and about practices with which they disagree.[6] Permissivist literature has mainly negative criticism of traditional education as its ideological foundation. When it comes to the task of constructing a positive philosophy permissivists find themselves in a difficult position since they must "permit" anything but restrictiveness. What permissivists have done, therefore, is to attempt to solve the problem by borrowing quite selectively from Dewey and Freud, mainly, and by manufacturing a new metaphysics on the basis of these borrowings. The character of the movement is heavily moral and, as already indicated, seems to derive most of its force from derogation—derogation of the older education, of subject matter, of teachers. The derogation is often concealed by words and rather vague, even mystical, writing. For example, Rasey says, "And we teachers. We teach nothing. We can no more teach than we can learn a child. We are onlookers while life teaches."[7] As with many such statements there is a kernel of truth here. But there is also obfuscation of the teaching-learning problem. A number of examples of derogation can also be found in Cantor's work. One of the best of these is his castigation of instruction which begins with definitions.[8] He implies that any instructor who uses definitions in approaching a subject is, ipso facto, a bad teacher. In another place, Cantor, like many other educators, derogates those who lecture. He says, "The instructor who lectures deprives the students of their right actively to participate in their class."[9] He then says, very significantly, "The instructor who is aware of his function refrains from using students for displaying his knowledge. He permits himself to be used, in a professional way, by them."[10]

The argument being advanced is that, if permissivism is basically a reactive doctrine it must also necessarily be essentially negative in tone and practice. The teacher must *not* do anything restrictive; she must *not* do anything—or think anything—traditional. To be deeply concerned with subject matter, for example, is questionable since it leads to "coercion" of pupils.[11] It seems evident that permissivist educators served a very useful purpose during the early days of reaction against the authoritarian practices of the past. (The battle is of course by no means yet won.) To continue to espouse a basically negative and reactive ideology, however, can be a defeat of the hard-won victories of a splendid educational movement.

Perhaps the most serious implication and end-result of extreme permissiveness is that it leads to manipulation of pupils. The very permissive teacher sets up few or no limits for her pupils. Few norms of behavior and learning are supposed to be teacher-determined. But a normless social situation is of course impossible; some norms or rules must always govern behavior. If the teacher does not supply the rules or norms, the pupils will. Fine! says the permissivist, and it is fine—to a certain extent. But the teacher is a basic authority ingredient of any learning situation. Many educators may dispute this and say that the learner, or rather, the learner group should be the basic ingredient. But the teacher is a guide to learning; she is the experienced group member who must take a leading role in directing group activities toward educational goals set at least partly by society. She is society's surrogate who must ensure, by norm and rule-setting, that the societal educational goals are reached. Now when she does not take this function, she puts herself into the unfortunate situation of being forced, consciously or unconsciously, to manipulate her charges. She *must* discharge the societal function; there is, by definition, no alternative. Pupils may take the responsibility adequately; they may decide to teach the societal goals. Then, again, they may not. And this cannot be left to chance, and any teacher knows it. Pupils, even by the age of six, are dimly aware of it, as Piaget's work would seem to indicate. The problem boils down not to whether or not there are norms—there are always norms —but to who sets the norms. Ideally both pupils and teacher should set them. Yet the teacher's role in norm-setting, again by societal definition, must always be dominant. Any other situation is sociologically and psychologically anomalous. To say that this is a violation of democratic freedom is semantic nonsense. Freedom is always relative; it is always bounded by norms and rules for behavior. As Dewey well said, ". . . guidance given by the teacher to the exercise of the pupil's intelligence is an aid to freedom, not a restriction upon it."[12] The argument can be rounded out with another Dewey excerpt.

> Sometimes teachers seem to be afraid even to make suggestions to the members of a group as to what they should do. . . . But what is more important is that the suggestion upon which pupils act must in any case come from somewhere. It is impossible to understand why a suggestion from one who has a larger experience and a wider horizon should not be at least as valid as a suggestion arising from some more or less accidental source.[13]

The above argument leads to the third point: that extreme permissivism leads to autocratic rather than, as supposed, to democratic thinking and practice. If the permissive teacher acts upon the precepts of a Kelley or a Cantor, she will find herself in a peculiar predicament. If the group will does not point in the socially desirable direction—and, again, any teacher will know this by the very nature of social norms which depend for their efficacy on being interiorized by all or most members of a society —she will be in the unenviable position of manipulating the group so that it will more or less fall into line. The famous expression, "Do we have to do what we want to do today?" while a humorous exaggeration, contains the kernel of this problem. Basically, and somewhat cynically, the teacher who is committed unilaterally to permissiveness must so manipulate the situation, herself, and the pupils that the goals of society which are her goals by definition since she is, at least in good part, a surrogate of society, are achieved. The manipulation comes in when the direction of educational activity strays too far from the societal goals. It should not be thought that this is a defense of education as a preserver of the status quo. No matter what position is taken on education's function, it still remains a fact, by the definition of education as a cultural phenomenon, that schools must teach at least a basic core of values, attitudes, skill, and facts. Variability will be very great in a democracy, naturally, but the common norm must be there.

In other words, the lines must be drawn somewhere, and it is the teacher acting for and as society who draws the lines. And the lines must be clear and unambiguous. To think or act otherwise is to lay the foundation for social and personal chaos. One good definition of a teacher is that he is a person working to put himself out of a job. This means, of course, that a teacher always should try to have his students develop as rapidly as possible into mature people who have learned what he knows, who have his understandings and more. To give a child too much freedom too soon, to force children to make choices they are really incapable of making, is to defeat this definition because, as Fromm has pointed out, we have to grow to independence through dependence, through self-love to love of others. Learning from teachers always has this symbiotic character. It is not undemocratic; it is natural and inevitable.

That an espousal of relatively extreme permissivism can lead to violation of the integrity of the individual follows from the argument on manipulation. Manipulation of pupils, if practiced systematically, is a violation of the integrity of both pupil and teacher for quite obvious reasons. The integrity, the wholeness, of any individual depends upon acting fairly consistently in accordance with both approved social norms and one's approved self-image. The manipulation is of course usually not perceived as manipulation. The teacher has herself been taught that the ideas she is trying to implement are good—and they are good. Democratic cooperation, participation in the learning process, and the like are good values. But the difficulty is how to achieve them. The group way, she has been taught, is the right way. She is also taught not to impose her will on children but to discover their needs and interests and to use these to achieve the learning objectives. All this, too, is good. But somewhere, some time, she must draw lines beyond which children cannot be permitted to go. To do this she sometimes must use methods which, in a permissivist framework, are not good, she believes. Thus there is a conflict. And the conflict between being democratic and autocratic cannot be resolved, for her at least, by a clearcut choice. She has no choice: she must be democratic. Yet to be democratic, she has learned, is to be permissive. Her only recourse is to use the permissive methods and still achieve societal objectives. And this often means doing things which are "coercive." She often ends up using "nice coercion." Children soon learn the rules of the game, and, as Riesman points out, they become skilled at conforming to these "nice" demands. They also become skilled at manipulating the teacher. But in the process both teacher and pupil lose some of their integrity since life and the classroom are not always so nice, so cooperative, so democratic, and in order to maintain the "nice" fiction, it is often necessary to practice mild but insidious deceptions on others and on oneself.

To complete the argument, we need to examine the relationship between permissiveness and conformity. When permissiveness is the *fundamental* guide of a teacher's thinking and behavior, pupils must pay the price of conformity. This is perhaps best understood by going through the back door. It can be agreed that in an autocratic setup the social situation is clear to all parties concerned—role relationships are clearly understood as are group norms. The pupils, for example, at least have something concrete to rebel against and, if necessary, to fight. But with the highly permissive teacher, whether manipulatory and autocratic or not, there is nothing to rebel against or to fight. A pupil may have a vague feeling of being used, and he may want to do something about it. But what can he do? Even the other pupils will disapprove of him if he goes against the "nice one." The pressures toward conformity are very strong in such situations. And the conformity goes beyond what was demanded under the outright and open autocratic setup: it is personal and moral as well as behavioral. The pupils should even think like the teacher, or rather, the teacher-pupil group.

Study of a number of contemporary educational writings shows learnings which clearly imply conformity to the group. In fact, permissiveness and group cooperation, as doctrines, usually go hand in hand in much of the writing. They seem to be basic tenets of a new orthodoxy. For example, Kilpatrick, in talking about the effectiveness of group education, says:

> How then is good character best built. . . . In the multitudinous social contacts there will inevitably arise situations of social stress. Under wise guidance the group should be led to see the issues involved and conclude as to just disposition of the dispute. Such a group conclusion no individual will permanently dispute. To defy his group seldom satisfies. *In the end he will accept* . . .[14] [Italics mine.]

Comment here is hardly necessary.

Along with these emphases goes a concomitant rather strong emphasis on emotional learnings. One gathers that the basic function of education is to foster proper emotional attitudes and the ability to get along with people.[15] It is here contended that this "sociometric" approach to education, as Riesman has aptly named it, is actually detrimental to democratic education, that it leads in effect, to autocratic practices. When the emphasis in a class is emotional, it is difficult for children to learn objective modes of thinking. They learn to focus on the rather slippery ground of affect and only secondarily learn to handle facts and things. It is not contended here that emotional learning is wrong. But it *is* contended that a *basic* emphasis on emotional learning is wrong. The emphasis in a classroom should be on work, on things, *and* on attitudes, but work should be central. Only thus is the child free to develop as a democratic human being. When the central emphasis is on feelings, especially feelings toward other persons, objectivity, independence, and autonomy become difficult or even impossible to learn and to achieve. This is because constant preoccupation with one's own and other people's feelings is an unstable and insecure ground on which to build a basis for learning to make objective and critical judgments of problems and issues since all of one's thinking becomes colored and perhaps distorted by interpersonal affect. This is a major defect of much of the practical application of group dynamics as well as of the classroom dominated by feelings. When one learns always to be concerned with the feelings of others and of oneself *as primary* in any situation, then one also learns to be careful and circumspect, to be always concerned with not promoting bad feelings. Such affect preoccupation effectively cripples any budding learning of how to approach problems objectively since one's approach to problems becomes strongly conditioned by irrelevant concerns such as what other people may think of your proposed solution of the problem. Questionable hypotheses, hypotheses that might jar the group and other people's feelings, are entertained timidly if they are entertained at all. Gradually one learns to be sufficiently sensitive to what will or will not disturb other people's feelings. There are always situations, in any problem solution and in any complex learning, in which it may be necessary for someone to say, "You're wrong; this is the right solution." But this is forbidden in the permissive, group-oriented classroom, strange as it may seem. The word "permissive" comes to mean to permit anything but that which will hurt feelings, which will disturb the nice cooperative atmosphere of the class group.

It can readily be seen that permissiveness in education is anything but permissive. Norms, rules of behavior, are set up in any situation. In the traditional classroom they are set up almost entirely by the teacher. In the permissive classroom, they are set up by the group which includes— or may not include—the teacher. In the former situation the norms are usually clearcut and well understood. They may not be liked but they are clear and unambiguous. And traditional classrooms are usually object or subject or problem-oriented. In the latter situation the norms usually lack clarity and definiteness; they are the rather amorphous product of an amorphous social situation where, theoretically, much is permitted but where, in reality, a great deal is restricted. Norms that are amorphous and ambiguous, however, are still rules of behavior, expectations about the right and wrong things to do. The trouble is that no one is clear as to just what is right, only what is wrong. It is wrong to be uncooperative, not a good group member, not nice. Anything else is right, provided it meets the needs and purposes of the group members. Such an inverted value scale is characteristic of extreme permissive groups, and it is no wonder that manipulation also becomes a characteristic. Manipulation is almost demanded by such a topsy-turvy social situation for, as indicated earlier, the group leader is responsible for achieving the external group goals. But she cannot impose her will; this would not be democratic. Thus she must manipulate the group except in the fortunate case when the group's wishes perhaps fortuitously coincide with the external group goals, i.e., with the goals of society.

The individual psychological consequences of permissiveness have been almost entirely ignored in this essay and can only be touched upon now. It was pointed out in the earlier paper on permissiveness that one of the cogent psychoanalytic reasons for permissiveness was to avoid frustrations to prevent the presumed consequences of frustration, aggression, and possibly mental ill-health. Fenichel has cogently discussed this problem, and I will not repeat his argument.[16] Suffice it to say that in the extreme permissive situation there is probably a good deal of frustration which cannot be dealt with since by definition it is not supposed to exist. Nobody is frustrated if almost anything is permitted everybody (except, perhaps, in the adult group when some members want to get the work done), but as we have seen everything is not permitted. There is a wide band of thinking and activity which is not permitted, even though nothing may be openly said about this *verboten* area: don't do or say anything which will hurt other people's feelings, which is undemocratic (or that anxiety-provoking word, authoritarian), which is uncooperative, which will prevent the group from reaching its goals and meeting its needs. Above all, don't be an unnice person who is hard to get along with. The autocratic implications of all this should be obvious. Like consensus unanimity thinking,[17] extreme permissiveness carries within itself the seeds of authoritarianism. Conformity, not rational conformity which is necessary for any social life, but irrational and emotional conformity and loss of freedom are the prices paid for this questionable product. Other prices, while not as high, are devastating to the individual, especially to the teacher. Guilt at not being nice, at not being sociometric, at not being a good guy is probably increasing among content-oriented teachers. Anxiety lest one say or do the "wrong" thing, lest one be undemocratic, lest one hurt someone else's feelings, lest one be obstructive (the older word is "argumentative"), lest one not appear right, or—most crushing to the teacher—lest one not be permissive, lest one not let whole children grow as wholes, lest one not be warm and loving, is also increasing. Again, the ultimate price of the permissive-group complex is freedom of the individual. Permissiveness, as preached in some educational literature, can be a corrosion of individual freedom, the freedom of the individual intellect to wander, to speculate, to be daring, to be imaginative, even to be radical. To permit too much is really to permit very little.

Many readers may think that the argument as presented is extreme. And it is. But it is believed that the tendency as outlined exists to an extent little realized by educators themselves. And what is worse, the idea that the philosophy being espoused may be questionable, may be deleterious to children and to teachers, is not even considered. Educators are also often not aware of the metaphysical quality of contemporary permissivist doctrine. Nor are they aware of its dogmatism. As Dewey aptly said, "It is not too much to say that an educational philosophy which proposes to be based on the idea of freedom may become as dogmatic as ever was the traditional education which is reacted against."[18]

A final word is in order. In a healthy democratic classroom the bounds and limits of behavior must be clearly known and understood by teacher and pupils. Pupils must understand authority. Authority of course does not mean authoritarianism. Nor is authority a dirty word. It is an inevitable concomitant of the social process. In the classroom it inheres in the teacher and only seldom in the class group. To be permissive, especially in an extreme fashion, is to blur and confuse the outlines of the class social situation. This does not mean that a teacher should not be permissive. The difficulties mentioned arise when permissiveness is espoused (explicitly or implicitly) *as a basic doctrine* of educational practice and is not something a teacher occasionally is. When it is espoused as a basic doctrine, it, like all other dogmatisms, leads not to democracy but rather to authoritarianism in the classroom.

Notes

1. For an excellent discussion of some of these points, see Ross Stagner, *Psychology of Personality,* 2nd Ed. (New York: McGraw-Hill, 1948), Ch. XX.
2. Arthur B. Moehlman, School Administration (Boston: Houghton Mifflin, 1940); Howard K. Beale, *Are American Teachers Free?* (New York: Charles Scribner's Sons, 1936). Many other references could be cited.
3. Careful scientific studies of authoritarianism in education are scarce, almost non-existent. This is probably a function of the difficulty of measuring such a complex phenomenon as authoritarianism plus a general touchiness of school people on the subject.
4. Fred N. Kerlinger, "The Origin of the Doctrine of Permissiveness in American Education," *Progressive Education,* XXXIII (1956), 161–165.
5. Fred N. Kerlinger, "The Authoritarianism of Group Dynamics," *Progressive Education,* XXXI (1954), 169–173.

6. See, especially, Earl C. Kelley, *Education For What Is Real* (New York: Harper, 1947), Chapter V *et passim,* and all of Nathaniel Cantor, *Dynamics of Learning* (Buffalo: Foster & Stewart, 1946).

7. Marie I. Rasey, *Toward Maturity* (New York: Barnes & Noble, 1947), p. 231. See, also, the same author's *This Is Teaching* (New York: Harper, 1950).

8. Cantor, *op. cit.,* pp. 145 and 153.

9. *Ibid.,* p. 174. See also, Earl C. Kelley and Marie I. Rasey, *Education and the Nature of Man* (New York: Harper, 1952), p. 86. This latter work is especially interesting because it is supposed to give the scientific foundations for the authors' educational beliefs. Of the entire list of 131 entries (footnotes), however, only four are reports of actual scientific research, and of these four perhaps one is a significant study.

10. Cantor, *op. cit.,* p. 174. Space limitations forbid citing other examples of derogation. In fact, the references for the points made have been kept to a few particularly clear cases. But many others could be cited.

11. Kelley, *op. cit.,* pp. 98–99.

12. John Dewey, *Experience and Education* (New York: Macmillan, 1938), p. 84.

13. *Ibid.,* pp. 84–85.

14. William H. Kilpatrick, *Group Education for a Democracy* (New York: Association Press, 1940), p. 130.

15. See *ibid.,* pp. 103–104, and Marie I. Rasey, *This Is Teaching, passim,* as examples.

16. Otto Fenichel, *The Psychoanalytic Theory of Neurosis* (New York: Norton, 1954), pp. 584–589.

17. Kerlinger, "The Authoritarianism of Group Dynamics."

18. Dewey, *op. cit.,* p. 10.

Philosophic Idealism in Rogerian Psychology

Richard W. Dettering

The Nature of the Rogerian Movement

The "non-directive", client-centered, student-centered therapy and teaching of Carl Rogers and his followers have begun to assume the proportions of a minor crusade in this country. A unique kind of Rogerian methodology has significantly penetrated the practices of counseling, psychiatry and education. The following this approach has already amassed is a tribute to its effect and to the meaning which it has come to have to thousands of able and alert professionals in these respective fields. Nor is it only the extent of influence which excites attention. The professed aim of the movement is revolutionary. "If education is most effectively conducted along lines suggested by client-centered therapy," writes Rogers, "then the achievement of this goal means turning present-day education upside down."[1] This combination of strong support and radical intent entitles some broad questions to be asked in both historical and philosophical, as well as psychological, terms. Where did this movement come from? Why did it arise at this time? Where is it going?

There are a few elementary features of the Rogerian movement which are clear at the outset. Its overt attraction has been to the most extreme antiauthoritarian elements of our culture. It is not only opposed to command and instruction, but also to admonition and advice. The movement is thus directly antagonistic to the classical heritage of moralizing and educating. It rejects any form of "realism" which would have the client or student adjust himself to any body of hard, inflexible facts—whether, they be external events, rational norms, or libidinous processes within him. And with even greater force, Rogerian thinking turns down any variety

"Philosophic Idealism in Rogerian Psychology," *Educational Theory*, 5 (October 1955), 206–214, has been reprinted with the permission of the author and of the publisher, *Educational Theory*. Richard W. Dettering is Professor of English and Education at San Francisco State College.

of Aristotelianism, Thomism or Rationalism which would induce the subject to follow, imitate or submit himself to some higher, imposed standard. The stress is all the other way—towards self-direction, self-discovery, self-realization. The reliance is placed entirely on the "fountain within", as Coleridge called it.

Thus it is not surprising to find among Rogers' converts and allies large numbers of psychologists and educators who have been sympathetic with the trends in "group dynamics", "action research", and "field psychology". The new phenomenalists like Snygg and Combs show by ample reference and quotation their abundant goodwill towards Rogers and his works. And receding one more generation, it is not unexpected that a large residue of "progressive educators", enticed by Dewey's repudiation of static absolutes, should find in Rogers a further culmination in their efforts to find truth and value only in the realm of experience. Rogers himself has said that his work "represents a rediscovery of effective principles of Dewey, Kilpatrick and others."[2] Surrounded by such an impressive array of modernists, the Rogerian school may well feel itself to be the latest vanguard of a personal liberation movement in recent Western thought. And this raises a preliminary question of great interest. If Rogerian psychology is the latest leader of a trend, what *is* this trend? How has the trend been exemplified in the past? What are its values and its philosophic rationale?

The Counterpoint in Pragmatism

We might well suppose, in view of the new alliances, that the experimentalist philosophy of Dewey and his followers would contain significant features consistent with Rogerian principles. And such seems to be the case. Dewey's passion for the continuity and unity of experience and nature, his integration of mind and body, is affirmed by Rogers and the field theorists with their concept of the interrelatedness of the phenomenal field. Both Dewey and Rogers believe in the dynamic character of human experience, in its constant movement and change. Both have seen within this matrix of flux, the possibility of freeing the individual and the emergence of a self-directive "purpose". And both have envisioned as the goal of this personal emancipation some kind of social cohesiveness; as Rogers has expressed it, "self-actualization appears to be in the direction of socialization, broadly defined."[3] These four broad similarities cannot be discounted; and they have undoubtedly given the Rogerian school a powerful momentum to ride within the immediate heritage of American philosophic thought.

But there is another side to the picture. Dewey represented a convergence of Hegel and Darwin, of dialectical idealism and empirical science. And it is the Darwinian side that we have been leaving out. Meiklejohn has exposed this conflict in forceful terms:

In two different social moods Dewey gives two different accounts of
the activities of problem-solving. One . . . is predominantly individualistic. The other is equally socialistic. . . . If we say that thinking takes
place as the result of "strain" in human experience, the most popular
and widely accepted pragmatic interpretation of that statement is subjective and individualistic. . . . This view regards a problem as solved,
for an individual, when, in the experience of that individual, the feeling
of strain out of which the problem came, dies away. The individual in
question is no longer disturbed. His problem is solved. . . . But (Dewey)
has also another account of problem solving which is far more difficult
to construe. . . . The strain of a problem, he often tells us, is not in any
individual alone. It is "in the situation." It is objective. It is social. And
this means that a problem may remain utterly unsolved even though
any given individual may have been freed from the strain of it.[4]

It is this social, objective, scientific aspect of Dewey's philosophy—his
Darwinian side—that we should now seek to compare with Rogers.

The Conflict Between Dewey and Rogers

Our task, at this point, is to find documentation for Meiklejohn's
analysis, such that we can establish points of comparison with the thinking
of Rogers. The Darwinian side of Dewey focuses on three major conceptions which we shall now examine in turn.

a. The Concept of Interaction

Dewey has written that "the word 'interaction' expresses the second
chief principle of interpreting an experience in its educational function
and force. It assigns equal rights to both factors in experience—objective
and internal conditions. Any normal experience is an interplay of these
two sets of conditions."[5] Now the problem in interpreting this statement
is whether the "interaction" is to be regarded as Darwin undoubtedly
would have regarded it—as an objective, scientifically reported phenomenon—or whether it is to be considered as itself a private experience
involving only two interacting aspects of the experiential field of any
given subject. Dewey may remain ambiguous here, but there is no doubt
as to where Rogers stands. For Rogers the individual reacts to the field
as he perceives it. Snygg and Combs also constantly inveigh against the
so-called "normative" or "external" approach of conventional psychology,
which, so they contend, views the subject's environment from the position
of the *outside* observer and therefore overlooks a considerable amount
of the stimuli *within* the subject's field and to which he is in fact responding. It is when we consider social interaction, especially in the educational
process, that the difference between Dewey and Rogers becomes clear cut.
Dewey always emphasized two-way participation between student and
teacher. The teacher at least *suggested*[6] and became an essential corre-
spondent in the relationship. However, even this much intervention would

violate Rogers' non-directive ideal. With Rogers the role of teacher or counselor becomes unusually restricted and suspends even the normal non-authoritarian habits of social intercourse; the weight is placed on interaction *within* the subject, not between the subject and agent. The agent serves not as a partner or active cooperator, but as a catalyst. He interacts as does a mirror. In terms of the measured activity of the agent, if nothing more, there is an important difference between the Deweyan and Rogerian learning situations.

b. Experiment and Consequences

The original pragmatism of Peirce led to Dewey's attention to the consequences of acting from given ideas. The anticipation of consequences stands on conclusions about the regularities of nature. The whole notion of "experiment" falls if there is no constant upon which to experiment. In a completely unpredictable universe an experimental act would be nothing more than a random expression. Kilpatrick has construed experimentalism as "the conception that we find out what to expect in life by studying experimentally the uniformities within experience."[7] Thus arises the "operational method" of testing and determining their meaning and truth-value. This is one of the cornerstones of experimentalist philosophy and has given it a unique role among modern systems of thought. But here again Rogers must demur. The introduction of socially acknowledged results as tests of therapy or learning smacks of the "external approach". Rogers does not wish to make such outside criteria matters of anxiety to either patient or therapist, student or teacher. Kerby-Miller has described this aspect of Rogers' thinking as "love *without* consequences." And although Rogers through his clinic has exposed some of the results of his technique, he is basically consistent with his maxim that "the best vantage point for understanding behavior is the internal frame of reference of the individual himself."[8] He stands opposed to *any* external imposition of norms, whether based on authority, custom, logic *or* consequences. It is contrary to Rogers' morality to assess the person from without; intersubjective must yield to intrasubjective verdict. The divergence here from the *social* side of Dewey's thinking is striking.

c. Conflict and Problem-Solving

Hegel's dialectical process mingled with the Darwinian struggle for survival to furnish the basis for Dewey's concern with conflict and challenge as a necessary factor in self-development. The belief that not only the specific solution, but the general capacity to solve, comes out of repeated, experimental and self-directed efforts to solve problems, emerged in Dewey's writings as a distinct and arresting program for promoting human education and growth. Whereas Hegel emphasized contradictions appearing in the process of reasoning which required rational reconciliation on a higher level, Dewey dealt with problems as ecological threats or frustrations to be coped with by the maximum expression of both mental and manual skills. The ongoing process is the same in both Hegel and Dewey; a solution merely means passing on to another problem. But unlike Hegel, Dewey did not think the business was structured and pre-determined in a diagnosable dialectic. Each problem would be new, fresh, contingent; but it would call for exercise of past training and the full use of knowledge, habits and abilities strengthened by previous problem-solving efforts. Certainly Dewey in his educational theory did not advocate *throwing* problems at students; but he did believe in the value of "upset-ting experiences" and he thought that the nature of living and growing up in society was a matter of facing and solving continual problems. Perhaps his most important prescription here was that the problem should be solved by the student and not by his teachers or elders. But then Dewey drew a fundamental distinction between "subject-matter which constitutes the problem and subject-matter that is supposed to resolve the problem. To discriminate and recognize cases of audition, vision . . . merely exposes a problem. No persistence upon the method that yields them can throw any light upon them."[9] In brief, while the problem may be *found* introspec-tively, in the private world of experience, it cannot be understood or solved except in social and scientific terms.

Rogers' thinking on this question shares the ethics of self-directed solution to problems. But unlike Dewey he would keep the problem within the subject's field, for both its comprehension *and* solution. The only prob-lem to be recognized by the teacher or counselor or society, is that which the subject freely verbalizes; and then society has no right to expect him to solve the problem or to solve it—or even to formulate it—for him. For Rogers the subject's expression of the problem is a complete self-fulfilling act; from the standpoint of the outsider, nothing more needs to be done. If the subject continues to work on the problem, this is his business for which the all-accepting counselor or teacher is ready to help. But the problem never really gets externalized, although its nature may get com-municated to society. For this reason Rogerian therapy and teaching dis-counts the problematic-situation as a socially acknowledged fact and relies instead on the self-determination of both problem and solution by the subject. This is contrary to the position of Dewey quoted above.

It would be possible to go beyond these three points of difference between Dewey and Rogers and discuss some of the problems Rogerian psychology would face in adjusting to the naturalistic and scientific basis of experimentalist thinking. But enough has been indicated to show a serious discrepancy in the respective descriptions of the teaching-learning situation. One opposition which seems to run through all these differences we have discussed is between an intersubjective and an introspective concept of knowledge. Here we must especially remember Dewey's criticism of the "introspectionist" view that "consciousness or experience is the organ of its own immediate disclosure of all its own secrets"—a view, he says, which arose with Descartes and Locke and was "foisted on psychology from without."[10] On this issue above all, Rogers must part with Dewey. Whereas Dewey relied ultimately on the consensus of the scientific community, Rogers rests on the process of self-disclosure.[11]

The Rogerian Adventure into Idealism

We have seen how the naturalistic and scientific theme in pragmatism is irreconcilable with the personalistic and subjective criteria which Rogers employs for both therapy and learning. On the other hand Rogers' concepts are consistent with the individualistic stress in pragmatism. But Rogers then proceeds to stretch this individualism far beyond the point that any legitimate pragmatist is likely to go. There are at least two important respects in which Rogerian thinking has treaded into idealistic ground.

a. The Concept of Self-discovery

Rogers has emphasized that "truth that has been personally appropriated and assimilated in experience cannot be directly communicated to another." He has found with "some relief" that Kierkegaard, the mystic Danish theologian, realized this too—"it made it seem less absurd."[12] Learning, then, cannot be provided from without; it is a process of "self-discovery". Now "self-discovery" is capable of an interesting ambiguity. Dewey too believed in "self-discovery", but he meant discovery *by* the self—discovery of data that were *not* the self. But another interpretation is readily possible. In this view "self-discovery" would mean not only discovery *by* the self but discovery *of* the self— it *is* the self which is discovered. Although Rogers may not have intended it, the main direction of his therapy indicates that this second interpretation is being used. In the current language of phenomenalist psychology the subject-object distinction is represented as an arbitrary and often transitory differentiation within the phenomenal field. It is only part of the perceptual field itself, as Rogers says, which becomes known as "reality". The distinction is tentative and may be changed with further reflection or development. In some cases, as with the therapist-patient relationship, according to a statement by Rogers,[13] the distinction may be lost altogether and the two individuals in effect merge. It is clear that this "self", originally a *part* of the "phenomenal field", has movable walls—it may *become the whole phenomenal field*. And in such a case *any* discovery would automatically be discovery of more of the "self". The mechanics here are akin to the epistemology of traditional mysticism, which involves a successive rejection of subject-object distinctions, ending in speechless identification with the cosmos. And so Rogers says:

> This whole train of experiencing . . . seems to have launched me on a
> process which is both fascinating and at times a little frightening. It

> seems to mean letting my experience carry me on, in a direction that I can but dimly define . . . The sensation is that of floating with a complex stream of experience with the fascinating possibility of trying to comprehend its ever changing complexity.[14]

The dynamics here are highly subjective—and auto-suggestive—and even that part of the "phenomenal field" called the "external world" is given no credit for pushing Rogers on. While there is a mystic surrender of the self and its controls here, the surrender, as with idealism, is not to an external world, but to a world that was in the self to begin with. The "self" disappears only in the recognition that it is everything; hence there is no "not-self", and "self" becomes meaningless. This is the process by which modern idealism has developed.

b. Self-development and Unfolding

The non-directive method places great weight on trusting the client or student, in encouraging his spontaneity and in maintaining that he already holds the answers within himself. Some of this credo is as old as Socrates, part of it was used by Dewey, but Rogers carries it about as far as it can possibly go. Now the Western idealist philosophers have differed on the amount and nature of external guidance and direction which should be afforded in the learning process, but there has been general agreement among them that the self contains within it the momentum for its growth and education. Brubacher has pointed this out especially with the Fichtean brand of idealism.

> Some idealists are inclined to exalt will rather than intellect or reason to the position of the Absolute. On analysis, they find that primacy must be awarded to a certain activity or striving as the heart of reality. This theory is notably different from the pragmatic in accounting for the activity principle in education. It puts education squarely up to the individual. Neither teacher nor parent, school nor church, can educate him. Only through a voluntary act of his will can he educate himself.[15]

Along the same line, there is an idealist tendency to stress the personality rather than the subject taught. As Horne puts it, "The main thing is to remember that we teach pupils, not subjects."[16] Education here, it is easy to see, moves closer to therapy. But perhaps most significant and reminiscent are the views of the great idealist and theistic educator, Froebel, who stressed the notions of "inner connection" and "self-revelation". Froebel founded the kindergarten—the child's garden where the children unfolded and blossomed like flowers. In the early nineteenth century Froebel wrote,

> The drawing of direct inferences concerning the inner life of childhood and youth from certain external manifestations of life, is the chief cause of antagonism and contention, of the frequent mistakes in life and education. . . . Therefore, education in instruction and training, originally and in its first principles, should necessarily be *passive, following* (only guarding and protecting), not *prescriptive, categorical, interfering*.[17] (Italics his.)

It would be hard to see how the non-directive educator and psychologist could fail to applaud the foregoing statements. The person who cannot be taught but can only learn, the self-enhancing, self-actualizing person of Rogers and the field theorists, seems to have attained an emancipation from the immediate environment and a dependence on "inner connection" that has historically been presented most vigorously in idealism.

Conclusions

We have tried to show initially that Rogerian psychology has made important departures from the social, scientific, environmentalist strain in pragmatism and experimentalism. Next, we have argued that is has stretched the subjective and individualistic side of pragmatism far over into the idealist camp. Let us return now to our original questions about what all this means.

First, we are presented with an interesting religious phenomenon. The Rogerian school would seem to be the first major expression in modern psychology of Protestant individualism. The theology which rejected the mediating formalism of the church and stood for direct, personal communion with God, which stressed initiative and self-reliance and abhorred institutional controls, finds its sophisticated counterpart in the little self-enhancing individuals of Rogers' clinic and Rogers' classroom. Far from being a pure weakness, however, this personalism is Rogers' greatest strength. It fits his methods into our religious and economic heritage and undoubtedly accounts for the easy shift so many people have made into his fold. As Kant, who started German idealism, has been called the philosopher of the Reformation, perhaps Rogers, somewhat belatedly, can be called its psychologist. But just as Western individualism has run into constant difficulty in times calling for great social responsibility and organized change, so non-directive therapy and education is apt to fall short of that often needed juncture of the individual with the group. Rogers' thinking is curious here. "Finally, the self-actualization appears to be in the direction of socialization, broadly defined."[18] As Rogers will not permit the counselor, teacher or society to motivate this socialization, he must count on some tendency within the individual to bring it to fruition, as the idealists counted on the individual will to evolve into the social will. Adam Smith, of course, had the same problem; and Rogers' uncaused socializing tendency could be regarded as the "invisible hand" of a laissez-faire psychology. The other problem here is solipsism, long a bane of idealistic philosophies. Rogers' denial of the positive role of the interacting agent makes this problem for him especially acute. If he and the "phenomenalist psychologists" insist on encapsulating the individual in his "phenomenal field", then they must posit some unexplained overlap or "pre-established harmony" between various persons' fields in order to account for socialization. But if they renig at such complete encapsulation they must acknowledge some intersubjective relationship, some norm or agent outside the individual. In either case, the dilemma is not solved.

Secondly, there is a neat factor of historical timing in the emergence and popularity of the Rogerian movement. Personalism in philosophy has always had a paradoxical kinship with certain forms of positivism, as both have stressed the superior validity of immediate, subjective experience. The refusal of Rogers to make interpretations beyond the given experience or to encourage his subjects to do so joins him in this traditional phenomenalistic approach. There are two points to be made about this kind of orientation. It has on the one hand a strong affinity with the mysticism of the East, where enjoyment of the "aesthetic continuum" of pure experience has been given priority over the theoretical interpretations and abstract meanings of experience.[19] And this is perhaps not all regrettable in a period when East-West communication is of rising moment. But on the other hand, such retreat into the privacy of consciousness or of given sense-data is typical in Western history only when traditional institutions, concepts and values are in a state of collapse; the absolute in such times is found within. As Northrup has expressed it:

> Whereas the Orient is for the most part continuously positivistic, the West tends . . . to be positivistic only during those revolutionary transition periods in its historical development when the traditional scientific and historical doctrine has broken down in the face of new evidence, and before the new, more adequate one has been put forward to take its place."[20]

It is hard to deny that we are going through such a period today, resulting from the collapse of the social values of the New Deal era and the disillusionment with post-war internationalism. One of the clearest symptoms of our contemporary epistemic regression is the sudden new modesty of the psychiatric profession, with its "not sticking your neck out" approach and its trend towards silent, permissive treatment along Rogerian lines. In education, too, scepticism, acceptance and "understanding"—"get the most out of the age of five"—are replacing the theoretic and moralizing strictures of "work for the night cometh". In this one respect, of course, Rogers' methods run counter to traditional Protestantism, with its utilitarian work-ethic; but the emergence of leisure in our society has rendered such frontier values obsolete and is drawing more heavily upon the passive, non-judgmental aspects of Protestant culture, represented best by the Quakers. When not much work needs to be done, experience gets assessed more for its intrinsic qualities—the depth of its religious content and its immediate and personal meaning. Such is the direction we seem to be taking. Appreciation of the aesthetic component of experience is supplanting our former explanatory and interpretative response.

The main impact of our argument is that the Rogerian movement is a symbol of much more than its adherents realize or are willing to admit. Its psychology is one of *enduring* life rather than *remaking* it—with something akin both to early Christianity and modern French existentialism. One need never deny the personal benefits and sense of relief that come from this doctrine. The cultivation of empathy, seeing the other person from his own inside, is a long standing humanitarian virtue. But whereas Dewey regarded it as the starting point of social co-operation, Rogers considers it the stopping point as well. Only in some kind of idealistic terms—of an "emergent mind" or a "natural self"—can such a position be justified. Otherwise it would seem to be wanting in the production of effective citizenship or social reconstruction. In view of the present world-crisis, the question is whether we can afford to try such an easy way out. Perhaps the answer is to improve our ability to make judgments rather than to lose it.

Notes

1. Carl Rogers, *Client-Centered Therapy* (Boston: Houghton-Mifflin, 1951), p. 385.
2. *Ibid.,* p. 386.
3. *Ibid.,* p. 488.
4. Alexander Meiklejohn, *Education Between Two Worlds* (New York: Harper & Bros., 1942), p. 128.
5. John Dewey, *Experience and Education* (New York: Macmillan, 1938), p. 38.
6. *Ibid.,* p. 84.
7. William Kilpatrick, "Philosophy of Education from an Experimentalist Outlook," *41st Yearbook, National Society for the Study of Education* (Chicago: University of Chicago Press, 1942), Part I, p. 44.
8. Carl Rogers, *op. cit.,* p. 494.
9. John Dewey, *Philosophy and Civilization* (New York: Minton, Balch and Co., 1931), p. 265.
10. *Ibid.,* p. 261.
11. Carl Rogers, "Classroom Approaches to Human Behavior" (Address at Harvard Conference, April 4, 1952).
12. *Ibid.*
13. Carl Rogers (Address at San Francisco State College, June 12, 1952).
14. Carl Rogers, *op. cit.,* "Classroom Approaches to Human Behavior."
15. John S. Brubacher, *Modern Philosophies of Education* (New York: McGraw-Hill, 1950), p. 313.
16. H. H. Horne, "An Idealist Philosophy of Education," *41st Yearbook, National Society for the Study of Education* (Chicago: University of Chicago Press, 1942), Part I, p. 172.
17. Friedrich Froebel, *The Education of Man* (New York: D. Appleton, 1887, trans. by W. N. Hailman), p. 7.
18. Carl Rogers, *Client-Centered Therapy, op. cit.,* p. 488.
19. F. S. C. Northrop, *The Meeting of East and West* (New York: Macmillan, 1947), p. 375.
20. *Ibid.*

Varieties of Alienation and Educational Response

Louis Goldman

The need to examine and analyze the concept of alienation has become acute in the last decade. In the first place, the phenomenon of alienation is probably manifesting itself more and more. Secondly, we find that many disciplines are now using the concept. Philosophy has begun to reexamine the works of Hegel[1] and Marx[2], and the rise of existentialism has brought the concept into new focus. Psychology and psychiatry, influenced perhaps by existential philosophy, have also begun to make liberal use of it. Sociological investigation, going back at least to Durkheim's work, has long been concerned with the social roots of alienation. Political science also shows an interest in the concept.[3] Literary criticism, naturally, has dealt with the idea.[4] None of these disciplines is bound to do what the others are doing, but it seems to me that we would all be better off if we spoke the same language. I believe the language that needs to be spoken is the language of alienation. This leads me to a final reason for analyzing this concept. Within education itself we find that our ideas have largely been shaped by our acceptance of some underlying metaphor. We are familiar with the conception of the educator as a potter molding inert clay. We are familiar with the image of the teacher as artist interacting with his material in some creative way.[5] We have seen, for example, Burns and Brauner[6] talk about the analogy of the jungle, the herd, the market-place, and the organism.

If we review the trends in the evolving language of education, we find more and more the use of terms borrowed from the profession of medicine. We have special *therapists* who do *diagnostic* testing. The teacher is a professional practitioner who may need *aides* of various sorts. The ideological focus has shifted to individualizing instruction and moving

"Varieties of Alienation and Educational Response," *Teachers College Record,* 69, 4 (January 1968), 331–339, has been reprinted with the permission of the author and of the publisher, *Teachers College Record.* Louis Goldman teaches philosophy of education at Wichita State University.

away from standardized programs, indicating that the emotional and intellectual "health" of the student, and not the needs of society, has become our first responsibility. In short, the language we are speaking more and more is shaping itself around the metaphor of the organism, which is another way of saying the metaphor is based upon the conception that education is analogous to medicine and is concerned with the integrity of wholeness of the individual. I suggest that, if this is the case and we are concerned with wholeness, we are necessarily involved with fragmentation.

In summary, therefore, we are driven by the reality of our situation, by the work of a number of related disciplines, and by the internal logic of educational discourse itself to a serious and systematic inquiry into the matter of alienation.

Mythic Versions

We are not the first culture to recognize that the human condition is one of alienation, fragmentation, imperfection, incompletion, or what you will. In the past this recognition usually was explained in some sort of mythological form. The Greeks certainly had an appreciation of man's predicament. You may recall that in Plato's *Symposium* the comic playwright, Aristophanes, is asked to speak about love. He replies by inventing a myth: Originally mankind had four legs and four arms and two faces looking in opposite directions. In this original state, man felt supremely blessed. He felt that because he could see everything around him—front and rear— he was omniscient. Because he could extend his arms and legs and literally roll along at great speeds, and was able to accomplish other anomalous physical feats, he soon felt that he was omnipotent. He became proud, and the cardinal sin for the Greeks was *hubris* or overweening pride. The gods became angry and wished to punish him. They did this by dividing him in two. At this point the question comes up, "What has this to do with the matter of love, which is what you should be talking about?" Aristophanes answered "everything." Love is simply defined as each of the severed halves going about in search of its better half. This conception, of course, is implied in much of our everyday speech and common idioms so that we hear the minister in church proclaiming to the bride and groom that they are now one.

The Hebrews, of course, with the myth of Adam and Eve in the Garden of Eden created the pattern by which we have subsequently analyzed and talked about man's state of alienation.

The myth can be analyzed into several phases or components, and it may serve as the model or the paradigm for analyzing other forms of alienation. (1) We observe that there is postulated an *original unity* of man and God; and that because of this state of perfection, man is blissful and ignorant. (2) We then have the *Fall* or the separation of man from that which has made him perfect. We are now dealing with an imperfect, alienated being who necessarily, because he is alienated, is discontented and seeks reunion—but who also, because of his imperfection, is incapable of perceiving without distortion or thinking without fallacy. (3) Thus, alienated man strives to overcome his alienation but chooses *inappropriate means* for so doing. This phase has as its theological equivalent the conception of *idolatry*. (4) To break the pattern of futility in trying to overcome his alienation, man must choose an appropriate means to overcome his alienation. It becomes necessary to introduce a new element. This can be either personal *revelation* or some form of collective *institutionalized insight* (i.e., the church or the school). Presumably through these means alienation may ultimately be overcome and the individual is once more at one (that is, he atones) with God.

Having thus exposed the framework of the concept of alienation, let us turn to a consideration of the varieties of alienation and their educational responses. This analysis will appear to be historical and progressive, but this is not necessarily the case. All forms of alienation may exist simultaneously and they may indeed logically and psychologically implicate each other.

Alienation from God and Nature

Schematically it is obvious that man can be alienated from (a) something beyond himself, (b) from other men, or (c) from himself, and that within each of these major types of alienation there can be various subdivisions. Let us look at man's alienation from something beyond himself, first as alienation from God and then as alienation from nature. American educational history begins with this form of alienation. From the Middle Ages through the 17th century, most men believed that man was created by God but has fallen and is miserable because of it. The Protestant revolution led men to believe that salvation is possible in a somewhat new way. Man could become one with God if he understood God's will. He could do this best not by trusting the interpretation of a priesthood or some other intermediaries, but by reading the Word of God in the Bible for himself. And so the Puritan schools were founded ostensively to teach people to be able to read the Word of God and, by so doing, to regain their oneness with Him. Thus, the *New England Primer* begins, "In Adam's fall we sinned all" and "Thy ways to mend, this Book attend." The Puritan ideal of using the schools to achieve oneness with God still persists in all parochial schools in America, whether they be Jewish, Protestant, or Catholic.

Now the 17th century also gave rise to the New Science which was by no means free of theological concerns. The figure of Spinoza best illustrates the transition from the older conception of man's alienation from God to the newer conception of man's alienation from nature. It began to appear to Spinoza and his contemporaries that the heavens and the earth and man himself were God's creation as much as the Bible itself, and that perhaps God's nature and God's will were better known by reading the Book of Nature. The familiar analogy of the watch and the watchmaker came into prominence. Surely, if we discovered a watch on the beach of a supposedly deserted island, we would know a watchmaker or a man necessarily had been there because the intricacies of the design of the watch were so marvelous that is inconceivable that such an instrument could have been created by chance. Likewise, when we discovered the intricacies and design in nature, we became convinced that there is an author of all of nature. And furthermore, just as we may infer that the mathematical relationships existing between the various gears in the mechanism of the watch must have been in the mind of the watchmaker, so we infer that the laws of nature tell us something of the mind of God.

These laws of nature may be written in the universal language of mathematics, free of analogy and mistranslation. So we move gradually to a concern with nature rather than with the Author, since we only know the author through his works. Indeed, we begin to see philosophers such as Spinoza questioning the need to separate God from nature and suggesting instead that the material world is one of the attributes of God. There we have a statement of the pantheistic position. If this is the situation, then we would say that man is alienated from God in so far as he is ignorant of the laws of nature.

We find a number of writers attempting to understand and explain man's apparent inability to grasp the essences of nature. Some suggest that our senses deceive us and that only through the intellect, free from the distractions of the senses, can we truly comprehend. Others suggest that our methods of receiving knowledge need improvement. Later the conception of nature changes somewhat, and it is the senses which give us an intuition or immediate knowledge of nature; it is our intellectual constructs which prevent us from seeing things as they are. We even have Francis Bacon attempting to systematize the obstacles to the understanding of nature, using the very language of the analysis in this paper when he speaks of the Idols of the market, the theatre, the tribe, and the den.

The conceptions of nature are various indeed; and I think it is safe to say that there is a separate educational response peculiar to each concept of nature and Fall. The standard curriculum in American schools from the 18th century forward is basically a response to the belief that man is alienated from nature. The curriculum includes geography to orient man to the spatial dimensions of his universe; history orients him to its temporal dimensions; mathematics and science relate him to the inner workings of the world. The assumption is that, by understanding what's what, or the nature of reality, man can see his relationship to it or his place in nature and, consequently, overcome his alienation.

Alienation from Others

Let us now turn to man's alienation from other men, which can be roughly subdivided into a consideration of (1) groups of men being alienated from other groups of men, and (2) the individual person being alienated from the human community at large.

Needless to say, individual groups of men have always been separated from other groups of men. The residents of the Island of Samoa are obviously separated from the residents of Hawaii, but it does not make much sense to claim that they are alienated from one another. Nor should we use the concept of alienation to describe the fact that one Germanic tribe was separated from another Germanic tribe or that one Italian kingdom was separated from another Italian kingdom. We can only intelligibly use the concept of alienation of *group from group* if there begins to develop an objective basis for a communication or union of some sort between the groups. Thus the Plymouth colony was not alienated from the settlements along the southern coast of the United States during the 17th century. But with the growth of common interests and needs dictated by political and commercial movements, the two realistically shared similar purposes in the newer context. It then makes sense to introduce the concept of alienation.

Now the special nature of the group itself is of secondary importance. We could, if we had time, consider the alienation of groups from each other on the basis of national origins, races, religions, age level, and perhaps sex. What is apparent is that the separateness of the groups need to to be modified to some extent; the *pluribus* must relate to an *unum*. Should we wonder why this alienation is not overcome; why in other words, the diversity becomes divisiveness in the face of obvious advantages to both groups, we can best answer by giving a synonym for idolatry: *ethnocentricity,* or the belief that one's provincial values are universal values. Obviously a brief reading of American history impresses us with the relevance of this analysis, for we are the melting pot or conglomeration of the most divergent imaginable groups of men. And we know that with each new group arriving on the American scene we do not always open our arms to these "huddled masses yearning to be free," but that we are hostile and that at best we grudgingly accept them. And we know the classical responses to hostility: the withdrawal into cliquish groups and the dogmatic counterassertion of one's own superiority—which is, perhaps, another way of saying ethnocentricism. Thus, we have the experience of the Catholics being driven against the wall in the 19th century and forming parochial schools; and we have American Irish out-Irishing their brothers in Ireland; and now we have black power and the Black Muslims.

The American response to this alienation of group from group was the Common School. Perhaps it succeeded as well as can be expected, but nonetheless it worked *within* the framework of white Protestant American groups. Within these boundaries it was a success, but it was a failure because of its boundaries. Today the so-called Common School has turned out to be more and more uncommon, and most of our deliberate efforts to reconstruct the schools have been to make it a truly common school. But of this books may be written. Let us now consider the alienation of the individual from any sense of community.

The Individual and Community

The alienation of the individual from mankind at large, or from *community,* is probably an even more recent phenomenon than the alienation of group from group, although both have as one of their major causes the accelerated rate of social change and the increased impact of industrialization and urbanization. A small, static society, in other words, is usually capable of making provisions for all of its members. A large, changing, specialized society can frequently generate social isolates. To understand this form of alienation requires some understanding of the basis for man's association with other men. Although there are perhaps infinite grounds for association or community, and although individuals may suffer alienation in an infinity of ways, for purposes of simplification we can assert that the *dominant basis for association in today's society is through occupations.* Thus alienation of the individual from community can focus on those who are unemployed or unemployable. Here we have three major sub-groups: (a) the very young who have not yet worked or have not had our substitution and preparation for employment, formal schooling, (b) the retired, and particularly the involuntary retired, and (c) the unemployed or unemployable mature man.

Preschool children (and even some school-age children) have probably suffered more from the shrinkage of the family from its previous extended kinship relationships to its nuclear structure, and from the growth of the automobile-dominated metropolis. There are less and less people, and especially other children, directly around a child growing up today, and it is more and more difficult and unsafe to reach other children. The predicament of the alienated child and an inappropriate response to his situation can be vividly understood by the images of *the sidewalk and the station-wagon.* The sidewalk symbolizes the avenue of communication between one child and another. In many areas this has vanished: either sidewalks are no longer built, as in some suburban housing developments, or the sidewalk has become too unsafe, as in many metropolitan areas. The response to the disappearing sidewalk is the mother-driven station-wagon. Instead of relying upon informal mingling of children, the image of the station-wagon implies a planned, structured mingling of children: the Boy Scout meeting at 7:30, the Little League game at 4, the music lesson at 5, etc. What is gained by structuring common activities for children may be lost by some of the concomitant results—the loss of spontaneity when games and recreation must be carefully scheduled and supervised, the early creation of the "organization man," etc. The increased numbers of nursery schools and Head Start programs is part of the same response to the deprivation of young children. It is very possible that these are not the most adequate responses, however, because they generate or contribute to the varieties of alienation from which the Organization Man suffers. More careful attention to the needs of children by city-planners and architects may be the real solution. Superior land-usage for informal recreation has been made by some of the New Towns in England, and in a few of the planned communities in this country.

Alienation from Oneself

Our final two forms of alienation are *from oneself*. Human nature may be variously conceived: for Marx, especially in his early writings, man was a maker, a doer, a creating animal. For Freud, man's impulses or libido or id was the basic element.

For Marx, *work* is capable of being a great good. Man *works out* his potentialities; he becomes man by doing, by actively exercising his varied abilities. With the division of labor so necessary to industrialism and with the control of the conditions of work divorced from the worker himself with the rise of corporate management and capitalism, work loses its meaning, becomes a necessary evil, and man is dehumanized or alienated. The trouble lies in the separation of the ruling class from the proletariat, of the decision-makers from the decision implementers, of the theoretical from the practical, or the head from the hand, of the white collar from the blue collar.

In this alienated situation, two distinct forms of education emerge: for the ruling elite, an education for decision-makers emphasizing theory, Greco-Roman virtues and the liberal arts; for the masses, a training in useful skills and Christian humility. Additionally, to compensate for the deadening, meaningless working hours, the alienated worker is attracted to diversions which create an illusion of life and vitality. He overconsumes food and drink. He is obsessed with sex. He creates a music and dance to titillate his senses. He makes a "fun culture" (to use Max Lerner's phrase) but underneath he is bored and suffers ennui. His idolatries are many, despite his discontent with work. He still glorifies the infinite accumulation of wealth and material goods though it has enslaved him; he glorifies education, but it is an alienated education of either theory *or* practice, and it reinforces his alienation: he strives for ever more "fun" or "kicks", though these always prove fleeting and unsatisfying.

To overcome this alienation of man from himself, Marx recommends a radical restructuring of the organization of our economy and society. The theoretical and the practical must interpenetrate. The decision-makers and the decision implementers must become one. There must be a dictatorship of the proletariat. Paralleling this, the two track education system must become classless by fusing the theoretical with the practical. The Soviets call this *polytechnical* education, and it has been the ideological foundation of Soviet pedagogy from Marx through Krupskaya and Krushchev. (Interestingly, many developments in the American economy surpass the Soviet ideals—unionism, profit-sharing, etc., and Dewey's "learning by doing" has its roots in egalitarian democracy as much as in the scientific method.)

Finally, following Freud's analysis, man can be alienated from himself in terms of his impulses, emotions, or affective life. The evidence for the existence of two selves in man, alienated from each other, is considerable. There is the dream life and the waking life; there are slips of the tongue; there is compulsive behavior. To understand the cause of the creation of an *unconscious* self alienated from a *conscious* self we only have to understand that man, to some extent at least, is controlled by the pleasure principle, that the expression of many impulses or emotions frequently lead to punishment and pain, and hence it becomes necessary to push down, or repress these difficult impulses. The repository of these impulses is the unconscious. The possible sources of repression are many. Perhaps prohibition against incest generates the earliest repression of affect between child and parent. Certainly, every society has its mores, its manners, its laws which prohibit certain kinds of behaviors and allow others. It also appears to be the case that primitive or savage societies have fewer prohibitions and consequent repressions than do more civilized societies.

The Life of Impulse

Obviously, as society becomes more advanced, people become more interdependent, live together in cities more, and have greater destructive powers (compare the spear of the savage with the H-bomb of civilized man). Because of this, civilization must exercise greater control over the impulsive life of citizens; it must, in effect, demand more repression and create discontent. Man is willing to sacrifice a great deal of his spontaneous expression for repressive civilization, however, because civilization gives him other benefits—security, a greater range of choices, etc. But Freud did not believe that man must necessarily be as self-alienated as he was. Although a conscious and an unconscious exist, it is possible to integrate the two. Unconscious or hidden motivations and impulses can be exposed by the techniques of psychoanalysis. We can at least *know* more about our other self, even though we still keep it in chains—and there is some ground for believing that the chains don't have to be as binding as we had believed. Freud's terse formulation of salvation, or overcoming alienation, was "where id was, there let ego be." In a sense psychoanalysis was re-education, and the therapist a teacher. A follower of Freud, A. S. Neill, has probably drawn the educational implications of Freud better than Freud himself. In *Summerhill*, Neill pictures an educational institution dedicated to overcoming this form of alienation in two ways: (a) create a permissive, though responsible, environment so that a minimum amount of repression takes place and (b) provide therapeutic help for those who have become crippled by too much repression.

We have tried to sketch the main forms of alienation and their educational consequences: the traditional school as a response to alienation from God; the academy, to alienation from nature; the Common School, to alienation of groups from each other; the nursery and adult education, to alienation from Community; the polytechnic school, to alienation from work; and *Summerhill,* or the guidance-dominated school, alienation from affect.

This taxonomy suggests further developments and correlations. For example, we might investigate the interconnections between the forms of alienation. We might ask the question, "Must man overcome all or certain of these alienations to be judged healthy?" We might develop the hypothesis that alienation may be a necessary aspect of creativity and growth, and not always an evil. We might look at the taxonomy historically and chart natural developments. We might suggest that each form of alienation is a distinctively different kind of problematic situation, demanding different methods of inquiry and generating different conceptions of knowledge and curriculum. Finally, we could ask ourselves if it is possible for any single school to take *all* forms of alienation seriously. Would the community school be that school?

Notes

1. Walter Kaufmann, *Hegel* (New York: Doubleday, 1965).
2. Erich Fromm, *Marx's Concept of Man* (New York: Frederick Ungar Publishing Co., 1961).
3. Sebastian de Grazia, *The Political Community: A Study of Anomie* (Chicago: University of Chicago Press, 1948).
4. Stanley Finkelstein, *Existentialism and Alienation in American Literature* (New York: International Publishers).
5. Israel Scheffler, *The Language of Education* (Springfield, Ill.: Charles Thomas, 1960).
6. Hobert Burns and Charles Brauner, *Problems in Education and Philosophy* (Englewood Cliffs, N.J.: Prentice-Hall, Inc., 1965).

PART II

Schooling

AN HISTORICAL PERSPECTIVE

Perhaps the beginning counselor can better understand the modern elementary school and its population if he views the school as an evolving historical institution. Although the institution of the elementary school is extensive and complicated, counselors can gain some insights into its nature by briefly viewing its origins, its changing curriculum, and the reforms that it has experienced.*

Early schools of our country reflected the motives and social conditions of the people. In New England, where a strong emphasis was placed on religion, the town school flourished, emphasizing reading, writing, and religion. Reading and writing were means to salvation. This school, which was the forerunner of the free school, was open to all students and was supported by common taxation. Dorchester, Massachusetts, in May 1639 was the first community to establish such a school.[1] From New York to Virginia, economics was a prime factor in education. Both private and pauper schools prevailed.[2] Governor Berkeley of Virginia related that in his state, as in England, each man enjoyed Christian instruction according to his ability to pay.[3] The governor was overjoyed that there were no free schools in his state.

Instruction in schools in the early colonies contained common elements. Reading, writing, religion, and laws formed the curriculums of early schools, and the alphabet and the Horn Book were the basic educational media. In 1683, however, Enoch Fower initiated the idea that it would be useful to have students "cast accounts"[4] so arithmetic was added to the curriculum. Textbooks that were used were Webster's *The New England Primer,* Dillworth's *A New Guide to the English Tongue,* and Nicholas Pike's *A New and Complete Arithmetic Composed for the Citizens of the United States.*[5]

Startling to the reader of history is the fact that during the early years of our country, an indenture system of work and

* This brief historical introduction to the elementary school does not serve as a thoroughly documented historical study. Instead, the writer hopes that it will initiate extensive study of the elementary school and the coming of guidance services to that institution.

training was prevalent. Paul Monroe dates this system back to 1660 and reports that as late as 1774: "The Boston Newsletter of 1746 advertises 'A few servants indentures for seven years and girls for four years.' "[6] Such a form of primitive education many times resulted in free student labor in return for the teaching of a few meager skills. No wonder the system died out!

At this time, the concept of the free school was developed which placed the responsibility for individual salvation with the person and substituted the authority of the Bible for the authority of the Church.[7] Thus, the need for education was created. The rebellion against the church began in Europe. In New England, the town school reiterated the authority of the Bible and the need for universal education to enable people to read the Bible. Yet the American public was not persuaded to adopt and support the town school. Instead, social forces made evident more strikingly the need for free education. Immigrants in desperate need of training in speaking, reading, and writing the English language were arriving from Europe. In the West, where democracy was a way of life, skills were needed to harness raw natural resources for survival. The westward movement called attention to the strong need for secular education. But, as Ellwood P. Cubberley points out: "The people were poor and indifferent to education," and as a result, "popular education was the dream of the reformer rather than the conviction of the people."[8] However, the land was productive and the people began to prosper. The Lancastrian system, which included the concept of student monitors, was introduced from England in 1806, and it made free education appear possible.[9] A revived concern for free education culminated in the enactment of the First Morrill Act, which gave land grants for colleges and universities. By 1862 the idea of public education was beginning to be accepted in the northern states and in some of the southern states.[10]

Arising out of the development of the free school was a concern for "the need of a broad, general, and diversified training, adapted to the needs of the future rather than to the needs of the present or past," which, according to Cubberley, became ". . . more ever evident."[11] As a result of this orientation, the curriculum expanded. Businessmen from Massachusetts petitioned the legislature of their state to include drawing in the public school curriculum.[12] Noah Webster and the Reverend Jedidiah Morse advocated the study of an American Universal Geography.[13] History, too, was suggested and eventually added, and Davenport's *History of the United States,* published in 1831, combined the study of history and geography.[14] Physical exercise was also added to the curriculum. Of major importance was the addition of science, or nature study, to the elementary school. This was introduced before 1850 and after the

Civil War it was firmly entrenched in the elementary school curriculum. So, the elementary school curriculum consisted of art, reading, writing, arithmetic, history, geography, science, and physical exercise. In addition, nursery schools were introduced to our country from Europe. Such "schooling" of the child, though limited in scope and extent, characterized education as a continuous, sequential process.

During this period when the curriculum was dramatically expanding, the country too was expanding. Education was characterized by public schooling for all and a striving to meet the political, cultural, and economic needs of the time. The country was characterized by the rise of the common people and the expansion of industry, until the Civil War marred that growth and expansion.

According to Edwin Grant Dexter, "The early elementary schools were extremely simple and unorganized."[15] Additions and modifications occurred, yet the schools remained highly authoritarian in nature, drawing on rote knowledge obtained from teachers and textbooks. As a result of the importation of educational ideas from Europe, those of Pestalozzi,[16] for example, the elementary school gradually began to change. The position of the reformers was stated by Cubberley: "Reading, writing, arithmetic, grammar, geography, and history, the staples of the elementary school curriculum, are really of little value except as they are closely related with the needs and problems of our social, civic, and industrial life."[17] John Dewey with his systematic attack upon the school and his philosophy of education based upon "the belief that genuine education comes through experience. . . ." became the leading school reformer.[18] His philosophy and writing dramatically changed the character of the elementary school from one of teacher-materials centeredness, coupled with strict obedience of students, to one of focus upon the children—their interests, ideas, and active participation. This change was of extreme importance, since it produced an atmosphere conducive to guidance and counseling in the elementary school.

Another important development in the history of elementary education was the National Education Association Committee of Fifteen's recommendation for professional preparation of teachers.[19] The need for training seminaries originally was suggested by William Russell in 1823 and had long been emphasized in the work of Henry Barnard; yet widespread implementation awaited the Committee of Fifteen's recommendation.[20] Furthermore, teacher training was given direction and continuity as strong emphasis was placed on child study and the understanding of children. This concern for children had special implications for elementary school counselors, since it established a need for guidance and the advent of a specialist in this area. Thus, the final step in the development of the elementary school, according to Hillway, was that "health and guidance units have been added. . . ."[21]

In summary, the elementary school has evolved from a rigid, limited institution providing reading and writing skills along with religious instruction to a complex unit of diversified offerings including guidance services. Such growth has reflected the social and political motives of the people and has been of an additive nature. So it is not presumptuous to conclude that many elementary schools may be in need of unifying curriculums addressing present-day needs of their children. The elementary school counselor may be the instigator and facilitator of change in the school. Also, though the counselor may focus on the elementary school—its curriculums and student body— care must be taken to recognize the importance of preschool or kindergarten education, so that smooth transitions may be made by all children in the sequential process of education. Indeed, the preschool is our beginning.

Notes

1. William Lucio, "Elementary Education-Development," in Chester W. Harris (ed.), *Encyclopedia of Educational Research,* 3rd rev. ed. (New York: Macmillan, 1960), pp. 412–421.
2. Edwin Grant Dexter, *A History of Education in the United States* (London: The Macmillan Company, 1914), p. 28.
3. Lucio, *op. cit.,* p. 413.
4. Dexter, *op. cit.,* p. 156.
5. *Ibid.,* p. 217.
6. Paul Monroe, *Founding of the American Public School System* (New York: Macmillan, 1940), pp. 39–42.
7. Lucio, *op. cit.,* 1413.
8. Ellwood P. Cubberley, *Changing Concepts of Education* (Boston: Houghton Mifflin, 1909), pp. 27–30.
9. *Ibid.,* pp. 30–31.
10. *Ibid.,* p. 34.
11. *Ibid.,* p. 51.
12. *Ibid.,* p. 39.
13. Ellwood P. Cubberley, *Readings in Public Education in the United States* (Boston: Houghton Mifflin, 1934), p. 276.
14. *Ibid.,* p. 280.
15. Dexter, *op. cit.,* p. 155.
16. Cubberley, *Readings in Public Education in the United States, op. cit.,* p. 302.
17. Cubberley, *Changing Concepts in Education, op. cit.,* 1413.
18. John Dewey, *Experience and Education* (New York: Collier-Macmillan Ltd., 1938), p. 25.
19. Lucio, *op. cit.,* 1413.
20. Henry Barnard, *Normal Schools and Other Institutions, Agencies and Means Designed for the Professional Education of Teachers* (Hartford, Conn.: Case, Tiffany & Co., 1851), p. 11.
21. Tyrus Hillway, *American Education: An Introduction Through Readings* (Boston: Houghton Mifflin, 1964), p. 180.

Guidance at the Preschool Level

Ruth J. Tasch

Introduction

At the preschool level "guidance" is more than a unidimensional concept. It has two components: developmental or preventive, and diagnostic and treatment. Both aspects have the same objective, namely, that for the development and maintainance of the healthy personality, the environment must be manipulated in such a way (i.e., by maximizing strengths and dealing with weaknesses) that the child can experience triumph over frustration. The goal is, in the end, to tip the balance between success and failure in favor of success* (9, 15, 16B).

There are three main thrusts in the developmental (preventive) approach:

> *(1) The School Program.* With the child's abilities used as a guideline, the daily program is structured in such a way as to ensure that the child will experience a reasonable amount of success in his daily activities.

> *(2) Teacher Behavior.* An offshoot of the daily program, and yet interwoven with it, is the role of the teacher, for she is the prime instrument in creating within the school situation a psychologically healthful climate in which the child can function in his encounters with the physical environment and his relationships with both his peers and adults.

> *(3) Parent Education.* Recognizing the pervasiveness of the parental influence and the limitation of the teacher's influence in

"Guidance at the Preschool Level" is an original article written for this book. Ruth J. Tasch is Associate Professor of Education at Wichita State University. She also serves as Institutional Coordinator of the Head Start Supplementary Training Program in Wichita.

* This is not to deny the value of the struggle in Erikson's (7) terms. Erikson points out that the negative aspects serve an important function in the final successful accomplishment of the developmental task (7, 8).

41

the guidance of the preschool child, the teacher works with parents (by involvement and education) to the end that the child is consistently enveloped in an emotionally and functionally sound environment.

Examination of the status of diagnosis and treatment brings a complex situation to light. Because of the many types of group settings in which preschool experiences are provided (e.g., the two-and-a-half-hour daily program, the two-and-a-half-hour program operating either two or three days a week, the Sunday school program, the twelve-hour day care program, etc.), and the diversity of auspices under which these "preschools" are sponsored (churches, private operators, United Fund, government agencies, etc.), a good deal of variation exists in the way in which help is sought and provided for the "problem" child.

(1) Parent Referral. Although most schools have a medical doctor on call for emergencies, when psychological problems arise with which the teacher cannot cope, the child may either be excluded from the classroom or the teacher may ask the parents to contact appropriate personnel (i.e., a psychologist, psychiatrist, guidance or diagnostic center, etc.).

(2) The Guidance Counselor. The guidance counselor has not been a routine part of the preschool staff. However, there have been some indications since the advent of Head Start that this picture may change. Head Start, from its inception, has included adjunctive medical and paramedical services in its program (19B).

(3) Newer Approaches. Recent experimental approaches are providing some innovative trends in teacher training (16B, 29), consultative services from "child development generalists" (16B), the psycho-educational team (25) in the therapeutic nursery school, and community mental health services for children and parents (16B).

The Educational Experience

Because there is yet so much unfinished business in the growth and development of the "before-school" child, the educational experience at the preschool level is a significant one. It has great potential. The chances for a positive outcome are good because of the malleability of the emerging personality.

The Daily Program

The kinds of encounters the child has with his preschool environment are crucial for his psychological well-being. The approach to programing permeates every aspect of the daily schedule whether it involves large muscle development; imaginative, cognitive, and sensory experiences; social interaction; or emotional growth. Therefore, the way in which the day-to-day activities in the classroom are mediated has important consequences for the child's mental health and personality development.

Ideally, the program should take into account the developmental status and developmental tasks of this age group from the choice and arrangement of equipment to the opportunities available to the child so that he may develop his sense of autonomy and initiative (in Erikson's sense (7)). Some examples illustrate this point. If the child is presented with a task involving finer motor coordinations, such as tying a bow on his shoelace, buttoning his coat, pounding a nail with a small head into a piece of hard wood, coloring a picture with directions to stay within the lines, or even singing a song beyond his vocal range, or, if he is asked to make fine discriminations of shape, size, and color before he is ready developmentally, he is bound to fail. If he is shown a two-dimensional picture of an object rather than given opportunities for sensory exploration of a three-dimensional object by means of touching, feeling, examining, tasting, stroking, looking at, listening to—in other words, *first-hand experience*—he is not likely to form accurate and sound concepts of the object.

If he is at the stage where he is slowly emerging from his egocentric world, and is asked to "share" and "take turns" before he is ready, or if he is exposed to too much stimulation either from activities or other children, the occasions for promoting a sound psychological environment are not realized. If, in other words, the net effect of a day in the preschool environment has provided more chances for failure than success, the consequences of frustration upon frustration will lead to the kind of child who develops a negative self-concept, gives up easily, has tantrums, will not undertake new tasks, and has fewer encounters with his environment. He fails to find the world a place of wonder, of invitation to venture, to try, to see, and to explore. The teacher will find him a difficult child to deal with. He may become sullen, withdrawn, unfriendly. On the other hand, if a child becomes boisterous, demanding, and destructive because he does not have enough challenge in his daily activities, his needs are also largely unmet, and the preschool environment has been unproductive. Thus, it is obvious that the daily program plays a significant role in the guidance of the preschool child through the care and deliberation with which the stage is set, that is, the arrangement and selection of equipment, and the attention given to the provision of an appropriate daily schedule.

Teacher Attitude and Behavior

Much has been written about the characteristics of a good preschool teacher (2, 12, 15, 20) and what her role is in the preschool situation. Katherine Read has referred to the nursery school as "a human relationships laboratory" (20). And so it is, the teacher being the pivot upon which the mental health of the nursery school turns (27).* She sets the emotional tone. It is her attitude of acceptance and understanding that

---

* See: Dena Stone, *Children and Their Teachers* (27) for some negative examples.

creates the climate within which preschool children can function. Ruth Updegraff (28) calls her the "key" to the child's environment.

ATTITUDE. The first requirement for becoming accepting and understanding is for the teacher to be nonjudgmental, by adopting a questioning and probing attitude, using the scientific approach, asking "why?" "how did this behavior come about?" searching for reasons.

BEHAVIOR. It is generally agreed in the literature that positive reinforcement works best at the preschool level. One of the most widely quoted prescriptions appears in Katherine Read's book (20) in which she lays down fourteen "guides" to speech and action (p. 91). The gist of her advice to the teacher is to state and act positively rather than negatively. This will help the child to see himself as a learner who can achieve. He will develop a positive self-image and will perceive the teacher as a helping and encouraging person—a person who will help him in developing cognitive skills as well as emotional resources for dealing with jealousy, anger, and frustration; who will guide his growth impulses and help him find ways to manage his negative feelings.

ASSESSING THE TEACHER. How does one become a master teacher? Efforts have been made to sort out the ingredients. In an early study (22) an attempt was made to discover what distinguishes the master teacher from the novice. One conclusion that was reached was that the inexperienced teacher either overreacts or does nothing. The skilled teacher is able to time her activity to produce the desired results.

Another finding in this study was that the beginning teacher is reluctant to become involved in emotionally tinged or psychologically toned activities. She either ignores them or turns to more neutral types of activities such as helping children with their clothing, straightening out the construction paper, or occupying herself in some other part of the room. The author questions whether by emphasizing this kind of activity teachers are not "evading rather than meeting up with the realities in the lives of children;" by spending so much time on physical and material care, does the teacher "leave little time and emotional energy for deeper psychological involvement with children"? (22).

A more recent study (16B) sought "to isolate and define factors which make a good teacher good" (p. 9). The authors are of the opinion that preschool teachers "are not sufficiently attuned to the implications of making themselves available to children emotionally" (p. 9). In an attempt to determine the factors involved, an instrument is being developed that will isolate teaching styles (16A). This instrument is still being improved. At present, the focus is on two aspects of teaching style: (1) During the class time, what areas of behavior does the teacher attend to (e.g., the child's relationship to the physical surroundings, to other children, to his own feelings, etc.)? (2) What degree of responsibility does she assume for the behavior of the children in her classroom (e.g., walking away from the child, watching the child, verbal interpretation of the child's feelings, etc.)? Two teachers' methods have been analyzed by this scale.

Although this procedure is still in the pilot stage, the authors think that the method holds promise of validity because "a researcher who knew nothing of the children, teachers, or teaching 'philosophies,' could demonstrate the same aspects of differences in style that were apparent to experienced professional observers who knew the teachers and their work very well" (16A).

It is through studies of this kind that we may eventually be able to pinpoint some of the variables operating in the preschool environment that can have implications for good or ill in the developing personality of the preschool child.

Working with Parents

The goal of parent education, as in other areas of guidance, is to help parents gain insights into their relations with their children that will stimulate them to provide opportunities for the child's optimum growth in all aspects of development.

Parent education, in one form or another, has been on the scene since 1880. With time its philosophy has changed from information-giving to actively encouraging attitude change, participation through "sharing" (5), and parent "involvement" at all levels of participation (decision-making, establishing policy, teaching, etc.) (19).

Implicit in this approach is the recognition that any effort on behalf of preschool children can be only moderately successful if the parents are not involved. Home is the child's primary learning environment, and the few hours a week spent in nursery school cannot effect lasting changes (15, 32). One expert (10) goes even a step further and asserts that for the middle-class parent, at least, "teachers need to help parents see nursery school as an extension of the opportunities which the home offers, not a substitute or competitor." And another (32) emphasizes the point that since parents and other family members make up the preschool child's world, "what happens to the child at school must be related to what happens to him at home." She points out that the child is also a family member. For these reasons, many nursery schools are becoming increasingly family-centered, with parents serving on important committees and participating in significant ways in the running of the nursery school.

Traditionally there have been three principal methods used in parent education: literature and other mass media, group programs for parents, and educational counseling (1A). However, they all share the same objective: to increase the parent's competence in dealing with his children through a heightened self-awareness, an improved understanding of the parental role, and a better understanding of the processes of child growth;

or, as Bettelheim (4) says, to help parents "find a way of living more at ease with the children in their care" (p. 5).

LITERATURE AND OTHER MASS MEDIA. By far the largest appeal to parents has been through popular literature (6, 17, 21, 23). This does not deny the importance of radio, TV, and films; however, literature has a longer history and has enjoyed a wide audience (3, 11, 13, 24, 30). Its main focus has been on problems of development (e.g., fears, discipline, temper tantrums, thumb-sucking, toilet training, eating and sleeping routines) and how to deal with them. More recently, newer approaches, such as behavior modification, have come into vogue, and there is now available a self-instruction manual whose stated objective is to "provide a technique for handling certain problems of child management" (26). This type of literature is presently proliferating (31, among others).

It is hard to measure the effectiveness of this information-giving approach except over a long period of time, when it suddenly becomes apparent that the emotional climate in child-rearing is now "permissiveness" whereas earlier it was Watsonian objectivity and, even earlier, "Victorianism." Indications at present seem to be that we are in for still another change.

DISCUSSION GROUPS FOR PARENTS. Meetings of one kind or another dealing with child-rearing also have a long history. Although large meetings have been one technique, the small discussion group seems to have been more fruitful in effecting changes in attitudes.* The literature on this subject has largely been devoted to the mechanics and processes involved in conducting such discussion groups.† This emphasis continues to occupy a central role. To illustrate, a recent book (1B) is devoted to a detailed analysis of the mechanics—the role of the leader, topics for discussion, setting the meeting, dynamics of group interaction, etc. Another (4) is more concerned with process. Bettelheim argues for the scientific attitude, probing for the reasons for the behavior: "Why does the child behave this way?" "What is behind the observed behavior?" "Why does the child want attention?" He evaluates this approach as successful because he found that those parents in his group who, four years earlier, were asking for the "right" answers, now tackled a problem by setting out to "discover what was wrong" (p. 16). (Parenthetically, it might be remarked that both parents and teachers can profit from such an approach.)

As the value of small discussion groups as an effective educational technique becomes recognized, the qualifications of the leader will assume

---

* Even though it has been highly refined in some areas, it is still not a widely used technique in others. A survey in the writer's community, where nursery schools are largely privately operated, indicated that this method was rarely used.
† There are some types of discussion groups that use prescribed material as the basis of their discussions, however. An example of this type of group is illustrated in Ethel Kawin's *Parenthood in a Free Nation* series (14).

a more important role, and most likely, training for this specialty will receive more emphasis.

EDUCATIONAL COUNSELING. Probably, counseling of parents of preschool children is a more common practice than is generally recognized, because so often it is carried out informally. At one time or another, a variety of specialists have been involved in this type of relationship with the parent: the clergyman, pediatrician, general practitioner, nurse, and preschool teacher. In the writer's community, a survey indicated that telephone conversations or informal conferences either before or after school, when the child was brought or called for, represented the most frequent type of contact between parent and preschool teacher. The casework literature seems to indicate that a good deal of attention is given to parent counseling, and presumably the educational component is not overlooked.

Auerbach (1A), in assessing the status of educational counseling for parents, suggests that it is still in its infancy. Its value is apparent when specific help with an immediate problem is needed and other means are either unsuitable or ineffective. It has the advantage of a one-to-one relationship, which is essential in some situations, and it can be used in conjunction with other methods. As a matter of fact, none of these approaches is mutually exclusive, and they often are used interchangeably. However, where one method seems more suitable for a particular individual than another, it is used.

NEWER APPROACHES. The advent of Head Start has made a significant change in much of the current thinking about parent education. The attitude expressed by Gilkerson (10) that the school is an "extension of the opportunities which the home offers" can refer only to the middle-class home. The opposite premise seems more accurate in relation to the disadvantaged home, and this is the rationale behind the big push for parent involvement. Guidelines for classroom participation (19A) state: "In order to provide permanent and lasting benefits to the Head Start child, parents must learn why the classroom activities are planned and conducted as they are. By participation and observing in the classroom, parents can learn to continue in the home those activities and practices that will provide an atmosphere conducive to learning." The mother derives from the classroom "understanding of her child through other children, new ways of handling her child, understanding how a child grows and learns, understanding how school and home work together to help the child" (19A).

Implicit in this, of course, is the notion that parental ideals for children will become more consonant with the teacher's ideals; that through the parent's ability to impart skills (helping children to use books, work puzzles, learn to discriminate shapes and colors, classify, develop concepts, etc.), the child will become a more efficient person, experience success, and develop a positive self-image.

To bring about increased parental competence (19C), a many-pronged attack has been launched to reach mothers who are not working as teacher aides in Head Start classrooms. Home visits have been made by teachers with a view to helping mothers develop more skills that will ultimately benefit their children. Experimental programs such as the one at Juniper Gardens, Kansas City, have been undertaken. In this program mothers were given detailed instruction and training in learning positive reinforcement techniques that they could then use with their own children.

Active parent-education programs are a part of each Head Start center's activities. Consumer education and other skills (budgeting, sewing, knitting, cooking) are taught. A parent coordinator is part of the Head Start staff. Mothers are encouraged to take out library cards.

Parents constitute at least half of the policy advisory committee of each center, and thus they are actively engaged in running the center, from approving the staff to approving the program. They are getting experience in decision and policy making—another aim of Head Start (19E, p. 14).

For those parents who work in Head Start centers, opportunities are offered for taking college courses through the Supplementary Training Program. Behind all this is the philosophy that upgrading their own skills makes them more competent parents (19C).

With these newer approaches to the problems of parenthood, the emphasis has changed from "parent education" to "parent involvement," which describes more accurately what is taking place today in working with parents of disadvantaged children.

Therapeutic Intervention

Related to the educational aspects of guidance is the assumption that early detection and treatment of emotionally disturbed children can serve a preventive function. For this reason the preschool years are most important.

There are several fundamental notions related to diagnosis and treatment that should be reviewed:

(1) Diagnosis depends on assessing the strengths and weaknesses that the child has demonstrated in coping with his life situation up to that point and then utilizing these in the service of therapy by developing a treatment plan aimed at reinforcing the growth-promoting processes and ameliorating the growth-retarding forces (9, 16B, 25).

(2) The younger the child, the more difficult it is to make an adequate evaluation (16B, 25).

(3) The child is a family member and the parents must be involved in any diagnostic or treatment plans. In diagnosis, the parents are the main sources of information (providing the devel-

opmental history, presenting the problem, etc.) (9, 16B, 25). This is one of the main distinctions between child and adult psychiatry (9). Effective treatment requires the participation of the parents because of the interdependence of parent and child (9, 25).

(4) A team approach is desirable both for diagnosis and treatment, since these are collaborative processes and utilize the specialized methods of several professional disciplines (teaching, pediatrics, psychology, psychiatry, social work) (9, 25). The pooling of observations of different workers strengthens the picture (18).

(5) Observation in a variety of situations is indispensable, for it gives a more realistic picture and offsets biased and subjective judgments. (This can be of inestimable value to parents and teachers as well as the diagnostician.)

(6) In diagnosis, account should be taken of the multiplicity of causes. Especial attention should be given to organic disorders since they frequently can explain the basis for a child's behavior (more so, perhaps, than an adult's). For example, it is the child's attempt to compensate for defective vision or hearing or motor control (4) rather than "wilful misbehavior" that may account for his actions. These can have later consequences in "shyness, resistance and emotional upsets" (18).

(7) Treatment, especially management procedures, carried out in the social setting of the preschool classroom is preferable to removing the child for individual therapy (16B).

Change comes slowly and, while exciting innovations are taking place in large, experimentally oriented institutions, in the small, privately operated school, many teachers struggle as best they can using the resources of the pediatrician, or, if available, the services of a guidance clinic. Pace-setting will remain the role of the well-endowed experimental facility, and since the experiments of today will become, it is to be hoped, the way of life for tomorrow, it would seem appropriate to close this paper with a report of an imaginative program being conducted at the Eliot Pearson Department of Child Study at Tufts University (16B).

Under a National Institute for Mental Health grant, a new specialty is being developed: the child development "generalist." This is a person with specific skills concerning the preschool child—skills in understanding the emotionally disturbed youngster and his family in the community. This generalist is more than a teacher, yet she will work with teachers and design management procedures and remedial play experiences for young children. She is more than a consultant, although she will make herself available to the teacher to observe, screen, and consult and help teachers work out intervention plans for problem children. These treatment programs are mediated through the classroom teacher rather than in individual therapy, which is never used. If a teacher works on an individual problem with the mother and child, she uses the school setting wherever possible.

There is a good deal of outreach into several clinics in neighboring communities. In one such (the Somerville Guidance Center), a pilot therapeutic nursery was established along these innovative lines. Teachers, besides teaching the group, maintained regular contact with the parents either by telephone or home visits. On these occasions, they focused on the problems of management at home, interrelationships of home and school activities, and appropriate school placement for the coming year. Parents were invited to observe both teacher and child through an observation booth in the classroom. There was a great variety of tasks that were performed, including the intellectual and mental-health screening of 300 Head Start children.

The authors think this preschool unit can be regarded as a model in community mental-health services for young children and their parents. It is a community-based diagnostic and treatment facility, and the directors feel that it "will bridge the gap between institutions as they exist today and a basic social system approach in primary prevention" (16B, p. 7).

These are some of the directions the newer approaches to diagnosis and treatment will take. The troubled youngster will not be isolated. He will be treated in the context of his group. Teachers will have expanded roles to play and will be called upon to try themselves in new and unexpected ways. There will be a new level of home-school cooperation. Working with "problem" preschool youngsters will become a mind-stretching, imagination-stretching, and exciting enterprise, and, in the final analysis, a rewarding experience.

Selected References

1A. Auerbach, Aline B. *Trends and Techniques in Parent Education: A Critical Review.* New York: Child Study Association of America, 1960. 37 pp.

1B. ———. *Parents Learn Through Discussion.* New York: Wiley, 1968. 358 pp.

2. Bacmeister, Rhoda. *Teachers for Young Children—The Person and The Skills.* Early Childhood Education Council of New York: undated. 18 pp.

3. Baruch, Dorothy W. *New Ways in Discipline.* New York: McGraw-Hill, 1949. 280 pp.

4. Bettelheim, Bruno. *Dialogues with Mothers.* New York: Free Press, 1962. 216 pp.

5. Beyer, Evelyn. *Sharing—A New Level in Teacher-Parent Relationships.* Washington, D.C.: National Association for the Education of Young Children, 1959. 10 pp.

6. Child Study Association of American Pamphlet Materials. 9 East 89th Street, New York, New York. Representative titles.

7. Erikson, Erik H. *Childhood and Society.* New York: Norton, 1963. 445 pp.

8. Evans, Richard I. Filmed Interview with Erik Erikson. Houston, Texas: University of Houston, 1964.

9. Group for the Advancement of Psychiatry. *The Diagnostic Process in Child Psychiatry.* Report No. 38. New York: GAP Publications, 1957. Pp. 313–355.

10. Gilkerson, Elizabeth. *Teacher-Child-Parent Relationships.* Brooklyn, New York: Early Childhood Education Brooklyn College Council, 1955. 10 pp.

11. Ginott, Haim. *Between Parent and Child.* New York: Macmillan, 1965. 223 pp.

12. Gore, Lillian L., and Rose Koury. *Educating Children in Nursery Schools and Kindergartens.* Bulletin No. 11, OE–20054. Department of Health, Education, and Welfare, Office of Education. Washington, D.C.: U.S. Government Printing Office, 1964.

13. Hymes, James L., Jr. *Understanding Your Child*. Englewood Cliffs, N.J.: Prentice-Hall, 1958. 188 pp.
14. Kawin, Ethel. *Parenthood in a Free Nation*. New York: Macmillan. Vols. 1–3. *Manual for Group Leaders and Participants*. Chicago: American Foundation for Continuing Education, 1966.
15. Langford, Louise M. *Guidance of the Young Child*. New York: Wiley, 1965. 347 pp.
16A. Braun, S. J., Mathilda S. Holzman, and Miriam G. Lasher. *Teachers of Disturbed Preschool Children: An Analysis of Teaching Styles*. Mimeographed. Presented at American Orthopsychiatric Association Meeting, 1968. 17 pp.
16B. Lasher, Miriam G., and S. J. Braun. *Preschool Teachers of Emotionally Disturbed Children*. Progress Report from July 1966–August 1967 to National Institute for Mental Health, United States Health Service. Mimeographed. 31 pp.
17. Human Relations Aids, 419 Park Ave. So., N.Y. 10016. Child Training Leaflets. 21 titles.
18. Murphy, Lois B. *Problems in Recognizing Emotional Disturbance in Children*. New York: Child Welfare League of America, Inc., 1963. Pp. 473–487.
19. Office of Economic Opportunity, Project Head Start. Washington, D.C.: U.S. Government Printing Office.
    (A) *Criteria for Evaluating a Head Start Parent Participation Program*, 1968, 0–296–983. Unpaged.
    (B) *An Invitation to Help*. 64 pp. Undated.
    (C) *Head Start Newsletter*. September 1968, v. 3, No. 5. 8 pp.
    (D) *Parents are Needed*. No. 6 of Rainbow Series, 1967, 0–247–830. 16 pp.
    (E) *Points for Parents*. No. 10 of Rainbow Series, 1967, 0–247–832. 28 pp.
20. Read, Katherine. *The Nursery School (A Human Relationships Laboratory)*. 4th ed. Philadelphia: Saunders, 1966. 371 pp.
21. Ridenour, Nina. *Some Special Problems of Children—Age 2 to 5 Years*. Philadelphia: National Mental Health Foundation, 1949. 72 pp.
22. Rigney, Margaret. *Practices of Teachers in Dealing with Preschool Children*. Unpublished Ph.D. dissertation, New York: Teachers College, Columbia University, 1952.
23. Ross, Helen. *Fears of Children*. Chicago: Science Research Association, 1952. 49 pp.
24. Ruben, Margarete. *Parent Guidance in the Nursery School*. New York: International Universities Press, 1960. 72 pp.
25. Selligman, Augusta. *A Day Residential Program for the Disturbed Pre-School Child*. New York: Child Welfare League of America, Inc., 1958. Pp. 16–19.
26. Smith, Judith M. and D. E. P. *Child Management (A Program for Parents)*. Ann Arbor, Mich.: Ann Arbor Publishers, 1967. 100 pp.
27. Stone, Dena. *Children and Their Teachers*. New York: Twayne, 1957. 280 pp.
28. Updegraff, Ruth. *Practice in Preschool Education*. New York: McGraw-Hill, 1938. 408 pp.
29. Sperber, Z., and H. Adelman. *Empirical Evaluation of a Training Program for Preparing Teachers of Emotionally Disturbed Pre-School Children*. Paper presented at American Orthopsychiatric Association Annual Meeting, Chicago, 1968. Dittoed.
30. Wolffheim, Nelly. *Psychology in the Nursery School*. New York: Philosophical Library, 1953. 144 pp.
31. Valett, Robert E. *Modifying Children's Behavior (A Guide for Parents and Professionals)*. Palo Alto, Calif.: Fearon Publications, 1969. 66 pp.
32. Woodruff, Myra. *Parents and Teacher Work Together*. Washington, D.C.: Association for Childhood Educational International, Leaflet No. 12, Nursery School Portfolio, 1960–61.

Changing Curriculum of America's Schools

John I. Goodlad

Today's educators have a formidable task in seeking to select what to teach, especially in cumulative fields such as the natural and behavioral sciences. If this accumulation is plotted on a time line, beginning with the birth of Christ, it is estimated that the first doubling of knowledge occurred in 1750, the second in 1900, the third in 1950, and the fourth in 1960.

Whether or not these are only rough approximations, they have impressed upon educators an inescapable fact, well stated by Professor Schwab of the University of Chicago: It is no longer merely difficult to select and package for instruction the most important bits and pieces of knowledge; it is impossible! The search is on for something more lasting than "the bits and pieces" emerging as residue from the advance of knowledge, something more permanent around which to organize learning.

Some of the guiding questions are old ones. What is worth knowing? What knowledge prepares for the acquisition of new knowledge? What kind of education is most likely to help individuals become self-propelling during a lifetime of learning?

Clearly, a massive reformulation of what is to be taught and learned in the schools of the United States is under way. Talk of the "new" mathematics, the "new" physics, and the "new" biology is now commonplace. Various scholarly groups and individuals, handsomely supported by the National Science Foundation—and, to a lesser degree, by private philanthropic foundations—have developed new course outlines and instructional materials for mathematics, physics, chemistry, biology, anthropology, economics, geography, English, and foreign languages. New

"Changing Curriculum of America's Schools," *Saturday Review* (November 16, 1963), 65–67, 87–88, has been reprinted with the permission of the author and of the publisher. Copyright 1963 Saturday Review, Inc. Dr. Goodlad is Dean of the Graduate School of Education of the University of California, Los Angeles.

textbooks are in wide use, both in this country and abroad. Tens of thousands of teachers and students in elementary and secondary schools have participated in the preparation and trial use of these materials. Many of these teachers and thousands more have attended institutes on the new content and how to teach it.

The beginnings of the current curriculum reform movement are commonly identified with the successful launching of the first Russian satellite in the fall of 1957. This spectacular event set off blasts of charges and countercharges regarding the effectiveness of our schools and stimulated curriculum revision, notably in mathematics and the physical sciences. But the roots of change go back further, to the years immediately following World War II. The recruitment of young men for the armed services had revealed shocking inadequacies in the high school science and mathematics programs of high school graduates. The problem was partly the limited quantity of work in these fields, partly the quality of what had been taken. The high school curriculum too often reflected knowledge of another era, not the scientific advances of the twentieth century. Recognizing their responsibility for this unhappy state of affairs, scholars in a few fields began to participate actively in what has now become a major curriculum reform movement.

Sometimes an individual took the initiative, sometimes a learned society (the American Mathematical Society, for example), prompted by a few articulate members. In either case, the subsequent course of events was surprisingly similar from project to project. First, a group of scholars came together to review the need for pre-collegiate curriculum change in their field. Then, in subsequent summers, scholars and teachers invited from the schools planned course content and wrote materials. These materials were tried out in cooperating schools during the regular school year and revised in the light of this experience. Meanwhile, in summer and year-long institutes, teachers were educated in the new content and methodology. Throughout, participants have been agreed, apparently, that new materials are central to basic curriculum change.

The current curriculum reform movement is now too far advanced to warrant the adjective "new." In some fields, notably mathematics, the first wave is about to be followed by a second. The "new" new mathematics is in the offing.

There is grave danger, however, in assuming that curriculum change has swept through all of our 85,000 public elementary and 24,000 public secondary schools during this past decade of reform. Tens of thousands of schools have been scarcely touched, or touched not at all, especially in areas of very sparse or very dense populations. Tens of thousands of teachers have had little opportunity to come to grips with what advances in knowledge and change in subject fields mean for them. Tens of thousands hold emergency certificates or teach subjects other than those in which they were prepared. In elementary schools, teachers with any appreciable backgrounds in science and mathematics constitute a species that is almost as rare as the American buffalo.

Suburban schools have fared well by comparison, with extensive participation in curriculum projects, ability to attract qualified teachers, and resources for providing in-service education. The gap between the haves and have-nots persists and, in some ways, is accentuated.

Curriculum planning is a political process, just as it is an ideological process of determining ends and means for education. Proposals must find their way successfully through the political structure into educational institutions or slip into obscurity. Almost without exception, those projects have had their genesis outside of the formal political structure, having been conceived primarily by scholars in colleges and universities who were joined by teachers from elementary and secondary schools.

Projects have been generously supported from funds that are predominantly federal in origin, testifying to the fact that the education of its youth is a primary interest of the nation. But the relationship among local, state and federal governments in the support and conduct of school affairs is a sensitive one that has materially affected the ways by which the various curriculum projects have entered the bloodstream of American education. Conditions of the grants have cautioned recipients against promoting their wares in any way; project directors have been limited to descriptive information, articles and, on request, speeches. But their efforts are in vain unless the benefits find their way to local schools and school systems. It is not surprising, therefore, that products, largely in the form of textbooks, often have been turned over to commercial publishers who have their own effective means of reaching state and local school authorities. These products now come into the schools through the expenditure of state and local funds. This whole fascinating series of events warrants further study.

The curriculum reform movement has been sharply focused on single subjects planned, generally, from the top down. This focus and the "national" character of the projects have attracted first-rate scholars into pre-collegiate curriculum planning. But these characteristics have also attracted scholars from fields not normally included in pre-collegiate schooling, who sense, apparently, a fresh opportunity to include their particular roads to the good life in the curriculum of elementary or secondary schools.

This competition among fields places severe burdens upon instructional time. Just how all of the subjects will share this time remains to be seen. Demands will exceed time, even if the school day, week, and year should be lengthened. Some subjects will have to be combined or left out —there is not room for twenty academic disciplines in the kindergarten. Arguments for the root nature and basic value of a discipline notwithstanding, problems of what subjects shall prevail are resolved largely in the political realm at federal, state, and local levels of educational responsibility, with national concerns largely determining the priorities today. Consequently, the humanities and social sciences will gain increasing favor with any appreciable reduction in world tension.

The strengths and weaknesses of the several projects stem in part from the nature of American education, with its characteristic strengths and weaknesses. For example, there is no single set of aims for America's schools; there are many. Therefore, each curriculum project is free to formulate objectives for its own particular segment of the curriculum. Some have; some have not. Rarely are objectives defined with such precision that one would know exactly what to evaluate in determining the success of a given project. It might be argued that those undertaking the various curriculum activities have no responsibility for the formulation of objectives; that local school districts set their own and gear materials to them. Each project is responsible only for setting forth what to teach in a given subject. But can ends and means be thus separated in any aspect of curriculum planning?

Although objectives are vague or not stated, documents describing the several projects express an almost uniform point of view. The current curriculum reform movement is seeking more in the student than the mere possession of information, however updated that information may be. The student is to sense *intuitively* the *structure* of a field. By "structure" is meant the concepts, principles, and methods that constitute the discipline. "Intuitive" refers to glimpses of abstraction that go beyond immediate practical experience. Sometimes the stated goal is for the student to think like the physicist or the historian.

Goals of this kind have a certain mystical quality. What does a student do when he senses the structure of a field intuitively or thinks like a physicist? How does a teacher decide that the student has acquired these commendable traits? And how are they best developed? Some project directors are deeply preoccupied with such questions. Others have brushed them aside, either because adequate answers appear to be hard to come by or because they believe that their programs already answer such questions reasonably well.

Most of the projects have sought to bring the student into the structure of the subject by identifying a few key concepts (number, quantity, energy, time, space, supply, and demand) which are to be developed persistently and with increasing depth over several years of schooling. The curriculum is thus organized into units, each unit progressing in difficulty and both reviewing and extending one or more concepts introduced earlier in the student's experience. Very often, the subject-matter is similar to that of conventional programs. But the treatment called for is different. For example, the textbook for grade 9 in the program produced by the School Mathematics Study Group concentrates on algebra, as is common in conventional curricula. Emphasis, however, is on the behavior of numbers rather than the solving of algebraic equations.

Some of the new programs depart radically from conventional content. Suppes and his associates, in their Experimental Project in the Teaching of Elementary School Mathematics at Stanford University, are developing their instructional materials around the concept of set. A set is simply any collection or family of objects. The putting together of sets of physical objects is a more concrete operation than the addition of numbers. According to Suppes, operations on sets—rather than the more abstract and difficult operations on numbers—permit the child to understand the way a number is related to a set of objects and lays the groundwork for the abstractions constituting mathematical thought. This is quite different from the arithmetic most of us learned in the primary grades!

Those involved in the various curriculum projects may have started out to reform the *content* of their fields, but few stopped there. In many instances, content has been pushed down or expectations for the year increased. There sometimes is provision for gifted high school students to go as much as two years into work normally reserved for college. Throughout, as noted earlier, emphasis is upon unifying concepts, principles, and methods of inquiry, with each successive topic designed to develop a central theme or element. Usually, subject matter is very carefully arranged— "programed" in the jargon of the trade—in a step-by-step sequence. Often, self-instructional programed workbooks accompany the familiar textbook. By means of these workbooks, students are able to work independently and at their own speed part of the time.

Perhaps the most comprehensive instructional package is that produced by the Physical Science Study Committee for a year-long course in high school physics. The first tool of learning is a new textbook, carefully developed by a team of outstanding physicists working in collaboration with high school teachers. Other tools include laboratory experiments and bits of simplified apparatus, a set of films, achievement tests designed to test the application of knowledge and techniques to new problems, a library of paperbound books on special and related topics, and a teacher's guide. Neither laboratory activities nor films are supplementary or for enrichment. Films demonstrate experiments that go beyond the confines of high school laboratories or otherwise provide a perspective not attainable in the classroom. Textbooks, films, laboratory experiments, and class discussions are planned to fit into a consistent, unified whole. With such tools so conveniently available, teachers' talk and chalk are extended as never before.

With grade placement of content determined, and with textbooks, teachers' guides, and supplementary materials published, some project directors see their work as nearing completion. Fearful that the relentless quest for knowledge in their own fields will pass them by, they are anxious to get back to research and teaching, usually maintained only with tag ends of energy during project years. Others, however, have become inescapably caught up in those fascinating learning and pedagogical problems that have alternately intrigued and frustrated psychologists and educationists. Patrick Suppes, for example, of the Stanford Institute for Mathematical Studies in the Social Sciences, as much a psychologist as a mathematician, wants to know what mathematics young children can learn, what they learn with ease and what with difficulty, and why. His materials on sets and numbers for the primary grades are little more than by-products of his central activity.

David Page, now of Educational Services Incorporated in Watertown, Massachusetts, is not enamored with the search for precise grade placement of subject matter. He seeks, instead, what he calls an "intermediate invention" of great power: power to stimulate an almost infinite number of mathematical operations, power to incorporate most of the basic mathematical concepts and principles, power to absorb and challenge children of vastly differing abilities. In one of his intermediate inventions, "maneuvers on lattices," children explore general rules, laws, and proofs for numbers through a simple table of numbers and a system of arrows variously pointing up, down, to left, to right, and diagonally. With the teacher's sweep of an eraser and scratch of the chalk, a new set of stimuli is on the board before the class. The limits of exploration and invention defy grade barriers. There is something here for children of all ages.

Although there are gross similarities in approach among the several dozen curricular projects now under way, probing reveals marked differences. Mathematics, with an array of projects embracing both elementary and secondary education, again provides an excellent illustration. Is mathematical insight enhanced by the verbalization of concepts? The organization of some projects reveals the careful coordination of mathematical operations and their verbal counterparts. Others, however, are casual in their concern for and approach to this question.

Beberman and his associates of the University of Illinois Committee on School Mathematics maintain that the early, often glib and incorrect, verbalization of mathematical concepts inhibits or distorts insight. They believe that precise verbalization is necessary for purposes of communication and proof, but this verbalization should come *only after* the individual has become thoroughly familiar with the generalization and has had adequate opportunity to test and refine it. "Precise communication is a characteristic of a good textbook and a good teacher; correct *action* is a characteristic of a good learner."

Mayor and his associates of the University of Maryland Mathematics Project seek a close and supporting relationship between the verbal and the operational components of mathematics. Both the sequence of mathematical operations and the appropriate vocabulary for them should be planned side by side and pedagogy designed to promote the simultaneous attainment of both.

Page, in the University of Illinois Arithmetic Project, is impatient with "the hindering verbiage (minuend, dividend, partial product, and the rest)'' of conventional arithmetic. He seeks what he calls "new frame-works for mathematical ideas" through which children are challenged to explore mathematics—to develop, invent, and extend. Page avoids technical language in his teaching, encouraging children to invent their own, which, he says, often is better. They will come to the use of precise language soon enough, he thinks, when situations demand appropriate communication.

One of the shortcomings of the current curriculum reform movement, running almost uniformly through the projects, is the poverty of data regarding their effectiveness. There are, indeed, gratifying testimonials from teachers and students who have been involved. But are students learning fundamental concepts better than they did in conventional programs? If so, does insight into these concepts provide increased power in dealing with unfamiliar problems? Are all students able to proceed satis-factorily and with satisfaction to themselves in the new mathematics, physics, chemistry, and biology, if allowed adequate time? If so, does this place a solid high school curriculum in these subjects within the reach of all?

Most of the testing to date has compared students in new curricula with students in the old, using test items based on the latter. This is hardly fair to the new ventures. Nonetheless, students in the new curricula have shown up about as well as their counterparts on these conventional achievement tests, except where vocabulary or other specific memory items were called for. In those few instances where students in new curricula have been compared with students in the old using items thought to be more appropriate to the former, students in the old have performed rather poorly.

The scarcity of evaluative data has been defended on the ground that an overwhelming job of curriculum reform had to be accomplished quickly. Time and resources have not yet permitted broad-scale appraisal. The argument has merit. Nonetheless, one must still regret the dispropor-tionate attention to evaluation in projects that sometimes have gobbled up as much as a million dollars a year, not collectively but individually. By and large, the several projects have been conducted apart from the regular teaching and degree-granting structure of universities. Consequently, there have not been the theses and dissertations that might have been stimulated otherwise.

Prospects for the future look somewhat brighter. Several projects have built long-term evaluation into their fiscal and personnel policies. Some have contracted with private testing agencies for the preparation of instruments appropriate to project goals. These provisions, in turn, should force the more precise definition of each project's goals.

The most significant question for the future is whether the current curriculum reform movement, long overdue, has built-in mechanisms to guarantee continuing self-renewal. Are present accomplishments to be enshrined within the covers of textbooks, there to remain (with periodic minor revisions) until some crisis precipitates another massive reform? The answer probably depends on whether or not highly competent, dedicated educators can either reproduce their own kind or attract successors of like competence and reputation into the enterprise. This, in turn, depends on the continuing intellectual challenge of that enterprise.

First-rate curriculum development demands the coordination of a vast array of resources: subject matter specialists, experienced teachers, educationists with a broad understanding of the schools, psychologists, programers, film makers, publishers, and skilled managers to get the most out of this talent. Experience has shown that scholars will participate for a few days during the year and for several weeks during the summer. But pre-collegiate curriculum building is not their primary interest. Nor is textbook writing a rewarded activity in universities. Some psychologists are interested in the learning problems involved but the contribution demanded of them usually is of an applied rather than a basic research nature. Most of the problems are of central concern to educationists but their interests usually cut across subject lines. They know only too well the difficulties of putting together all the separate subjects so that a reasonable and realistic curriculum emerges. Further, they are more than a little skeptical about establishing pre-collegiate curriculum building as an ongoing university enterprise in view of their own long-term frustrating efforts to have such activity recognized as important by the academic community. If the current effort is to continue with vigor, it must either become established within the research and development framework of universities or be taken over by new institutions capable of reaching both the resources needed and the schools.

Whether the controlling agencies be universities or other nonprofit institutions, they must exert influence on the education of teachers. Today's teachers came up through the programs which they are now being asked to replace. The college curricula from which they graduated are in need of wholesale reform. To expect these teachers to depart radically from what they know best is expecting a great deal. Many are making the change—and experiencing a sense of adventure in doing so. But the big change in pre-collegiate schooling will come about in twenty years when today's children in changing schools are teachers—provided the present momentum of reform is maintained.

It is fair to say that the current curriculum reform movement has not yet developed effective means for influencing content and pedagogy in those colleges and universities preparing tomorrow's teachers, school leaders, and teachers of teachers. Until it does, it will not provide for continuing self-renewal.

A Cooperative Approach to Reading Disabilities

Coker J. Denton

The counselor and reading consultant have similar interests and responsibilities in helping the pupil and classroom teacher create an ecology for learning. Although the interests and responsibilities are similar, there are jurisdictional boundaries in treating reading disabilities that should be defined and respected. Such respect of jurisdictional boundaries should enhance the cooperative team approach to the remediation of reading disabilities.

The Reading Process

Reading is a psychological-physiological process that serves as the common denominator for the entire curriculum. A disability in one or more of the three basic skill areas—word identification and recognition, understanding the structure of writing, or basic locational skills—can cause moderate to severe anxiety for a youngster. Thus, it is important that the classroom teacher, the counselor, and the reading consultant understand the jurisdictional responsibilities and strive to coordinate and complement each others' efforts.

The critical period of reading development, in terms of the instructional process, is in the primary grades. From the psychological standpoint, the youngster must want to learn to read. He must believe that reading is a meaningful activity. From the physiological standpoint, the youngster must develop the skills of visual discrimination of the printed symbol and auditory discrimination of the sounds of the language. Thus, the two most important objectives for beginning reading instruction are (1) to create an

"A Cooperative Approach to Reading Disabilities" is an original article written for this book. Coker J. Denton was formerly Assistant Professor of Elementary Education and Director of the Reading Center at Wichita State University. Presently, he is Associate Professor of Education at Northeastern State College of Oklahoma, Tahlequah.

avid interest for reading and (2) to help the child to achieve mastery of the sound-symbol relationship.

Causes of Reading Disabilities

In simple terms, a cause of a reading problem can be anything that is detrimental to the objectives of reading instruction. Causes of reading problems generally fall into three broad categories: physiological factors, psychological or emotive factors, and instructional factors. Table 1 summarizes some of the more common causes.

Those factors that are generally regarded as physical should be referred to qualified medical personnel for diagnosis and treatment. The counselor and reading consultant should avoid the explicit or implicit diagnosis of a reading problem as having a physical cause. If a physical cause is suspected, the referral should be made and judgment withheld until the medical report has been received. The reading consultant and counselor are not conducting themselves in a responsible professional manner when they suggest to a classroom teacher or parent that a child has not learned to read because of ocular-manual laterality, or because he may be dyslexic, or may be suffering some other physical disability, when no medical examination has been obtained. The counselor and reading consultant can enhance their mutual trust by respecting the jurisdictional boundaries of the medical profession.

The Elementary School Counselor

Emotional disorders have long been credited as contributing factors to reading disabilities. Jastak and Jastak have pointed out that the child with inherent or intrinsic emotional disorders normally excels in the language arts.[1] However, the child who is experiencing extrinsic emotional disturbances in his environment at the critical time of learning basic skills may fail to learn to read. The counselor should be aware of the distinction between intrinsic and extrinsic emotional disturbances and their relationship to reading. The elementary counselor or school psychologist is the most qualified of the professional team to determine if there are extrinsic emotional disturbances at work in the child's environment, and he may make suggestions for their alleviation.

Table 1 suggests possible causes of extrinsic disturbances that might have an adverse effect upon a child learning to read. The counselor should examine the home and school environment of a pupil experiencing difficulties to determine if one or more conditions exist or existed at the critical time of beginning reading instruction.

The counselor should be responsible for supplying such specialized information as pupil-potential estimates, results of psychological tests, and personality assessments. The counselor should also, in conjunction with

TABLE 1
Causes of Reading Disabilities

Physical Factors	Emotional Factors	Instructional Factors
A. Poor vision	A. Intrinsic emotional disorders	A. Instructional breakdown
B. Poor hearing	1. Autistic	1. Mobility of child
C. Auditory-visual shifting	2. Schizophrenic	2. Mobility of teacher
D. Ocular-manual laterality	3. Paranoid	3. Rigidity of teaching
E. Neurophysiology-synaptic transmission	B. Extrinsic disorders	4. Inadequate teacher experience
F. Neurological organization	1. Parent-child relationships	5. Inadequate materials
1. Genetic	2. Peer relationships	B. Transfer of learning breakdown
2. Trauma causes	3. Marital discord in the home	1. From reading instruction to literature
3. Environmental deficiencies for devel-opment	4. Reaction to difficulties or failures in the initial learning task	2. From reading instruction to literature to the content area
G. Dyslexia	5. Teacher-pupil relationship	C. Attitudinal breakdown
H. Perceptual dysfunction		1. Failure to effect commitment to the reading process
I. Auditory dysfunction		2. Failure to effect commitment to the learning process
J. Tactile dysfunction		
K. Speech disorders		
L. Intellectual deficiencies		

Source: Leo Schell and Paul C. Burns, *Remedial Reading. An Anthology of Sources* (Boston: Allyn & Bacon, 1968), pp. 29–106.

the classroom teacher and reading consultant, provide the basic direction to the counseling services to be provided the child and his family. The counselor should assume the role of team leader, coordinating the professional services of the classroom teacher, reading consultant, and medical resources.

The Reading Consultant

The reading consultant should be knowledgeable in the instructional processes for teaching basic and developmental reading skills. He should be the most qualified of the team to determine if there has been a breakdown in the instructional process and to make recommendations for improving the instructional process.

Table 1 suggests possible causes of instructional difficulties. It is entirely possible that the breakdown in the instructional process causes more reading difficulties than physical deficiencies and emotional disturbances combined. The school must provide a flexible instructional program that will permit the child to learn to read regardless of his physical handicap or emotional problem. The discovery that a child has a specific problem should challenge the school to find a way to teach him. Once the problem is understood, the child must be taught to read. The reading consultant best contributes to the professional team approach by providing for better instructional processes for reading.

A Suggested Team Approach

The classroom teacher has the basic responsibility for the environmental comfort and reading success of the child. When a problem in learning is first suspected or detected, the teacher should confer with the building administrator and make referral to the elementary counselor.

The school nurse should provide the preliminary screening for vision and hearing deficiencies, and she should explore the pupil's background to determine if other physical causes for the problem might exist. If the preliminary screening indicates the need for further medical examination, the referral should be made to the proper medical personnel.

The counselor should confer with the classroom teacher and the reading consultant as to further diagnosis. The exploration of environmental variables, the determination of pupil potential, and any psychological testing should be done by the counselor. The reading consultant should be given the responsibility for determining the pupil's strengths and weaknesses in basic reading skills.

When all the data have been collected, decisions should be made as to procedures for making the teaching-learning process more effective. If physical impairments are discovered, the proper adjustments should be made. If environmental disturbances are detected, a team decision should be made as to possible procedures for alleviation.

Regardless of the original cause, instructional adjustments must be made. The pupil, perhaps, should be given individual help, or the instructional method should be changed from a "whole-word-symbol" approach to a "phonetic-symbol" approach or to a "linguistic-pattern-symbol" approach. Perhaps enough emphasis has not been given to making reading a truly meaningful experience for the child. This suggests offering more in-depth literature exposure, possibly through the medium of the tape recorder. Most children can be taught to read, provided remediation is started early enough and can be administered over the necessary extended period of time.

Summary

A team approach should be adopted toward the remediation of reading difficulties. The elementary school counselor should assume the role of team leader, coordinating the skills of the other team members. Each member of the team should respect the jurisdictional boundaries. The counselor and reading consultant should avoid the explicit or implicit crediting of reading difficulties to physical causes until a medical diagnosis has been obtained. The reading consultant should confine his activities to the instructional processes and leave the assessment of pupil potential, psychological tests, and personality to the elementary school counselor. The elementary school counselor should avoid dictating instructional processes and emphasize collecting needed data.

Note

1. J. F. Jastak and S. R. Jastak, *The Wide Range Achievement Test: Manual of Instructions* (Wilmington, Del.: Guidance Associates, 1965), p. 35.

References

Doland, G. K. "Counseling as an Aid for Delayed Readers," *Journal of Reading,* 8 (November 1964), pp. 129–135.

Fennimore, F. "Reading and the Self-concept," *Journal of Reading,* 11 (March 1968), pp. 447–451.

Gardner, J., and Ransom, G. "Academic Reorientation: A Counseling Approach to Remedial Readers," *Reading Teacher,* 21 (March 1968), pp. 529–536.

Gillham, I. "Self-concept and Reading," *Reading Teacher,* 21 (December 1967), pp. 270–273.

Kilanski, D. M. "Reading and Guidance Centers," *Reading Teacher,* 21 (May 1968), pp. 754–757.

Neal, C. M. "Relationship of Personality Variables to Reading Ability," *California Journal of Educational Research,* 18 (May 1967), pp. 133–144.

Wattenberg, W. W., and Clifford, C. "Relation of Self-concepts to Beginning Achievement in Reading," *Child Development,* 35 (June 1964), pp. 461–467.

The Process-Oriented Science Curriculum in Elementary Schools: Guidelines for Guidance

John M. Nickel

Introduction

The role of the elementary school counselor in bringing about change in science teaching is that of a catalyst. The dynamics of this catalysis imply a change in the teacher first, but not primarily. The primary thrust must be to help children process the "mega-data" they receive daily from their world. However, teachers must be changed before children can be allowed by the teachers to change. In mediating this change in teachers for the benefit of children, the elementary counselor acts as facilitator. The counselor's stance cannot be one of approachable aloofness. His role must be one of mediating change, first in teachers and subsequently in children.

The curricular hardware in elementary school science is available now. This hardware is materialistic in structure. It invokes artifacts from the child's environment upon the child, and the child is led to utilize and develop ways of thinking processively about the "stuff" being considered. Several elementary school curriculum projects are available for school personnel to scrutinize. A cursory inspection of the *Report of the International Clearinghouse on Science and Mathematics Curricular Developments,* compiled by J. David Lockard at the University of Maryland,[1] will exhibit in excess of seventeen American projects for grades K–6

"The Process Oriented Science Curriculum in Elementary Schools: Guidelines for Guidance" is an original article written for this book. John M. Nickel is Associate Professor of Science Education at Wichita State University. Also, he is Director of the South Kansas Science and Mathematics Project, Title III—ESEA, and consultant for the Engineering Concepts Curriculum Project.

alone. A number of projects are reported from foreign sources. This paper will discuss briefly only three of these projects, selected by the writer to display the concept of processiveness.

Generally speaking, few teachers in the elementary schools have any in-depth science training. Superintendents of schools will generally indicate that only a few elementary school teachers possess more than the minimum college science and/or mathematics training presently required for teacher certification. The number of semester credit hours required in Kansas, for instance, is twelve hours total in the areas of mathematics and the physical and biological sciences. Many teachers certified before the early fifties possess credit in only one college course in science and mathematics. At least one authority—James Conant—has stressed the need for a minimum of fifteen hours in mathematics and science for teachers in the intermediate grades. However, with the present level of training in science, teachers are reluctant to attempt any program in these subjects beyond having the pupils read the book and work the examples. This practice is prevalent throughout the United States. Major steps have been made recently to develop new curricular materials and equipment for use at the elementary school level. However, without the support of the elementary classroom teacher, essentially none of these improvements reach the children. In the final analysis, instruction in science is far inferior to that in any other subject taught in the elementary school.

The New Science Program

Of critical importance to school personnel is the question: How can we upgrade our elementary science program? In making the decision to adopt and support an elementary science program, the science specialist in a school district, the guidance counselor, the teachers, and the children should be involved. The following questions are suggested as guidelines:

(1) Is the new program educationally sound?

(2) Is the new program psychologically sound?

(3) Is the new program consistent with current scientific knowledge?

(4) Does the new program appeal to the classroom teachers who will implement it?

(5) What does the new program do for the children?

Each of the new elementary school science programs has been developed through the combined efforts of scientists, science educators, educational psychologists, and classroom teachers. These programs reflect the combined efforts of hundreds of individuals, not two or three, as has been the case in textbook writing. The development of the programs has involved extensive writing, testing, revision, continued evaluation, and modification to produce a workable program—but not a finished, static product. Revision and updating continue.

Textbooks stress the findings of inquiry to the exclusion of the process of inquiry. The new programs use the findings of inquiry as vehicles to teach the process. Consequently, both findings and processes are important. The teacher is the key to the success of any instructional process. Information available indicates that teachers who have worked with new curricular materials in science are enthusiastic to the point of wanting to continue using the materials. Butts states, "The effectiveness of curriculum innovation is directly dependent upon the preparation of the teacher. Where, how, and when is the teacher to secure this preparation? Change on the part of the teacher is at least dependent upon the degree and amount of administrative support for that change and the opportunity to experience and practice the 'new look' in the role that the teacher plays in the classroom. The opportunity for experience and practice must be part of the teacher education program directed by competent leadership staff." He continues, "The development of [teachers] is a crucial step in the process of implementation."[2] Butts states that an in-service training program has been designed to correct two faults:

> *(1)* Inadequate academic background to use the curriculum innovation, hence the need for a program to increase teacher competence in the subject area.
>
> *(2)* Inadequate teacher strategies to foster inquiry and individual responsibility in learning, hence the need for a program to increase teacher competence in teaching strategies for inquiry.[2]

What should science do for the child? "Science should provide the child with a set of skills that will enable him to explore anything that can be subjected to observation and investigation," relates Blankenship.[3] The present curricular projects have the potential to equip the child with these skills. The *AAAS: Science. A Process Approach* attitude toward science education is represented by the following excerpt from the statement of purposes and objectives, prepared by Professor William Kessen of Yale University with the assistance of a panel of consultants of the American Association for the Advancement of Science Commission on Science Education:

> Science is best taught as a procedure of inquiry. Just as reading is a fundamental instrument for exploring whatever may be written, so science is a fundamental instrument for exploring whatever may be tested by observation and experiment. Science is more than a body of facts, a collection of principles, and a set of machines for measurement; it is a structured and directed way of asking and answering questions. It is no mean pedagogical feat to teach a child the facts of science and technology; it is a pedagogical triumph to teach him these facts in their relation to the procedures of scientific inquiry. And the intellectual gain is far greater than the child's ability to conduct a chemical experiment or to discover some of the characteristics of static electricity. The procedures of scientific inquiry, learned not as a canon of rules but as ways of finding answers can be applied without limit. The well-taught child will approach human behavior and social structure and the claims

of authority with the same spirit of alert skepticism that he adopts toward scientific theories. It is here that the future citizen who will not become a scientist will learn that science is not memory or magic but rather a disciplined form of human curiosity.[4]

The Elementary Science Study program is described thus:

Primarily we hope to develop more meaningful science materials for use by children. Our program is a highly individual experimental one in which all children have access to the materials for open-ended rather than teacher or textbook directed investigations. Careful attention is given to all materials used so that all equipment looks like materials which are normally accessible to children in their own environment and not imposingly "scientific." A mixture of university scientists and master teachers work together in our laboratories and in classrooms to test and revise their ideas before the materials are used equally successfully in middle-class surburban and low socio-economic areas, large cities and small towns, and in a great variety of different situations.[5]

The purposes and objectives of the Science Curriculum study are stated as follows:

SCIS usually capsulizes its purposes as the development of scientific literacy. But it is important to delineate exactly what we mean by that term and how we hope to achieve this goal. The most obvious meaning of scientific literacy is a sufficient knowledge and understanding of the fundamental concepts of both biological and physical sciences for effective participation in twentieth century life. The role science plays in society is continually increasing in importance and will not be decided solely by the scientist but also by the non-scientist. To make wise decisions, the non-scientist will have to have an understanding of the real nature of science.[5]

A second implication of scientific literacy is the development of a free and inquisitive attitude and the use of rational procedures for decision-making. In the Science Curriculum Improvement Study (SCIS) program, children learn science in an intellectually free atmosphere where their own ideas are respected, where they learn to test their ideas by experiment, and where they learn to accept or reject ideas, not on the basis of some authority, but on the basis of empirical data. It is to be hoped that some of this experience will carry over to other areas of life and incline the children to make decisions on a more rational basis after weighing the factors, or evidence, involved more objectively.[6] Comments from children involved in the kind of approaches sketched here may be represented by the following: "When we learn it this way, we not only learn science, we also learn how to learn."

Summary

Science for elementary school children should be based on inquiry, experimentation, and open-ended teaching, using materials readily available from the child's own environment to develop a free and inquisitive attitude toward the concepts of the natural sciences. The elementary school guidance counselor has the potential to facilitate change.

Notes

1. J. David Lockard, *Report of the International Clearinghouse on Science and Mathematics Curricular Developments.* 1967. A joint project of the American Association for the Advancement of Science and the Science Teaching Center, University of Maryland.
2. David P. Butts, *Manpower Development,* Science Education Center, University of Texas (mimeographed manuscript), n.d.
3. Jacob W. Blankenship, "Elementary School Science for the 70's: Myth 'or Reality." Speech made at the Science Conference, Salina, Kansas, September 27, 1968.
4. Paul B. Sears and William Kessen, "Statement of Purposes and Objectives of Science Education in School," *Journal of Research in Science Teaching,* 2 (1964), p. 4.
5. Lockard, *op. cit.,* pp. 224–225.
6. *Ibid.,* pp. 338–339.

The New Social Studies and Elementary School Guidance

John H. Wilson

No part of the elementary school curriculum enjoys the degree of ferment and change that is being experienced by the social studies. Following in the shadow of science, math, and the language arts, where bold, new changes have taken place, the "new" social studies discipline evidences major changes in curriculum content and instructional strategies. Social studies projects, at the national level, are becoming more numerous and comprehensive, with stronger financial support.

The Social Studies—A Definition

There are as many definitions for the social studies in the elementary school as there are social studies texts for prospective teachers concerned with the subject of methodology. Each author selects the explanation of social studies that best complements his particular approach to instruction and learning in the subject. A common theme—human relations education —provides the direction for the definition of social studies that will be used in this article.

Instruction in the social studies involves an effort extended by the classroom teacher to help young learners understand the relationships they have with other human beings and the relationships they have with the remainder of their environment. This effort is enhanced by the knowledge, perception, and experience the teacher can draw from each of the social science disciplines, i.e., history, geography, anthropology, sociology, political science, economics, and psychology.

There are major organized ideas, or generalizations, that can be gleaned from these disciplines. An understanding of these can result in a more accurate appraisal of others' behavior, as well as provide aid and skill

"The New Social Studies and Elementary School Guidance" is an original article written for this book. John H. Wilson is Associate Professor of Elementary Education at Wichita State University.

in self-analysis. In short, social studies is the directed study of certain aspects of the social sciences for competence in human relations.

Objectives of Social Studies Education

Although competence in human relations remains the general objective for social studies, a clearer delineation of particular goals must be given. These objectives fall into the categories of: (1) knowledge or understanding, (2) attitudes and appreciations, and (3) skills.

Knowledge or Understandings

The effective social studies program will give an understanding of: the historical events that have shaped men's lives; the way our geographical location plays a part in our lives; the political and economic systems under which we and others live; other people of the world, beginning with our neighborhood; the influence social institutions have on our lives; and our and others' behavior.

Attitudes and Appreciations

The learner in a well-designed social studies program will be given many opportunities to develop values, appreciations, and attitudes that characterize the open-minded, sensitive, rational citizen in a democratic setting. Belief in and demand for the welfare of the individual are of paramount concern.

Skills

Individual and group inquiry skills are accentuated. Locating, gathering, and using information intelligently is taught in many instructional settings. Critical analysis, organization, and presentation of material are other important skills.

This very brief statement of the objectives of social studies for the elementary school learner is incomplete without an explanation of the approach that is suggested for meeting these goals. Traditionally, social studies instruction has been designed to explain the "what" of man's behavior. What has man been? What are his institutions? What is his relationship to others? A most important part of the "new" social studies is in the rephrasing of these questions to "why." Why has man been as he has? Why has man formed these particular institutions? Why has man related to others in the way that he has?

Instructional Strategies

The expository, textbook-centered social studies class is being vitalized with exciting new instructional practices. Multi-media presentation of materials, enhanced by a wealth of extra-text information, is becoming the rule. The ability to solve problems, think critically, and use the scientific method is emphasized in the problem-solving approach to learning. Other creative teaching strategies embody dramatization, role-playing and role-reversal, sociodrama and structured dramatization, puppets, open-ended and problem stories, bibliotherapy, and film problems.[1] The key to the changes in instructional practices is "involvement" of the learner. The learning situation is no longer teacher-centered, with one-way conversations. Students are encouraged to become active participants in the learning act, often to the point of planning, executing, and evaluating whole units of instruction. The role of the teacher could be more accurately defined as a guide and resource person in this setting.

Other Trends in the New Social Studies

The new directions for elementary school social studies are accompanied by other interesting trends. One such trend, found in most new social studies programs, is the more *formal* inclusion of all of the social science disciplines. Certain themes are stressed in focusing on the major ideas that are identified with each discipline. Complementing this trend is the move to place emphasis on the structure of key generalizations and methods of inquiry that have been cited by scholars as especially important. Words, concepts, concept clusters, and then generalizations are carefully developed, couched in social studies content. Student inquiry is promoted. Education in citizenship and cross-cultural understanding is gaining impetus, as are in-depth studies and improvement of the thinking processes. Independent study skills, earlier introduction of topics, and current affairs are other trends that have gained favor in the new programs.[2]

Selective Functions of the Social Studies[3]

The content and methodology of social studies instruction are relevant to the work of the elementary school guidance counselor. An important goal of counselors *and* social studies instructors is to provide information and skills that enable a student to understand himself and his relationship to others. The manner in which a study of the social studies can contribute to this objective follows. A brief comment about the function of each social science discipline that is included in the social studies and an example of how the development of one generalization can contribute to self-awareness are provided. Effective instruction in social studies at the elementary school level elucidates several such generalizations.

History

From the study of history, students gain insights into the many factors that shaped the past and present and that provide clues for predictions about the future. The student can learn the important lessons that most dependable answers have their beginnings, at least, in the historical review of the problems and that history is the report of people's behavior in strategic and unique situations. The results of this behavior are available for analysis, and it is hoped that learners can gain skill in predicting the consequences of their own actions because of this understanding of others' actions.

The teacher may choose to develop the generalization that a community is a product of its past and is restricted by its past. The learner should come to grips with the notion that he behaves as he does partly as a result of being a product of his particular community and its history. An understanding of this influence on his behavior will provide the learner with a clearer perception of himself as well as the knowledge of why others react to him as they do.

Geography

The study of geography concerns the causes and consequences of the location and spatial arrangements of things on the earth, man's home. Interrelationships between the physical earth and man's behavior are studied by developing an understanding of the physical earth itself, mental-image maps of spatial arrangement, and areal association. The student should learn that people are different in the way they use earth spaces or areas.

An important part of the development of one generalization in geography is the understanding that some communities are in farming regions, some are in fishing areas, some are in the forests, and some are in places where there are many factories. Each elementary school child is a member of a community and tends to behave according to the expectations held by most members of that community. That is to say, his geographic location affects his personality development. A knowledge of this natural tendency to mimic his peers helps the learner understand his and others' ways of life better.

Anthropology

Anthropology helps the learner bridge the gap between his self-concept and understanding of the social order by linking the biological and social sciences; it is a comparative study of man and his works. It focuses upon how culture is adapted to serve man's needs on the one hand and how man adapts to the cultural conditions on the other. Learning the techniques and observations of the anthropologist can help elementary school children achieve a sympathetic objectivity in exploring their own as well as other cultures.

A major anthropological idea concerns the similarity of people's needs and desires, no matter where they live. The ways in which different people satisfy their needs and their ways of living may be quite different from those of the student, but one is not necessarily better or worse than another, only different. Studies of others' cultural traits will aid in the development of tolerance and help to promote acceptance of self and others.

Sociology

Primarily the study of man's behavior in groups, sociology probes the functions, organization, changes, and interactions involved in group living. Characteristics of various groups found in society are compared and examined, with the emphasis placed on the influence these groups have on man's behavior. Data are collected and analyzed to aid in the accurate prediction of man's social behavior.

It is important for young learners to understand that people from many diverse social, economic, ethnic, and national groups have located in the United States. To understand the people, it is imperative that the structure of their groups be understood in relation to one's group. Children will gain a more accurate understanding of themselves in the process of comparing their group life with others.

Political Science

Man's political behavior and the area of social life concerned with consent, control, power, and authority are studied in the political science discipline, an important aspect of social studies. Both the opportunities and obligations of citizens in a democracy are treated.

Elementary school youngsters soon learn that rules and regulations are a part of community life everywhere and that the development of self-discipline enhances group and personal living. Experience with membership in "political" organizations within the school setting can provide additional insights that help learners appreciate the influence these groups have on their behavior.

Economics

Determining how limited resources can be utilized to serve almost unlimited wants of human beings is a major concern of the study of economics. Revealing how man's behavior is, in a sense, controlled by the values and beliefs of economic institutions in a highly industrialized society helps learners understand individuals' motivations and life styles more perceptively. A practical understanding of economic affairs can help elementary school children see their role in the larger economic system.

In our economic system, how much a person can earn and thus demand in goods and services is determined in accordance with how skilled he is and how much his skills are needed. Elementary school students can use this and other economic information as they begin to make inferences and draw conclusions about the influence man's economic condition has on his behavior.

Psychology

Included in many of the new social studies programs, psychology includes study of many of the following concepts and key ideas: individual differences, the senses, attitudes, motives, interests, the control of feelings, effective ways of learning, perceptions of self and others, and social roles. A more complete understanding of the many influences exerted upon one's behavior will give important insights to elementary school youngsters experiencing the quest for self-understanding. Couched in the social studies curriculum, this information is significant to the learner as he relates his own experiences to the study of others' lives.

The development of the generalization that individuals take different roles in different groups and situations can help a young learner understand his changes in behavior and attitude in differing situations. Virtually all social studies programs present these disciplines in an interdisciplinary manner, melding the organized ideas into the appropriate content at the level of readiness determined for each grade level. One important consideration is that unrelated "facts" from each discipline are not taught. Instead, the factual knowledge that learners must possess is developed to assure an understanding of important concepts, and these concepts are further developed to contribute to an acquisition of the major generalizations of each discipline. The disciplines are all interrelated, and any understanding of one discipline will assure some knowledge of others.

Some Implications for Counselors

Counselors can take advantage of the content of the social studies curriculum as well as the strategies of instruction that are employed by the classroom teacher as they seek ways to help young learners gain more accurate self-appraisals. Some suggestions follow; however, their successful implementation depends on a good working relationship between the counselor and the teacher.

1. A careful examination of the influence that is exerted upon a person's life because of the social institutions he and his family belong to can be achieved through role-playing.[4] Role-reversal activities, where one tries to perceive another's view of certain situations, can accentuate the child's understanding.

2. Learning about problem solution as approached by a historian can give the learner invaluable insights into his personal problems. The counselor can use a "case-history" or a socio-drama approach, calling on real or imaginary cases that inconspicuously delve into personal concerns.

3. The new social studies not only presents important anthropological understandings, it also gives students opportunities to practice the methods of study employed by anthropologists. The most productive study of other

cultures involves living in another culture and experiencing its unique characteristics. Counselors and teachers can use life-drama teaching techniques to help students gain important vicarious experiences with subcultural groups with whom previous contact may have been causing behavioral problems.

4. Other techniques that are of value to both the social studies teacher and the counselor include: (a) unfinished stories with human-relations overtones; (b) a film or filmstrip story with special significance for a single student or a group, which can be stopped occasionally for discussion and interpretation; (c) cartoons and comic strips that speak to identified problems; (d) bibliotherapy; the selection of a book or article that relates to an individual's concern; (e) dramatization which can help identify an emotional problem or provide insights into its possible solution; (f) field trips that can give experiences and information about situations that may be threatening to individuals or whole groups.

Summary

An understanding of the major ideas of social science disciplines is a useful tool for the student to utilize in attaining an objective and perceptive understanding of himself. Competent human relations must begin with an accurate perception of self and proceed to an understanding, appreciation, and tolerance of others. Thus, with the goals of social studies education so closely aligned to those of the school guidance counselor, their partnership seems a "natural."

When the counselor understands the nature of the instructional strategies employed by the classroom teacher in social studies, he can make helpful recommendations for special learners. The teacher can enlist the help of the counselor when he interprets the behavior that results from instruction in social studies sessions. The results that can accrue from a planned working relationship between these two agents of the elementary school are yet untapped.

Notes

1. James A. Smith, *Creative Teaching of the Social Studies* (Boston: Allyn and Bacon, 1967).
2. John U. Michaelis, *Social Studies for Children in a Democracy* (Englewood Cliffs, N.J.: Prentice-Hall, 1968).
3. Wisconsin Department of Public Instruction, *A Conceptual Framework for the Social Studies in Wisconsin Schools* (Madison, Wis., Department of Public Instruction, 1967).
4. Fannie R. Shaftel and George Shaftel, *Role-Playing for Social Values* (Englewood Cliffs, N.J.: Prentice-Hall, 1967).

PART III

Guidance in the Elementary School

ORIGINS AND GROWTH OF
ELEMENTARY SCHOOL GUIDANCE

To borrow Hermann Ebbinghaus' description of psychology, one can say that guidance has a long past, but a short history. In the form of advice, understanding, and help for children, guidance goes back to the beginning of man. This concern has reiterated itself down through the ages. William Stern relates: "at every period of human civilization, we find care, education, and instruction of the child . . . now we suddenly discover we have wandered blind and deaf for thousands of years."[1] Through insights gained from the behaviorial sciences, elementary school guidance enhances the growth, development, and instruction of children.

Many factors, such as Comenius' *Orbis Sensualium Pictus,* have contributed to our understanding of children.[2] Darwin's and Pestalozzi's observations of infants initiated systematic study of the child.[3] Preyer's study, at Leipzig, of the mind of the infant and Millicent Shinn's *Biography of a Baby* contributed to our understanding of the mental functioning and development of the child.[4] The psychology of Sigmund Freud, with its emphasis on the early years of life, provided impetus and direction for personality study,[5] and G. Stanley Hall's enthusiasm for child growth and development gave international emphasis to that field. Thus, by 1904, when Freudian concepts were shocking the world, societies for child study were developing in Britain, France, Germany, and the Scandinavian countries.[6] In addition, events from the field of testing and measurement contributed to the guidance movement. A psychological clinic for diagnosing mentally handicapped children was opened at the University of Pennsylvania in 1896.[7] At Columbia, James McKeen Cattell worked to measure individual differences.[8] In France, in 1905, Binet devised a test comprising a series of tasks to measure mental abilities. Later, Louis Terman revised this test, which became very popular in this country. All these events in psychology and measurement provided foundations for the guidance movement.

The guidance movement was formally launched in 1908 in Boston when Frank Parons established the Vocation Bureau at the Civic Service House.[9] During that year, Clifford Beers published his book *A Mind That Found Itself.*[10] The following year, in Boston, the first counselor-teacher in the elementary school was appointed.[11] In Chicago, in 1909, Dr. and Mrs. William Healy established a clinic for children,[12] and in Cincinnati, in 1911, Frank P. Goodwin organized a guidance program for the schools of that city.[13] All of these events contributed to the early establishment and development of guidance.

However, it was William Burnham who defined elementary school guidance and its place in the educational process.[14] He consistently advocated a position that is linked with and reflected in present-day guidance and counseling in the elementary school. His tenets included the necessity of a positive learning climate for the child, mental health services for the teacher, and guidance for all children.

Growth of elementary school guidance units across the country was very slow. In 1928, when Lillian B. Gordon conducted a survey of elementary school guidance programs in seventy-five selected cities, she found that sixteen cities had guidance programs, but that only six programs were developed to the point that counselors were placed at individual schools.[15] As late as 1944, well-developed elementary school guidance programs were not common. In Los Angeles County, California, for example, there were four directors but no counselors.[16] After thirty-five years of existence, the spread of elementary school guidance was still sporadic. However, during the late 1940s and early 1950s, this situation began to change. In 1954, in Los Angeles County, California, a follow-up study revealed thirty-two elementary school guidance directors and seventy-two counselors.[17] During the 1950s, Goedeke surveyed school counselors in major cities. In his survey of fifty-two major cities (these were defined as cities with populations of 200,000 or more), he found that only 9.6 percent of these cities had full-time elementary school counselors.[18]

Additional impetus was given the movement in 1958 with the enactment of the National Defense Education Act, which provided for counselor training and equipment. The independent support of elementary school guidance continued, and major textbooks in the field continued to appear. Anderson, in 1967, investigating elementary school counseling in Washington, identified ninety-three elementary counselors.[19] Only 28 percent had attended a National Defense Elementary Guidance Institute, and 84 percent had been assigned to their job since 1965. This indicates, as Meeks has said, that "one of the most important trends in guidance is the growth of organized programs at the elementary level."[20] This conclusion was shared by McKellar.[21]

In summary, the history of elementary school guidance is closely related to child study in the field of psychology, to events in the development of educational psychology, and to the mainstream of the guidance movement. For forty years, growth of elementary school guidance was extremely limited. Moderate growth originated in the early 1950s. During the late 1950s and the mid-1960s, however, elementary school guidance mushroomed into a major development.

Notes

1. Gardner Murphy, *Historical Introduction to Modern Psychology,* 2nd rev. ed. (New York: Harcourt, Brace and Company, 1950), p. 389.
2. Paul Nash, Andrea M. Kazamias, and Henry J. Perkinson, *The Educated Man: Studies in the History of Education Thought* (New York: Wiley, 1965), p. 171.
3. Murphy, *op. cit.*
4. *Ibid.*
5. *Ibid.,* pp. 390–391.
6. *Ibid.*
7. *Ibid.,* p. 9.
8. *Ibid.,* p. 164.
9. John W. Brewer, *History of Vocational Guidance* (New York: Harper & Brothers, 1942), p. 59.
10. Joseph William Hollis and Lucile Ussery Hollis, *Organizing for Effective Guidance* (Chicago: Science Research Associates, 1965), p. 16.
11. *Ibid.,* p. 15.
12. Ruth Martinson and Harry Smallenburg, *Guidance in the Elementary School* (Englewood Cliffs, N.J.: Prentice-Hall, 1958), p. 8.
13. Hollis and Hollis, *op. cit.*
14. Verne Faust, *History of Elementary School Counseling* (Boston: Houghton Mifflin, 1968), pp. 11–16.
15. Martinson and Smallenburg, *op. cit.,* p. 10.
16. *Ibid.,* p. 13.
17. *Ibid.*
18. Milton Thomas Goedeke, "Operational and Supervisory Practices in Large City Guidance Programs With Special Reference to a Comparative Analysis of the Baltimore Schools," unpublished Doctor's dissertation (George Washington University, 1957), p. 141.
19. Marjorie M. Anderson, *The Extraordinary Growth of Elementary Guidance in the State of Washington* (Olympia, Washington: The State Department, April, 1967), p. 1.
20. Anna R. Meeks, "Guidance in the Elementary School," *Journal of the N.E.A.,* 51 (March 1962), 30–32.
21. Rebecca L. McKellar, "A Study of Concepts, Functions and Organizational Characteristics of Guidance in the Elementary School as Reported by Selected Elementary School Guidance Personnel," unpublished Doctor's dissertation (Florida State University, 1963), pp. 100–132.

The Father of Elementary
School Counseling

Verne Faust

While it is not always easy or possible—and, some would argue, not necessary—to trace a movement to its original source or leader, to do so where feasible seems to add momentum to the movement. Armies, social reforms, political ideologies, all seem somehow to require an image or images in the form of special men in whom the members of the movement can invest unusual powers of foresight and insight. These men penetrate the frontier where others have not trod, fearing to do so without leadership.

William Burnham

Perhaps more than any other figure, William Burnham can be named as the pioneer of what has become today the elementary school counselor. While his more than ordinary contribution, *The Normal Mind,* came in 1924, it was not until two years later that Burnham (1926) wrote *Great Teachers and Mental Health,* which established him as the father of what was to become modern elementary school counseling. Later, Burnham (1932) made still another contribution in *The Wholesome Personality.*

We are indebted to Percival Symonds (1959) for discovering among the morass of publications and mental health movements the singular figure of W. H. Burnham. Symonds portrays Burnham as the human behavior scientist who, probably more than any other one person until his time, perceived the role of the human behavior specialist in the schools as extending beyond a focus on crisis children, testing, and clinical diagnosis.

Prior to Burnham, what had existed in the form of a mental health effort, such as that which grew out of Clifford Beers' *A Mind that Found*

"The Father of Elementary School Counseling" has been reprinted from *History of Elementary School Counseling,* chapter 1, copyright © 1968 by Verne Faust: Reprinted by permission of the publisher, Houghton Mifflin Company. Dr. Faust is Professor of Education at the University of Miami, Coral Gables.

Itself (1908), was more clinical and never really became related to students in the educative process. In fact, the National Association for Mental Health, founded the year of Beers' publication, did not, as Symonds noted, "pay much attention to children or schools for a period of 15 years" after its founding. Until the time of Burnham's publication in 1926, practically all that had been written on the major principles and concepts of therapeutic behavior for children studiously neglected viewing them within a framework of the normal educative process. Publications centered on *certain* children (usually those with behavior problems) rather than on *all* children.

Burnham's "Learning Climate" Emphasis Versus Other Emphases of the Twenties

Symonds (1959) also called attention to the fact that "papers in the 1920's by such well-known persons as Fernald (1922), Taft (1923), Mateer (1924), Maxfield (1924), Haggerty (1925), Walter (1925), Mohlman (1926), Blatz and Bott (1927) . . . and Wile (1929) dealt with mental hygiene in the school, but it should be noted that the emphasis of all these early writers was on the problem of correction." The approach was basically clinical, diagnostic, and treatment-oriented, and the subject was largely the responsibility of psychologists, social workers, and psychiatrists. The elementary school counselor who was to appear in the sixties was not even dimly seen in the twenties.

The Teacher as the Key Figure for the Child

The writers of the twenties observed that children in the nation's schools were living on a sort of highway that took its toll in intellectual and emotional destruction. As a result of the mental health movement and the impetus of Clifford Beers' book, these writers proposed to treat these children. No one, however, thought to take the children off the highway. No one, that is, until Burnham came along and in an organized way called for building a new curriculum world for children. "Burnham was the first to see," Symonds again noted, "that mental hygiene in the school is a matter of relationship—a relationship with two poles—the teacher and the pupil. His book *Great Teachers and Mental Health* showed that the teacher becomes the key figure in the diadic relationship."

Burnham did not receive the kind of credit due him until Symonds brought his efforts into focus through an almost equally unnoticed and important article in 1959. But it is quite likely that Burnham's creative view of the role of the human behavior specialist focusing on the *learning* of *all* children in the schools contributed substantially to the new image of the elementary school counselor who was to emerge in America in the middle sixties. It is true, of course, that sporadic and incomplete calls for a commitment of guidance and counseling to the *educative process* had been heard during the late teens and twenties from persons other than Burnham.

But no one proposed them, however, on the elaborate basis which Burnham afforded the times.

Burnham's Entreaty and the Modern Counselor

By present standards, Burnham's publications were both primitive and modern. His profundities were often placed between almost zealous exhortations bordering on religious rather than scientific boundaries. Remembering the times in which he wrote and the level at which the psychology of behavior stood, we must assess Burnham's insights for the schools as remarkably innovative and up-to-date. An examination of his thinking discloses that he was open to and aware of most bodies of data available on human behavior at the time. He earnestly attempted to arrange on the continuum behavioristic notions at one end and, at the other, the model presented by psychoanalysis. He also incorporated the findings of physiology from a psychosomatic stance, as well as at the same time conceptualizing the existence of a self-system.

On the very first page of Burnham's initial book (1924) he began to examine the child in the elementary school. In speaking of educational objectives, he contended that "The child's first business is to grow and develop. Everything else can wait, but the demands of health are imperative." A sense of the developmental approach as the vehicle most basic to learning pervaded much of what he wrote. It should be remembered that Burnham was speaking of physical health and development as well as of affective growth, inasmuch as this was at that time a problem equal to that of effective personal adjustment.

Eight years later Burnham (1932) was suggesting, however briefly, one of the pivotal contentions of the new elementary school counselor: *only with health, primarily in terms of a relatively conflict-free personality, can intellectual functioning remain effective and unimpaired.*

Burnham was fully aware of the relationship of the effective personality (which he characterized by the then popular term, "mental hygiene") and central nervous system functioning, including the critical learning process of attention. He pointed out this relationship to educators. "Physiological studies, both before and during the War," he noted, "have placed mental hygiene upon a solid scientific basis. What occurs in the brain when the mind thinks, was the problem attacked long ago by the great Italian physiologist, Mosso. And a long series of investigations since have shown definite physiological changes correlated with mental work. ... The simplest test of these changes is the increased pulse rate that accompanies attention."

Some forty years prior to the appearance of the modern elementary school counselor, Burnham was saying that "One of the greatest advances in child hygiene in recent years is the insight that mental hygiene is quite as important as somatic hygiene, and that objectively excellent methods in hygiene, important rules of health and significant teaching, all avail nothing unless right mental attitudes and right habits of healthful mental activity are developed. Thus in connection with every school subject, even every lesson in child hygiene, and every form of motor training, the dictates of common sense and the plain techniques of scientific mental hygiene are to be considered. . . ."

Still speaking in 1924, Burnham noted that, not many years before, only common sense and the rudiments of subjects were all that were considered necessary for the teacher. However, he was now recommending to the teacher that "Theoretically, one should know the genetic point of view, mental-age levels, educational psychology, experimental pedagogy, the problems of retardation and acceleration, group psychology, group pedagogy, and mental hygiene."

From Theoretical to Operational Translations

Burnham moved a considerable distance between his first book (1924) and his third (1932) in translating his concepts operationally into the schools. In his earliest work he was laying down what he called the basic principles of "the preservation and development of an integrated personality." On the jacket of the volume that appeared eight years later, it was noted that Burnham was translating his material into operational approaches for the schools. His work, it was said, became "not theoretical guidance" alone.

Much of what Burnham wrote was directed to the critical role of the teacher in the effective functioning of children. He did this even though he overtly recognized the home—the parents—to be of first importance, and the school second, in the well-being of the child. Principally, Burnham addressed himself to teachers and the learning processes. He wrote of the immense difficulties of teaching, "the responsibility placed upon the teacher, and the demands of the professional self, which . . . is not infrequently in conflict with the other selves of the individual personality, together with the conflict arising from survivals of childish attitudes, the imperative impulses of one's individual ego, and social ideals." Still further, Burnham noted that "we teachers are handicapped by many limitations—the force of custom and tradition, the educational machine, the exigencies of class instruction, of grading, of marking, of promotion, of supervision, of official rules and regulations, and the like. Most of all perhaps we are limited by the conventional habits of our own thinking."

Burnham emphasized areas of teacher functioning which suggested support for the modern elementary school counselor's efforts in teacher counseling, or sensitivity training. "Thus the teacher who is a mental hygienist comes also to know more about himself, his own mental attitudes, his own emotional pitfalls, his own defense mechanisms, and the like." The modern counselor could not find a more explicit way of expressing the need for making teacher counseling or teacher group processes available in the schools than Burnham did over forty years ago. "A training in mental hygiene enables the teacher also to recognize the various defense mechanisms in children by which they dodge their work, escape the tasks necessary for their mental development, and acquire attitudes of shirking difficulties, of insincerity and deception, that mean inhibitions and disintegration of personality. . . . It is difficult to recognize the way to prevent them. Here especially the teacher is helped by mental hygiene."

Counseling teachers about the learning climate, in regard to teacher-child relationships, was succinctly expressed by Burnham in a single statement: "They should learn that their own feelings do not necessarily have any relation to reality."

Affective-Cognitive Processes

Finally, Burnham's first axiom for *all* education, around which it was implied that school personnel should be functioning, was his contention that "all sound education depends on the healthful and efficient functioning of the human brain and mind." In achieving these ends, he maintained that "It is not necessary that teachers should be specialists in clinical psychology; it is not necessary for them to make mental measurements; as a rule this should be done by specialists, trained psychologists or psychiatrists; but teachers should have a knowledge of children and normal mental attitudes and interests, as well as a knowledge of the common mental mechanisms and the pitfalls that threaten human reason and mental health alike."

Other Early Writers

While Burnham was calling for an all-out effort to place the guidance worker strategically in the center of the educative process, other writers were calling on a much less elaborate basis for essentially the same kind of direct, frontal confrontation with the learning process. For example, in 1918 the Committee on Vocational Guidance called for a view of curriculum as inseparable from guidance. The counselor, or other guidance worker, was to describe what it is that youth are like in the learning environment of the school: these data should then provide the fiber out of which the cloth of curriculum should be woven (Miller, 1961).

This suggestion was but one of many sporadic and nonsystematic efforts to move counseling away from the periphery of the child and teacher in the educative process. Again it appeared that only Burnham had, in any important way, urged that the human behavior specialist in the school deal more centrally with the learning effectiveness of all children. The impact of his effort was felt so much that professional counseling began to reflect this new position. Some thirty years later Miller (1961) wrote that "in the late 1920's and through the 1930's guidance was in danger of being so absorbed into curriculum revision in particular, and into the educational effort in general, that even a congressional investigating committee would not be able to recognize it as a function existing in its own right."

The Thirties and the White House Conference as a Reflection of Burnham's Pioneering Efforts

While other writers of the teens and twenties were focusing on the remediation of the behavior problem of children, Burnham was, to reiterate, pioneering beyond a clinical, school psychology approach, declaring that the child-teacher relationship, as the essence of the learning climate, was to be given major emphasis. It can only be inferred, of course, but there is reason to believe that the White House Conference on Child Health and Protection in 1930 was influenced, perhaps more than anyone knew, by Burnham's shift of attention a few years earlier to all children in the learning climate.

Symonds examined the section titles that came out of the Conference and found them to be "positive" or in keeping with Burnham's noncrisis-oriented focus. These section report titles included "The Mental Hygiene of the Present Curriculum" and "Mental Health of the Teacher" (Averill, 1930); "Contribution of Mental Hygiene to the Curriculum of the Future," "The Hygiene of Instruction," and "The Training of Psychological Counselors" (Watson, 1930); "Pupil Placement" (Strang, 1930); "Organizing the School for Efficiency" (Almack, 1930); "The Guidance Program of the School" (Brewer and Kefauver, 1930); "Special Psychological and Psychiatric Service for Problem Cases" (Symonds, 1930); and "School Relationships with the Home in the Interests of Mental Hygiene" (Fisher, 1930). As well as the eminent psychologists such as Percival Symonds among the White House consultants, familiar names in the history of guidance, counseling, and education can also be recognized, including Ruth Strang, John Brewer, Grayson Kefauver, and Carlton Washburne.

The term "mental hygiene" has been replaced today largely by "developmental emphasis." The same meaning appears to be generally referred to when counselors speak of "a noncrisis approach" and "a counselor for *all* children and not simply the deviant or special child approach."

Note that one of the section reports (by Symonds) dealt specifically with the deviant or special child and indicated that special personnel, such as psychologists or psychiatrists, would receive this type of referral.

Symonds himself was making an effort to find a way for school personnel to build a world for children in the school where they might learn at effective levels (1939). He seemed to be saying that the child's primary world with the parents in the home might not be meeting his needs for learning effectively in school. At any rate, he wrote a chapter, "Psychology of Parent-Child Relationships," in which he treated "teacher-pupil relationships" pretty much "in the role of the substitute parent." Twenty-five years later the new elementary school counselor would probably not be attempting to build effective learning climates through making parent-substitutes of teachers; but he would be working toward the same ends, and in many cases doing it chiefly through the teacher.

As it turned out, however, the momentum generated by a number of writers during the thirties, and by Burnham between 1926 and 1934 in particular, was insufficient to get elementary school counseling off to a full-fledged flight into the ultimately prevailing winds of the educative process. If the counseling vehicle got off the ground at all, the flight was no more (and no less!) than that of the Wright brothers. Counseling really went nowhere, except perhaps to the other end of the field. But the design for flight, in its unsophisticated, primitive way, had been at least sketchily blueprinted. Future, more elaborate flights into space were to be made. However little the pilots were conscious of it, those flights were to some extent based on Burnham's earlier contemplations.

Partial Bibliography

Beers, Clifford. *A Mind that Found Itself.* Garden City: Doubleday, 1908.

Blatz, W. E., and E. A. Bott. "Studies in Mental Hygiene: I. Behavior of Public School Children," *Pedagogical Seminary and Journal of Genetic Psychology,* Volume 34, 1927.

Fernald, W. E. "Inauguration of a State-Wide Public School Mental Clinic in Massachusetts," *Mental Hygiene,* Volume 6, 1922.

Haggerty, M. E. "The Incidence of Undesirable Behavior in Public School Children," *Journal of Educational Research,* Volume 12, 1925.

Mateer, Florence. *The Unstable Child.* New York: D. Appleton-Century Company, 1924.

Maxfield, F. N. *Mental Hygiene and the School Program,* Addresses and Proceedings of the National Education Association, 1924.

Mohlman, D. K. "Educational Guidance in a Mental Health Program," *Welfare Magazine,* Volume 27, 1926.

Symonds, Percival. "Mental Health in the Classroom: Historical Perspective," *The Journal of Social Issues,* Volume 15, 1959.

Taft, Jessie. "The Relation of the School to the Mental Health of the Average Child," *Mental Hygiene,* Volume 7, 1923.

Walter, R. "The Functions of a School Psychologist," *American Education,* Volume 29, 1925.

Wile, I. S. "Mental Hygiene in a Public School," *Mental Hygiene,* Volume 13, 1929.

The Concept of Culture and
Its Significance for
School Counselors

Eleanor Leacock

The culture concept, central to the field of anthropology, is becoming increasingly familiar in the social service fields. When properly applied, the idea of "culture" can be extremely useful for the understanding of behavior and the breaking down of many barriers to effective communication. However, like most ideas, it can also be distorted, and defeat the very purpose it should serve. This paper will discuss the appropriate use of the culture concept, and indicate the way it can be distorted when incorrectly applied to differences between children from "middle class," economically well-off homes, and children from economically marginal or insecure homes.

True cultural insight enables us to see behind superficial, socially patterned differences to the full integrity of an individual. It prevents us from misinterpreting behavior different from that to which we are accustomed. To take an example from American Indian culture, people working with Indian children have found that they often do not respond well to teaching techniques that depend on the desire to do better than one's peers on a test, to answer a question more capably, in short to compete successfully. Where Indian societies have retained roots with the past they are still pervaded by a cooperative spirit, and children feel uncomfortable in competitively structured situations, at least insofar as learning is concerned. This is often misinterpreted as a lack of desire to learn, but an awareness of cultural differences reveals that the motivation for learning is present, but that it is being inhibited rather than encouraged by teaching practices foreign to Indian culture.

"The Concept of Culture and Its Significance for School Counselors," *Personnel and Guidance Journal,* 46, 9 (May 1968), 844–851, has been reprinted with the permission of the author and of the publisher, the American Personnel and Guidance Association. Eleanor Leacock is Professor of Anthropology at Polytechnic Institute of Brooklyn.

The persistence of such responses was brought home sharply to me when I assigned oral reports, seminar style, to a college class of bright, argumentative students. One of the girls, who had seldom spoken up in class, asked for permission to write rather than deliver her paper. I was unsuccessful in my attempt to persuade her to try the experience of oral delivery. She later told me that the course had given her insight into her reason for declining, and to the discomfort she had always felt in school. Her father was Indian, she said, and though there was little of an ongoing Indian community in Connecticut where she was raised, nonetheless the style of American Indian discourse had persisted in her family. For her, discussion should not involve the rapid-fire, essentially competitive argument to which we are accustomed. Instead, it should involve measured, considered statements, and—so difficult for us—attentive listening. Each person should listen patiently to everyone else, and the attempt should be at reaching consensus rather than winning an argument. Therefore, this student had always felt uncomfortable in classrooms, with their built-in competitive atmosphere.

Thus, learning and exchanging knowledge are conceived differently in different cultures. So, too, are traditional styles of behavior between adults and children. Teachers working with Puerto Rican students often find that a child being reprimanded does not look at them or respond to their statements. They may think the child sullen, rebellious, or rude. In the cultural terms of the child, however, he is expressing acquiescence and respect. Understanding this culture difference enables a teacher to see behind socially patterned behavior to a child's actual feelings, and to relate to him as an individual.

Misapplication of the Culture Concept

However, the awareness that such differences exist can lead to their exaggeration and misapplication. Such is often the case with the "culture of poverty" described for economically underprivileged and minority communities. Unfortunately, "lower class culture" is fast becoming a new stereotype behind which the individual is not revealed more fully, but instead is lost. Indeed, the "old fashioned" but sympathetic and insightful person, who is skeptical of "all this talk about culture," and asserts that what really counts is the individual child, is more correct than those who have gone overboard with distorted expectations for "cultural" differences. Such a person knows intuitively that, although people act and react in terms of learned patterns for behavior, which may differ, nonetheless *all people respond positively to respect and real interest.* The study of man's many and varied cultures indicates that in this regard all human beings are alike. Further, while there are differences among class, religious, national, and racial groups in this country, all are part of a total "American culture."

An example of what can happen when the concept "culture of poverty" is carried too far is described in Estelle Fuch's *Pickets At The Gates*

(1966). A principal in a school that had shifted from predominantly white to Negro in the course of several years, wanted to prepare his new teachers, fresh from college, for the children they would be teaching. Drawing from the literature on the "deprived child," he wrote a letter stating that, compared with children from middle class homes, the school children would be poor financially, academically, and socially. Many would be on welfare; the school lunch would be the best meal they would get. Their mothers would be so busy with their "broods" that the individual child would be lonely. Often there would be no fathers in the home, and there would be no organized family activities. The children, he continued, would come from noisy atmospheres, and would not hear the quiet voice of the teacher until trained to give attention. They would have received no encouragement to achieve, and socially, economically, and culturally would be poor and not ready for school. This was true, he stated, of poor groups generally; the same characteristics found among our Negro and Puerto Rican families are found in Appalachia, among the hillbillies of the Ozarks, and among Mexican-Americans.

The unfortunate principal continued the letter with specific directives for handling these children and, proud of his efforts, sent a copy to each new teacher and also to the president of the PTA. He was shocked, hurt, and puzzled when irate Negro parents, active PTA'ers working hard to see that their children got the best education possible, promptly organized a picket line in front of the school, distributed a leaflet describing the principal's insulting attitude toward their children, and demanded his ouster.

The principal had utterly ignored wide variations within the Negro community. Further, by taking all the negative aspects of poverty and grouping them into a composite picture of all the children, he had drawn a picture that could only be false and damaging. It is one thing to say that in a poor community one would expect to find more bitter, angry, and withdrawn children, and greater difficulty mastering school lessons because of the tremendous objective difficulties with which many children are coping. It is quite another to say that children from poor families generally are uninterested in learning—an inference that unfortunately can so easily become a convenient rationale to excuse inadequate teaching and unequal school facilities in low income areas. Many are the working class families who aspire to a college education for their children (Purcell, 1964). Many also are the hard-working mothers without men at home, facing combined difficulties of bad housing, long hours, low pay, and inadequate community facilities for their children, who nonetheless give them a great deal of love, respect, and encouragement.

Wrenn (1962, pp. 31–32) warns against making premature judgments about family atmosphere based on demographic features alone. He writes:

> . . . whatever the facts about birth rate, family size, and divorce, there are widely varying and deeply held opinions on these topics in any community . . . There is little evidence that a small family or large one

per se provides the "best" climate for child growth. Economic capacity to support the children's social and educational needs is a factor, but so also is the love support the child receives, the integrity of the family unit, and the general psychological climate of the home.

Counselors should be knowledgeable about the interrelationship of such family factors and be slow to prejudge the home. . . . A counselor . . . needs to be wary of coming to conclusions about a family which may deviate from his stereotype of a "good" family.

Some literature on "disadvantaged children" begins to sound as if broken homes are the exclusive property of the poor. I have to comment here on the fact that in a parochial nursery school one of my children attended, half of the "white, middle-class, Protestant" children in one grade were from broken homes, several were quite emotionally disturbed, and the mother of one was dying of acute alcholism. Yet expectations for the children's performance were high, and the children were on the whole living up to them.

Culture Concept as a Tool

Does this mean the "cultural" dimension should be abandoned entirely by the school counselor who is trying to help children from working class homes? The answer is no, *if it is used as a tool for reaching and understanding the individual as an individual, not for burying him behind generalizations about a group.* "Culture" refers in part to the general style of interpersonal relations and related attitudes that are traditional in a given society. It does not refer to the infinite variety of ways each individual feels and responds in dealing with his own life circumstances. In addition, the notion of cultural consistency becomes fuzzy when it is applied to class differences in our society. True, any definable group has what can be called a "culture." One can speak of the "culture" of different institutions—hospitals have different "cultures" on the whole from schools, and both from business houses. Within certain general patterns of "school culture," each school develops its own traditions. One can even speak of a certain "classroom culture," developed during the short lifetime of a common experience shared by a teacher and a group of children.

However, when one talks of anything as general as "working class culture" or "lower class culture," one must do so warily, and define what one means. On the one hand, it is part of American "culture" as a whole; on the other, the "working" or "lower" class includes many national, regional, religious, rural-urban, and income variations. Finally, as stated above, one is only referring to certain very general expectations for attitudes and behavior—one is not talking about how the individual incorporates these into his total self.

At present we know more about these general expectations for attitudes and behavior within the so-called "middle class" than we do for the "working class." Therefore, the best use that can be made of the culture concept is as a tool enabling the counselor to understand his own "values," —or, as others may see them, biases. He needs as open a mind as possible when attempting to develop rapport with children who are bitter, angry, or withdrawn, and with their families. Conrad Arensberg and Arthur Niehoff (1964), writing a manual for Americans overseas, felt that the basis for giving people insight into other cultures was to give them some understanding of their own unquestioned assumptions about how people should be motivated and how things should be done. They discuss the cluster of attitudes involving time, work, and money, historically based in the Protestant Reformation, and changing with time, but still functioning. Time as a commodity to be apportioned and either "spent well" or "wasted"; work as an activity important for its own sake, as well as a means to an end; money as a measure of personal worth (hence people's embarrassment about revealing their salary)—these tie together in a specifically American pattern based on the assumption that effort leads to success. This pattern was well suited to a frontier country where hard work did indeed lead to financial success for many, and where the many more for whom it did not are forgotten. That effort will succeed is one of the most treasured of American beliefs. For "middle class" Americans, where it is more or less true, and for those from working class homes who have moved into a higher social status, it is so central a belief that they cannot empathize with those whose experiences have rendered it meaningless. On the whole, they are unable to see life in any other terms and hence are unable to communicate with children to whom the notion that effort will be rewarded has become an empty platitude.

Sensitivity with regard to his own attitudes enables the counselor to put himself in another's place—to *understand* rather than jump to a conclusion. On this basis, he is better able to assess materials he will be using, to evaluate forms of discourse he is employing. Do the filmstrips he is planning to use with a parent group deal realistically with the problems they are facing, or do they take a naïve and superficial approach that will only be a slap in the face? (This would be true of many psychologically oriented films geared to families living in quite comfortable circumstances.) How does the counselor introduce and evaluate test materials? What kinds of questions does he ask children who are in trouble? How meaningful is their experience to the counselor? How are children's problems reinforced by the role defined for them in the classroom? When the world is seen in their terms, do the children who appear unreachable reveal themselves as actually waging a desperate struggle for a sense of identity and self-respect?

Counselors already know the limits of testing and the fact that a child should not be assessed on the basis of test information alone. They also know that children from low income homes will generally do less well than those from middle income homes, even on the Rorschach and other projective tests of personality. Differences in previous educational experience of children, including familiarity with tests, and a bias in constructing and interpreting tests (a matter presently of concern to testing services) are partly responsible.

The problem of motivation is also important, as indicated by a study of the effect upon test scores of money incentives as compared with praise. Klugman (1944) tested a heterogeneous group of children twice, using the revised Stanford-Binet, and the second time offered some of the children money rewards for good scores. Whereas scores on a second testing generally rose somewhat, there was no demonstrable difference between the scores of those white children who were offered a money reward and those who were not. However, the Negro children given money rewards showed definitely better performances than those to whom praise was the only incentive. Now they had something real to work for!

How Not to Win Friends

An example of how a "middle class" cultural bias can hinder communication is afforded unfortunately by an "Inventory" of a "Child's Background of Experience and Interest" in an otherwise fine New York City guide for counseling (Board of Education of New York City, 1955–56). The first heading is "Fun at Home," the second, "Reading Fun." The child is asked about favorite activities at home, according to the sample questionnaire, and then, "Do you read aloud? To whom? Does anyone ever read to you? How much of your free time do you spend reading for fun? What kinds of books do you like best? What books have you read this term? How many books do you own?" Anyone who has worked in a low income neighborhood will recognize that this is hardly the way to establish rapport with a hurt and angry child.

The next topic is "Your Pet," with questions like, "Have you a pet? Who takes care of it?" Then, "Do you take lessons outside of school?" and, "Making and Collecting Things: What things did you make? What things do you want to make soon? What collections have you started?" Only then does the schedule come to less biased topics—helping around the house, friends, radio, TV, movies. The sensitive counselor would know that such questions could only further alienate a child from poor circumstances who is embittered and confused, and has been referred for help.

The consistent bias of school readers with their blond, suburban world that completely negates the existence of urban workers, and especially dark-skinned workers, has become a matter of concern. The presentation of life as a series of amiable and quite vapid incidents where all is "sweetness and light" is unhealthy not only for middle class children; it has become clear that it is especially hard on underprivileged and minority group children. Fortunately there are attempts to redress the situation. Illinois has a broad enough guidance program to plan improvements in texts and materials along these lines; Detroit has for some time been addressing itself to this problem; and the Bank Street readers picture urban scenes that include Negroes and Puerto Ricans as well as whites engaged in all manner of activities. However, it takes a long time to change a whole system of text-books, and it is important for counselors, where it is part of their responsi-bility, to help introduce more varied materials into classroom libraries. This can be particularly helpful where there is an individualized reading program.

Another instance where the very existence of working class and minority group children is denied—but one that lends itself easily to im-provements—involves the use of classroom walls. One can still enter class-room after classroom in our public schools without seeing a Negro adult or child pictured on the walls, and this extends to Puerto Ricans, Oriental people, Mexican-Americans. Classroom walls carry a clear message to the children as to what is and is not of value, and here an unhealthy message is being conveyed to children, white as well as nonwhite. Nor is this message fundamentally altered by posting a picture of Frederick Douglass during Brotherhood Month, along with a painting of a Negro and white child happily running hand in hand. A subsidiary message is only being added: pay lip service to the family of man at the appropriate times.

Creative Children

A final point to develop in relation to cultural bias concerns the ques-tion of lost talent and creative children. Sometimes the more creative children are withdrawn, concentrating on their private thoughts, but often they are "difficult" or "rebellious" from a teacher's point-of-view (Wrenn, 1962, pp. 55–56). Generally, in handling too large a group it is a tempta-tion for a teacher to value and lean heavily on the more conforming chil-dren. Unless she knows how to use the questions raised by more creative children, and feed them into discussions that are meaningful for the class as a whole, creative children become a problem to her.

When a creative child is from a low income home his difficulties are compounded, and his creativity is more likely to be channelled into unpro-ductive rebellion. We have already mentioned the denial of his very being by classroom materials and exhibits. He is also likely to receive more punishment for transgressions in behavior than is a middle class child. First discussed by Davis and Dollard in their *Children of Bondage* (1940), this aspect of school life for children was further documented by Hollings-head in his *Elmtown's Youth* (1949). He gives in detail one incident in which a working-class youth was literally driven out of school in the course of an episode stemming from initial lateness, although a worse record of lateness had been ignored in the case of a wealthy boy (Hollingshead, 1949, pp. 185–198). In *Education and Income* (1961), Patricia Sexton carries the point further, and shows the extent to which differential punishment and other inequities for middle and low income children permeate an entire urban school system, and in *The American School* (Sexton, 1967) she summarizes more recent studies of these inequities.

The study of classroom life carried on by the present author under the auspices of the Bank Street College of Education revealed another type of punishment disadvantaged children experience to a greater extent than middle income children. This is the subtle but pervasive derogation of their personal experiences, which, unfortunately, can be conveyed even by kind and well-meaning teachers. For example, in one classroom an eight-year-old Negro boy talked eagerly and at length about the planes he had seen at the airport. The lesson was on transportation, and one would expect the teacher either to open up the child's account for class discussion, or to question him further. Or she might simply have said, as observed in other classrooms, "How wonderful," or "Good," and asked another question— unimaginative, perhaps, but at least approving. Instead, the teacher asked, "Who took you?" She was clearly puzzled, since children in this neighborhood presumably did not go on trips. Deflated, the child answered, "Day Care," and the incident was closed. A little enough episode, but when repeated many times in the course of a week, the result would well be what was witnessed in a higher grade in the same school—children listlessly sitting through the day.

When interviewed, the teacher said she felt the "middle class" content of school readers was desirable since there was nothing in the children's lives on which learning could be built. At least, she said, the readers held up an image of something better (a professional and suburban life), to which the children could aspire. It never occurred to her—nor does it to most teachers—how undermining this would be to Negro children for whom the "something better" was not only largely unobtainable, but also totally white. Given this, plus the other kinds of denial mentioned, one could only expect a self-respecting Negro child from a low income environment to meet school personnel with suspicion and growing anger. Many children express this passively through resistance of learning; others, especially those who have been deeply hurt at home as well, are moved to active rebellion.

The Counselor's Responsibility

It becomes the counselor's responsibility to help reach these children and, whereas one can be depressed at the difficulties of the task, one can, on the other hand, be impressed by how many of them appreciate and respond to the honest concern of a sincere and emphatic counselor. However, to return to the question of creativity, it is sometimes the potentially more creative children, those who in the long run might have more to offer, who give the counselor the hardest time, more consciously challenging him, putting him to the test. Thus a counselor, overburdened though he may be, must be wary of giving up too soon with a very difficult child. But he must deal with the reality of the child's total life situation, and not gloss over problems of inequality and discrimination with a wishful belief that individual effort will necessarily win success. One cannot expect to help a socially disadvantaged child simply to "conform," and this is even more true of a deeply thoughtful and sensitive child. The counselor must instead help him learn that certain forms of rebellion are pointless and self-destructive, whereas other forms are meaningful.

Wrenn writes that the school counselor must be " 'radical' in encouraging individualism . . . while at the same time he helps the student see the need for living within present societal expectations. . . ." He goes on to say that counselors are often accused of encouraging conformity, and it is indeed their responsibility to help students "learn systematically what is now known, to build a solid foundation of understanding the present." This is not an end in itself, however, but "the *means to the end* [italics his] of creating the new and of being oneself. To understand the present and be dissatisfied with it enough to change it . . . *is to complete the process* [italics his] of which present knowledge and socialization are but introductory steps" (Wrenn, 1962, p. 79). Marie Jahoda touches on the same point when she writes of positive mental health as involving "environmental mastery," in the sense that "hard reality" is not seen as "unchangeable and only the individual as modifiable" (Jahoda, 1958, p. 60). The individual must see himself as capable (along with others) of modifying environmental factors. In the last analysis, it is only on the basis of such an understanding that socially disadvantaged children really can be reached —precisely because they are *socially* disadvantaged—and this is not only for psychological reasons, but for ethical ones as well.

The School as a Social System

The concept of culture also has relevance for a totally different aspect of the guidance counselor's functioning, i.e., his role in the school as a social system. Here he has much in common with the applied anthropologist, for both are faced with an impossible task. Both must relate positively and constructively to virtually all members of a social system in order to enable the system to fulfill its functions more adequately. The counselor's role involves helping teachers and children communicate more effectively with each other, likewise teachers and parents, and even parents and children. It also involves smoothing the channels of communication throughout the administrative structure in relation to myriad special services. Above all, his responsibility is to help children relate to schooling more positively, and to encourage their willingness to be taught as the school sees teaching them. Inherent in his role is the implication that he must do this without stepping on any toes, taking his lead from the principal's and teachers' ideas and desires, always being helpful, not threatening or irritating any-

one. Nor should he overstep his position with regard to teaching, which is
the teacher's responsibility, or individual therapy, which is the school psychologist's province (if there is one), or administration, the task of the
principal and his assistants. Yet his contribution to the school as a whole
should be substantial.

As to what the science of anthropology has to offer, it is in part to
generalize about what the good counselor has already learned from his own
experience. As an innovator, he will have learned that many other things
besides the intrinsic desirability of an innovation will determine whether
or not it will be accepted. He will also have learned not to be unduly discouraged if he meets what seems to him totally unreasonable resistance to
an innovation he feels essential. And he will have experienced the fact that
success does not automatically lead to encouragement and praise. Insofar
as he is socially wise, the counselor—like anyone working in an institution
—will know that, while irrationalities vary from school to school, they are
characteristic of "bureaucracy" in general. He will know that the better he
understands his own institution, and the clearer he is in his own mind
about what he wants to accomplish, the readier he will be to develop the
most favorable avenues for broadening his program. He will have sized
up the "decision-making structure" of his school—the role played by the
principle in relation to the older group of teachers, and the influence of the
senior teachers as compared with that of new appointees. He will have
assessed the sources for support of aspects of his program. He will be wary
of being caught between diverse interest groups in the school, and of being
forced to decide which to please or displease.

The anthropologist and sociologist rephrase this everyday experience
of the counselor in terms of recurrent patterns in the operation of bureau-
cratized structures. Merton (1964) developed the point that the "manifest"
functions of an institution—in this case the education of children—are not
the same as the "latent" functions, or the various social and cultural pressures that operate as an institution perpetuates itself and attempts to
expand its area of influence and control. For example, the concerns with
job security, with promotion, with status and prestige, result in sometimes
more hidden, sometimes more open jockeying for position in all institutions.

Furthermore, from a teacher's point-of-view, record keeping, management problems, and other "custodial" duties are constantly competing with
the task of *teaching,* and each day presents the problem of trying to
accomplish more than can be done. Any change in routine is thus a burden,
unless it clearly and immediately reduces the tasks to be carried out. However, innovation usually involves a great expenditure of time and energy
now, with it is to be hoped, reduced time and energy—or at least increased
success—later. Further, teachers have all too often had a backlog of experience with unsuccessful innovations. Thus, they are often "unreasonable"
from the counselor's point-of-view, while the counselor may be seen as
quite unrealistic from the teacher's point-of-view.

The wise counselor recognizes that, generally, teachers and administrators, although trying to do the best job they can, respond to all manner of pressures and drives other than those related to the best education for children. If he is really wise, the counselor will be able to assess his own limitations in this regard in the same terms that he assesses those of others. Before assuming their ineptitude or lack of interest, he will look for a "sociological" explanation rather than a more individual one for an existing irrationality, and on this basis seek a way to overcome the obstacle.

References

Arensberg, C. M., & Niehoff, A. H. *Introducing social change, a manual for Americans overseas.* Chicago: Aldine Publishing Company, 1964.

Davis, A., & Dollard, J. *Children of bondage.* New York: Harper & Row, 1940.

Fuchs, E. *Pickets at the gates, a problem in administration.* New York: Free Press, 1966.

Guidance of children in elementary schools. Curriculum Bulletin, 1955–56, No. 13, Board of Education of the City of New York.

Hollingshead, A. B. *Elmtown's youth.* New York: Wiley, 1949.

Jahoda, M. *Current concepts of positive mental health.* New York: Basic Books, 1958.

Klugman, S. F. The effect of money incentives versus praise upon the reliability and obtained scores of the revised Stanford-Binet test. *Journal of Psychology,* 1944, *30,* 255–269.

Merton, R. K. *Social theory and social structure.* New York: Free Press, 1964.

Purcell, T. V. The hopes of Negro workers for their children. In A. B. Shostak & W. Gomberg (Eds.), *Blue-collar world.* Englewood Cliffs, N.J.: Prentice-Hall, 1964.

Sexton, P. C. *Education and income, inequalities of opportunity in our public schools.* New York: Viking Press, 1961.

Sexton, P. C. *The American school, a sociological analysis.* Englewood Cliffs, N.J.: Prentice-Hall, 1970.

Wrenn, C. G. *The counselor in a changing world.* Washington, D.C.: American Personnel and Guidance Association, 1962.

Guidance in the Elementary School

Anna R. Meeks

One of the most important current trends in guidance is the growth of organized programs at the elementary level.

The urgency of the demand for guidance in the elementary school has become greater as the greater complexity of modern living has increased the pressures which can be factors in a child's maladjustment and which hinder learning. Teachers have seen, for example, that emotional pressures upon the child by the school, his parents, or his peers may create an emotional block which will prevent his learning to read until, through counseling or other help, the block is removed.

More significant than the recognition of the usefulness of guidance in the correction of maladjustment has been the acceptance of guidance as an integral part of the whole educational program. Guidance is now regarded as much more than a privilege accorded the maladjusted; it is also needed by other children and requires programs that have as their major objective helping all children to be at ease with themselves and with others.

Such an approach calls for a carefully organized program of services within the individual school, supplemented by services provided through a central office staff. Helping children meet their personal, social, educational, and vocational needs is facilitated by participation of administrators, teachers, parents, guidance specialists (counselors), school nurses, school psychologists, and community agencies.

The principal is responsible for policies, organization, and leadership. Through effective and democratic leadership, he promotes an over-all school climate in which guidance can be effective. The teacher is a participant in and not merely a recipient of guidance services for his pupils. He shares with the counselor many responsibilities including the identification

"Guidance in the Elementary School," *Journal of the NEA,* 51 (March 1962) 30–32, has been reprinted with the permission of the author and of the publisher, the National Education Association. Anna R. Meeks is Professor of Education at Oregon State University, Corvallis.

of children with special needs. In identifying these children and in fulfilling his key role in guidance services, the teacher makes use of his own observations, anecdotal records, sociograms, informal interviews, and the insight gained from study of his pupils' autobiographies and other creative forms of expression.

The counseling process in the elementary school differs from counseling at other levels only in its use of some specialized techniques which are particularly suited to the developmental level of the younger child. The counselor's office with its toys, pictures, and books offers a relaxing situation in which the child can handle his tensions, face his concept of himself and others, and learn to live with himself and his fellow classmates.

The uncommunicative child may be able to talk to the counselor on a toy telephone, or may express his hostile feelings by abusing a toy. No attempt is made to diagnose emotional problems or to structure therapy sessions through toys, but their use has a legitimate place in the counseling of elementary children, as the following example shows.

One day fourth-grader Mary came into the counselor's office and stood looking at the toy shelves. Apparently she was not ready to talk about whatever was troubling her but soon she began manipulating two hand puppets, one representing a baby; the other, a little girl. "That's Buddy and this is me," she explained and proceeded to let Buddy beat her badly in a vigorous fight.

On subsequent visits to the counselor, Mary repeated the puppet act several times. When Mary's mother visited the school, the counselor told her about the fights and got this startled reply, "Come to think of it, that baby is licking the whole family! It's time we took him in hand."

Armed with new insight, the mother and the counselor were able to help Mary see herself as a valued person. The teacher, in turn, was able to help her find more satisfaction in her school work.

Of course, had Mary's emotional troubles been more deep-seated, the counselor would have referred her to other specialists. Or, if Mary's problems had been common to those of several other children in her school, she might have been counseled with them in a group, rather than individually.

Small groups of intermediate children often benefit from talking together in the counselor's office. They discuss their school experiences, help each other recognize strengths and weaknesses, and decide how they can improve their strengths and remove their weaknesses. In working with these groups, the counselor will supplement unstructured conversation with effective methods of group work, such as sociodramas and role playing.

In some cases, group counseling is especially effective with underachievers.

A fifth-grade teacher, for instance, was troubled by the fact that two of his boys, Ted and Billy, were not working up to their ability. When he mentioned this to the counselor, he found that she had just scheduled some weekly sessions for five other boys from intermediate grades who were also underachievers. Ted and Billy would be welcome to join.

From these sessions, the boys emerged with a greater sense of responsibility and new confidence in their ability to learn.

Effective though group counseling may be in correcting some results of underachievement, it is far better to prevent underachievement from ever becoming a problem by early and continuous identification of children with superior mental ability.

As pointed out at greater length in the chapter I wrote for the study, *Guidance for the Underachiever with Superior Ability* (published by the U.S. Department of Health, Education, and Welfare), bright children share with all children the many needs that are met by guidance services. In addition, they have unique needs arising from their superior ability. They may need help in their relationships with less mature children; routines and drills may become irksome and cause them to lose their motivations for learning; adult expectations for the academically able child may exert pressures which adversely affect the pupil.

The guidance process can also have important bearing on another aspect of underachievement. While there has been a wide acceptance of a readiness level for reading instruction, many schools have failed to recognize that there are readiness levels for all types of learning and that an individual child may have wide differences in readiness levels, as Johnny's story illustrates.

Johnny's reading-readiness score indicated he was ready for formal reading and should make good progress in school. After a few weeks, however, he was having difficulty in both reading and arithmetic. Constantly urged by his parents to do better, he had become an unhappy, confused child.

Miss Brown, his teacher, consulted the counselor and after studying all the factors in his case, they concluded that his reading-readiness score reflected his rich home background more than his mental maturity and that it did not indicate readiness for all learning. When the parents had the situation explained to them, they stopped pressuring Johnny to make rapid progress, with the result that he was able to lead a more comfortable and realistic school life.

The concept of readiness for learning in this broader application needs the greater clarification that can come through child study and through extension and intensification of elementary-school guidance.

Certainly, the problem of the underachiever with superior ability will be greater at the secondary and college levels if guidance has been lacking or ineffective in early school experience.

To sum up, the elementary-school counselor is a professionally trained person with depth of understanding and knowledge in child development, theories of counseling, group dynamics, classroom teaching, curriculum trends, school administration, public relations, and the organization of guidance services.

These requirements explain in part why well-trained counselors are in woefully short supply. The main reason, however, is that few school budgets have adequately allowed for counseling services, particularly at the elementary level. Even the provisions of the National Defense Education Act of 1958 were specifically written for secondary schools.

These facts notwithstanding, I believe that in the next ten years, elementary-school guidance will grow rapidly. It is essential, however, that such guidance not be a pale replica of secondary-school guidance. Rather, the two programs must complement each other and provide continuous coverage for each child from the school's first contact with him until he goes from high school to the right college or the right job.

A Rationale for the Elementary
School Counselor

Merle M. Ohlsen

Recently we have heard a lot about elementary school counselors. Some teachers and principals are enthusiastic about the idea. Others have doubts; they often ask such questions as: What will be his qualifications? With whom will he work? How will his work effect what I do? Wouldn't it be better to reduce class size and relieve teachers from some of their non-teaching duties so that they could give pupils more individual attention rather than to employ counselors? Ferris (2) asks some of these questions; he also expresses the fear that having a counselor work directly with the pupils would damage the close relationship that usually develops between an elementary teacher and his pupils. Those who have seen what elementary school counselors can do for pupils, parents, and teachers take the opposite view (1, 5, 6, 7, 8, 10, 13, 15 and 16); they believe that the counselor enhances the development of a close working relationship between a teacher and his pupils. They also believe that he helps pupils by counseling them, by consulting with their teachers, and by counseling their parents concerning the children's problems. In other words, they believe that he fulfills functions that we cannot expect teachers to fulfill.

Principals' Perceptions

Though he recognizes the need for an elementary school counselor's services, Waetjen contends that most elementary school principals would oppose the idea of employing counselors. (14) In part, he thinks that the resistance to specialists arises out of specialists' failure to adapt to the elementary school setting. He also believes that it may stem from the idea that teachers can handle all the problems that arise within their classrooms. As

"A Rationale for the Elementary School Counselor," *Guidance Journal,* 5 (1966), 53–60, has been reprinted with the permission of the author and of the publisher, Ohio State University. Merle M. Ohlsen is Professor of Educational Psychology at the University of Illinois.

he sees it: "The challenge to elementary school principals is twofold: first, to examine their resistance to having counselors in the elementary schools; and second, to differentiate the organization and functioning of the elementary school so that the counselor may emerge." (14:62) It is his hope that the research and demonstration centers selected by the Research Commission on Pupil Personnel Services will help solve these and other similar problems.

McDougall and Reitan deplored the idea that no one had systematically surveyed the opinions of elementary school administrators and used their opinions in developing elementary school guidance programs. (9) From their survey of elementary school principals' opinions (from Idaho, Oregon and Washington) they found:

> . . . that the majority of responding principals favor the viewpoint that elementary guidance be concerned with specialized services to individual pupils rather than general curriculum guidance for all pupils. Preference is also expressed by the majority for personnel engaged in full-time guidance rather than a combination of part-time teaching and guidance duties. Seventy-five per cent of the responding principals favored special certification for elementary guidance personnel and a majority also favored additional salary beyond the teaching salary schedule.
>
> The reaction of the principals was solicited regarding problems in establishing elementary guidance programs. The most frequently mentioned problems were in the areas of program, finance, gaining school and community acceptance for the guidance program, and obtaining adequately trained elementary guidance personnel.
>
> Principals expressed their judgment concerning the major differences between elementary and secondary school guidance. Areas mentioned most often were the greater emphasis on the preventive aspects of guidance at the elementary level; the lesser need for occupational and vocational guidance in the elementary school; the need for more parental involvement at the elementary level; and the need for understanding developmental problems peculiar to childhood and pre-adolescence. (9:353)

In other words, these elementary school principals have a pretty good idea of what should be expected of the elementary school counselor. At least their ideas agree with the authors cited earlier who react favorably to having such a person employed in the elementary schools. If these principals accurately reflect the attitudes of most principals, then the climate for introducing the elementary counselors is more favorable than Waetjen (14) perceives it to be.

The Teacher's Contribution

Important as the principal's perception is, attention must also be given to what the effective teacher contributes to normal development of children. He recognizes the importance of teaching subject matter, but he also knows that having children memorize facts and practice basic skills is not sufficient. He tries to get children excited about learning by exhibiting interest in the intellectual activities that excite them, by raising challenging questions, by helping them learn to challenge others and evaluate others' ideas as well as their own, and by helping them locate and use information in making decisions. Besides increasing their desire to learn, he tries to improve their ability to educate themselves. He also tries to understand his pupils; to help them understand and accept themselves, including what they have a right to expect from themselves; to help them understand, accept, and work with important others such as classmates, parents, and teachers; and to help them discover and develop special interests, abilities, and aptitudes. He is interested in his pupils as individuals and he is able to convey to them that he is interested in them. He is aware that what children learn is a function of their needs, community and family backgrounds, previous educational experiences, and the atmosphere within the classroom as well as their learning potential. He recognizes that he must be concerned about both the conative and cognitive aspects of learning.

Expectations from the Counselor

Based upon the above definitions of the elementary school teacher's responsibility for guidance, the elementary school counselor should be expected to help the teachers to further normal social, emotional, and intellectual development of his pupils, to better understand his pupils, to discover and try to remove blocks to learning, to make effective use of such school specialists as the school psychologist, school social worker, remedial teacher, and speech therapist, and to refer certain pupils and parents to out-of-school personnel and agencies for treatment. In fulfilling these functions the counselor consults with teachers, counsels children, and counsels parents concerning their children's school adjustment problems. Since he is primarily concerned with normal children and the prevention of serious school adjustment problems, he does short-term counseling, tries to help teachers discover problems early, and tries to help them improve the learning atmosphere within the classroom.

A Working Relationship with Children

Like those who counsel adolescents and adults, the elementary school counselor tries to develop an accepting, trusting relationship with his clients. He uses his knowledge of the counseling process, of human behavior, and of each client and his environment to try to understand each client's problems as the client sees them, and in the elementary school, to try to help the child, his parents, and his teacher to understand the forces at work within the client and his environment. At the same time, the counselor recognizes that insight in and of itself is not sufficient, and for many clients it is not necessary (3); these children can learn to change their behavior without understanding why they had problems.

One of the unique characteristics of this relationship is the counselor's ability to listen—to make a personal investment in each client, and at the same time to maintain separateness. When a counselor is at his best he can feel deeply with a client without experiencing countertransference. Moreover, he is able to convey this commitment to his clients and his expectations from them. He also is able to convey to children what they may expect from him, including his willingness to talk to them whenever they have something bothering them and they want to talk to someone privately, they must realize that they can seek assistance without waiting for a referral from an adult. Contrary to what many authors have said, staff members in the Illinois demonstration centers have found that children will seek help on their own when such action is accepted by teachers and counselors. Apparently elementary school children trust counselors more quickly than either adolescents or adults, but counselors tend to have greater difficulty communicating with them than they do with older clients. Kaczkowski believes that children's limited vocabulary accounts for a large part of this difficulty. (5) Often a child does not know the best word to express a feeling, or he knows only a single meaning for a word which has many meanings and the counselor assumes another meaning, or he uses a word incorrectly and the counselor assumes a correct meaning for the word. Nevertheless, these counselors have found that even primary school age children can better convey verbally what bothers them than any noted authors have indicated. True, the counselor must listen very carefully, be patient and try to help the client fumble for words, or even teach the client new words to express his feelings. On some occasions the counselor also must use play materials to communicate, but not as often with normal children as psychotherapists have indicated one must with disturbed children. Further support for this idea comes from Moustakas. (11) He describes play therapy as a form of preventative mental hygiene for normal children.

What do these normal children talk to counselors about when they seek a counselor's assistance? They talk about a wide variety of problems from "I can't learn to read," or "My teacher doesn't like me," to "My little brother messes up my homework," or "My new puppy was killed." When, for example, a child thinks that his teacher does not like him, it helps just to have another adult at school listen to him and try to understand him. All some very young children need is more experience in relating to adults and help in discovering that all adults who accept them do not have to relate to them as their mothers do. The typical normal child requires only a few sessions in order to help him and his teacher and/or parents identify and remove his blocks to learning. When, however, the counselor concludes that a child cannot be helped with a few individual sessions, perhaps he should ask himself whether the child could be best helped in a group. Children who are shy, or have difficulty making friends, or have difficulty participating in class discussion, or have better ability than their performance indicates often can be helped in small groups.

Counseling Parents

In counseling parents the same basic relationship is required. The principles for counseling adults apply, but at the same time school counselors will have to try to limit themselves to helping parents deal with their children's school adjustment problems. Other problems will have to be referred to other agencies. This writer believes that eventually such services will be provided by agencies jointly supported by the local school district and mental health agencies. Now much can be done to help parents prevent school adjustment problems through cooperative efforts of school and community mental health personnel to provide group counseling for parents and seminars on child rearing for parents. Often the latter can be provided through the local school district's adult education program.

Consulting Teachers

Functioning as a consultant for teachers is a very important aspect of every counselor's work, but it takes on more than the usual significance at the elementary school level. Most elementary school teachers work within a self-contained classroom in which they are the primary source of influence outside of the home for an entire school year. Fortunately, the typical elementary school teacher cares about his pupils, and he tries to understand them. Hence, he is quick to recognize the need for help from a counselor who can appreciate what he is trying to do for his pupils and who also will try to emphathize with him. To benefit fully from what this counselor has to offer him, the teacher must trust the counselor—must believe that he can talk freely without fear of being criticized or evaluated. However, he will appreciate the counselor's help in criticizing and evaluating himself. Thus, the counselor must not be a line officer in the administrative staff. Though he uses his counseling skills to establish a relationship which is very similar to that which a counselor establishes with his clients, it is different. Rather than helping a teacher deal with his personal problems, the counselor tries to help the teacher discover why the pupil for whom the teacher sought assistance feels and behaves as he does; to help the teacher discover how he feels toward the child; to help the teacher discover and remove the blocks to learning, and often this requires visits to the teacher's classroom as well as private conferences with the teacher and case conferences with several teachers (13:182–187); and where appropriate, to help the teacher make a referral to a school specialist or to an out-of-school specialist.

The counselor also consults teachers when he needs assistance in understanding his clients. In fact, asking teachers to help him is often the best way for a counselor to develop a relationship which encourages teachers to seek his assistance, but it must not be done for that purpose. If is done merely for the purpose of manipulating teachers into seeking his help, teachers will see it for what it is and resent it. Counselors do need teachers' help in understanding their clients, and they had better seek teachers' aid only when they genuinely feel the need for it. There is no substitute for sincerity.

Professional Background and Preparation

Of the questions noted at the beginning of this paper that teachers and principals often ask, only two remain to be answered: (1) Wouldn't it be better to make the classes smaller or to relieve teachers of some of their non-teaching duties so they could give more attention to their pupils rather than to use the funds to employ counselors? and (2) What will be the counselor's qualifications? Granted, reducing class size and providing other assistance to reduce time in nonteaching functions would enable most teachers to work more effectively with their pupils. However, such change would not alleviate the need for counselors. The duties defined in this paper for counselors require specialized professional preparation which most teachers do not have.

With reference to the qualifications of the elementary school counselor, McDougall and Reitan found that the elementary principals whom they polled also recognized the need for elementary school counselors to have special preparation not ordinarily required of teachers. (9) If one looks at the responsibilities that principals would like most for them to assume (counseling children, consulting parents, helping teachers learn to use appraisal techniques to understand children and to identify children with special talents, and interpreting the guidance program in the community), one can readily understand why they prefer persons with elementary school teaching experience and want them to have special preparation in such courses as principles of guidance, individual testing, tests and measurements, and counseling theory.

Hill and Nitzschke reported that most master's degree level persons in elementary school guidance (and that is about the level of training of qualified persons at present) come chiefly from the elementary school teaching ranks. (4) Even as late as 1961 they found that few graduate institutions had well-defined programs for the preparation of elementary school counselors. Major emphasis in the preparation programs existed in the areas of psychological foundations, guidance principles, counseling theory, and analysis of the individual. Moderate emphasis was placed upon the practicum, organization and administration and research. Minor emphasis was placed upon information service, group work, social foundations, and remedial work. Nitzschke's findings on required courses suggest that graduate programs are similar today. (12) However, he did note an increased concern for preparation of elementary school guidance workers.

Conclusions

Finally, there is an important job to be done by the elementary school counselor and it is one which teachers cannot be expected to do. Moreover, special professional preparation is needed to prepare him for his work with pupils, parents, and teachers. At present more attention must be given to developing graduate programs to help elementary school counselors meet their professional responsibilities. More attention should be given to mental hygiene, personality development, the study of group process, group counseling methods for both children and parents, and the practicum, including in addition to supervised counseling, specific assistance in learning to function as a consultant to teachers and to apply their knowledge of group dynamics in helping teachers understand the forces at work within their classrooms.

Laymen are beginning to recognize the need for this service, and they are doing something about it. In the current session of Congress, Congressman Gibbons introduced a bill (House Bill 11322) to provide these services for at least primary school children. Though Congressman Gibbons defined the job to be done much as this writer defined the role of the elementary school counselor, he gave his specialist the title of child development specialist. The point is that funds for these services may soon be provided. Hence, the counseling and guidance profession must be prepared to act quickly and wisely in the interest of children. Professional leaders must cooperate in defining the job to be done, in planning graduate programs for the many persons who will be needed to fill the jobs, in recruiting and selecting persons for the training programs, and in using these specialists wisely once they are placed in the schools. Beginning with demonstration centers like those sponsored by the Guidance Department in the Office of State Superintendent of Public Instruction in Illinois shows great promise as a method for introducing these programs.

Bibliography

1. Brison, David W. "The Role of the Elementary School Counselor," *The National Elementary School Principal,* XLIII (April, 1964), 41–44.
2. Ferris, Robert R. "Guidance in the Elementary School: A Teacher Can Do Best," *National Education Association Journal,* LIV (September, 1965), 48.
3. Ginott, Haim G. "Play Group Therapy: A Theoretical Framework," *International Journal of Group Psychotherapy,* VIII (1958), 410–418.
4. Hill, George E., and Nitzschke, Dale F. "Preparation Programs in Elementary School Programs," *Personnel and Guidance Journal,* XL (October, 1961), 155–159.

5. Kaczkowski, H. R. "Role and Function of the Elementary School Counselor," Paper read before the Mt. Zion Conference for Illinois Demonstration Center Personnel and Consultants, June 8, 1965.

6. Lambert, H. S. "Program of Guidance in Eight Elementary Schools," *Guidance for Today's Children: Fifty-third National Elementary Principals' Yearbook*, 1954, 225–236.

7. Leiter, Sarah L. "Guidance in the Elementary School: A Specialist Is Invaluable," *National Education Association Journal*, LIV (September, 1965), 49.

8. Mahan, Thomas W. "The Elementary School Counselor: Disturber of the Peace," *National Elementary School Principal*, XLIV (February, 1965), 72–74.

9. McDougall, William P., and Reitan, Henry M. "The Elementary School Counselor: As Perceived by Elementary Principals," *Personnel and Guidance Journal*, XLII (December, 1963), 348–354.

10. Meeks, Anna R. "Elementary School Counseling," *The School Counselor*, X (March, 1963), 108–111.

11. Moustakas, C. E. *Psychotherapy With Children.* New York: Harper & Row, 1959.

12. Nitzschke, Dale F. "Preparation Programs in Elementary School Guidance—A Status Study," *Personnel and Guidance Journal*, XLIII (April, 1965), 751–756.

13. Ohlsen, Merle M. *Guidance Services in the Modern School.* New York: Harcourt, Brace, and World, 1964.

14. Waetjen, Walter B. "Counseling Services for the Elementary School," *The National Elementary Principal*, XLIV (February, 1965), 59–62.

15. Wilson, Frances M. "Realities in the Guidance Programs in Elementary Schools," *The School Counselor*, III (1956), 41–44.

16. Zeller, R., and Garber, R. "Demonstration Centers for Elementary Guidance," Mimeographed guides for Demonstration Center Counselors and Consultants, 1964.

Guidance in the Elementary School: Child-Centered Procedures and Techniques

Gwen Nelson

No sadder word of tongue or pen, than these—"it might have been." Clumsy poetry perhaps, but an apt expression of a real challenge to education in general and to elementary guidance services in particular. Johnny might have been a better reader—had someone discovered his acute hearing loss in the early grades. Mary might have had a more pleasing personality—had she been helped to overcome her shyness and timidity. Jim might have made a real contribution to society as a doctor, a lawyer, or educator—had his elementary teachers recognized his hidden scholastic potential. Many adults might be living more productive, satisfying lives—had they been helped to develop reasonable goals and adequate self-concepts.

Even more challenging is the recognition of the child as a bona fide individual. A common notion in our society is that children are merely tools to accomplish adult purposes. One of the major goals of the schools and of society appears to be the acceleration of adulthood—or at least early conformity to adult standards. Courses of study are designed to produce responsible voters, competent parents, productive wage earners, and intelligent consumers—all adult activities. The prospect of a child becoming an adult without first having been properly conditioned for the role is a constant source of anxiety for most grownups.

The fact that youth is a temporary state—most young people outgrow it—seems to justify little concern for the child as a child. Even the problems of childhood and youth are lightly regarded. Although no research

"Guidance in the Elementary School: Child-Centered Procedures and Techniques" was presented at the Invitational Conference on Elementary School Guidance held in Washington, D.C., March 31–April 2, 1965, and is reprinted with the permission of the author. Gwen Nelson is President of Cowley County Community College in Arkansas City, Kansas.

evidence is available that indicates a positive relationship between chronological age and the gravity of personal problems, adults are prone to label the emotional conflicts of children as "just the problems of growing up."

Moreover, youngsters are commonly used as scapegoats—that is they often are blamed for the mistakes of adults. A dramatic illustration of this indictment is the furor raised about the quality of education immediately after the Soviets launched Sputnik. While labor unions continued to press for shorter work weeks and Chambers of Commerce complained about high taxes, the schools were severely criticized for "softness" and "frills." Even staid educators were caught up in the ensuing "quest for quality" that required stiffer courses, more homework, and fewer electives. While a basic function of the educative process is to promote growth, this forcing of "top growth" by restricting the root system is recognized as a short-term expedient even by horticulturists who specialize in producing beautiful, early blooming—if short lived—plants.

Recent years have seen significant changes in educational programs designed to meet the needs of pupils living in a dynamic, demanding society. As environmental pressures mount from the population explosion, status awareness, urbanization, expanded technology, and automation; it is not unreasonable to expect that schools will be forced to consider new, more sophisticated approaches to resolving mental health problems.

The most efficient and well-trained teacher cannot be expected to assume the full responsibility for teaching expanded content to increasingly heterogeneous groups of pupils and also serve as a counselor, psychologist, social worker, and school nurse. At no place is the problem so acute as in the elementary classroom. Already charged to provide a "firm foundation in the fundamentals for learning"; the elementary teacher is reminded that "dropouts originate in the elementary school," that more pre-teens suffer from hypertension diseases than ever before, and that patterns of personality development become fairly stable in early adolescence.

In a society oriented to quick, simple solutions to problems, the failure of such techniques as "guidance through the curriculum" to provide the proper psychological penicillin has been very disappointing. Even the proponents of "every teacher a counselor" at the elementary level are beginning to recognize the limitations of the typical, overloaded classroom teacher. Administrative demands for early identification of the gifted and the press for accelerated formulation of educational and vocational plans have only aggravated the problem.

The concept of a guidance specialist providing direct services to individual pupils is becoming more and more acceptable. Properly trained professionals who owe a minimal allegiance to subject matter areas or administrative procedures are appearing more frequently on the educational scene. While debate rages over the function, the role, and even the title of such personnel, certain basic techniques and procedures identify and distinguish these guidance specialists.

Some Basic Considerations for Elementary Guidance

The purpose of a program of elementary guidance is to provide both corrective and preventive services that promote proper child growth and development. While most guidance programs appear to be crisis oriented, the prevention of pupil problems through developmental procedures is much more justified in a public school setting. The motives prompting preventive programs are no less practical than humanitarian. While the concept of conservation of human resources may appear idealistic at first glance, only a cursory examination of well-documented evidence supports the economic justification for elementary guidance services. As with most other maladies, early diagnosis and treatment of mental illness are most effective and economical.

Practicality and economy suggest the necessity for increased activity in primary prevention as opposed to secondary or tertiary care. This position is supported by the following observation from the 1950 White House Conference on Education: "The school, as a whole, has an opportunity and responsibility to detect the physical and mental disabilities which have escaped parental or preschool observations and which would prevent development of a healthy personality, and to initiate the necessary preventive and remedial services. . . ." (22)

In the foreword to the reprint of a series of studies in mental health originally published by the American Personnel and Guidance Association, R. H. Felix, Director of the National Institute of Mental Health, reports:

> Since the end of World War II, school systems have become one of the largest employers of mental health personnel. During this period, the growing interest of educators in the mental aspects of their work has led to a marked increase in research and program development in this field. At the same time, the mental health professions have been intensifying their interest in schools as a vital place to study the development of children and new ways of reaching children before they develop serious problems. (6)

The responsibility of the schools for providing elementary guidance services is highly related to the conditions within the school program that may precipitate emotional problems. While schools have little jurisdiction over most "high risk trauma" or "life crises," the more subtle effect of certain elements of the school environment cannot be ignored. A major problem, often researched but little understood, is that of sex differences in learning. An elementary school program tailor-made for little girls only contributes to the increasing proportion of maladjusted boys.

Children and youth are confronted with many minor crises or trauma situations during the school year. The effect of certain school practices—grading, grouping, promotion, retention, and honor rolls—upon personality development can be serious for some pupils. The elementary guidance specialist must work directly with pupils, but he cannot ignore the total school environment that contributes so much to the growth and development of children.

Techniques and Procedures Employed by the Elementary Guidance Specialist

Guidance is everybody's business. But just as in most other activities, what is everybody's business soon becomes nobody's business without proper organization and coordination. It is useless to argue the primacy of the home, the school, the church, or other agencies in the guidance function. A more reasonable approach is to analyze the procedures and techniques used by each agency, and attempt to minimize needless duplication and overlap.

It is impossible to present an exhaustive description of techniques and procedures used by the elementary guidance specialist. As with other human endeavors, there can be no "cookbook" or pat formula for operation. In our efforts to describe the unique function of the guidance specialist we must not be apprehensive about borrowing techniques used by the school social worker, the school psychologist, the school nurse, or even the classroom teachers.

While it may be possible to differentiate procedures on the basis of corrective or preventive services, it is impractical to do so. The philosophy of the elementary school is developmental. That is, school personnel must accept each child where he is and try to provide appropriate services for helping him to attain acceptable goals. This concept of guidance goes beyond the prediction of potential problems and their remediation to a planned program provided for all students to promote better mental health and school adjustment. Within this frame of reference, the function of the guidance specialist is described below under the headings of child study and child adjustment procedures.

• • •

Basic Data Form Outline

School history
    Attendance record
    Grades
    Standardized test data

Personal information
    General health
    Special activities
    Personality ratings

Family information
    Marital relations of parents
    Siblings (age, grade, abilities)
    Special environmental conditions

Most of the information for initiating the case history will be available from permanent records or from teacher files. Such information as anecdotal records, communications with parents, and school contacts with courts or other community agencies should supplement the basic data form and conferences should be conducted with other professionals who may have knowledge relevant to the case.

In a complete case study all of the pupil data obtained during the child study procedures are organized in a systematic fashion to facilitate the analysis and diagnosis of the problem and to suggest appropriate adjustive action. Although it is not advisable to construct a comprehensive case history for each subject, this technique is one of the most primary procedures employed by the guidance specialist.

Observation

The behavior and adjustment of a pupil should be considered within the context of his environment. Often it is desirable to observe the child in the classroom, on the playground, or at home, prior to a personal interview, in an attempt to identify certain environmental influences. A trained observer may recognize significant behavioral symptoms that provide a clue to the development of the child or to crisis situations. Facial tics, squinting, head turning, the lifting of the knees, excessive squirming, and patterns of withdrawal or aggression when related to the activities in which the child is involved often suggest underlying causes of certain behavior.

Although the "critical incident" observation technique pioneered by Flanagan (7) proved somewhat cumbersome for the classroom teacher to use, the principle of a systematic recording of observed pupil behavior has significant advantages for the guidance specialist. This technique provides for the recording of "critical incidents" of pupil behavior according to categories of: responsibility and effort, integrity, sensitivity to others, group orientation, or other relevant headings.

Another program of systematic observation is described in a guidance handbook by Kough and DeHaan (19). A summary roster is suggested that permits the recording of characteristics of gifted and talented pupils; emotionally, socially, and educationally maladjusted pupils; and physically handicapped pupils. Lists of identifying characteristics are related to potential behavior such as leadership, creativity, and dropping out of school.

Although seldom as dramatic as portrayed in Sherlock Holmes or Charlie Chan detective stories, the observation skill can provide significant clues to the causes of certain pupil behavior. It is important that the guidance specialist have a solid background in child growth and development, and be alert to typical behavioral symptoms, to utilize fully the observation technique. Publications of the Gesell Institute (9, 10, 11, 12, 13) are especially helpful in developing this insight.

Interview

The counseling interview with the child provides an opportunity to establish rapport both for counseling therapy and for evaluation and diagnosis. Many times the initial interview may be conducted in a very informal setting—on the playground, during a casual stroll, as an outgrowth of a group activity, or at a time when the teacher has asked the pupil to "help Mrs. Jones sort some cards." This is not to suggest that it is always necessary to "sneak up" on a client, but one of the pupil characteristics that often precipitates a referral is a suspicion of adults. One successful interview technique involves helping a child to disassociate himself from his own problems in order to promote free discussion and objectivity as a third person.

Seldom will the "now what's your problem," or the "third degree," or the "exhortation" approach contribute much to the counseling interview. Children are often so concerned about giving the "right answer" that the guidance specialist must be especially perceptive and take every care to establish a noninstructional relationship with a subject.

Certain structured interview aids are available and the competent guidance specialist will develop techniques which include the use of doll families, modeling clay, coloring sheets, and other projective devices. It is not necessary to utilize such "gimmicks" with every child, but an understanding of the principles of these techniques enhances even a casual visit with a pupil. Space limitations prevent a comprehensive discussion of the counseling interview, but several references are cited in the bibliography that can help the guidance specialist develop this vital tool for pupil appraisal and therapy.

Individual Analysis

Although a professional course in individual analysis is often devoted to the mastery of individually administered intelligence tests, in practice the procedure of individual analysis is much broader. Several instruments are available for the purpose of assessing mental, physical, and emotional development on an individual basis; but the tool is secondary to the examiner in this process. A competent examiner will emulate the professional safe cracker by sandpapering his evaluative fingertips to a fine degree of sensitivity. As in the counseling interview the guidance specialist must read between the lines and be attuned to every verbal and physical response of the subject.

The Gesell Institute (9, 10, 11, 12, 13) has developed an excellent procedure for evaluating the total development of young children. An advantage to this approach is that it attempts to assign appropriate weightings to the several aspects of child development. Rather than providing merely an expression of intellectual level, or the physical maturity, or the emotional development of a child, the schedule combines these factors to suggest a "developmental age."

Old stand-bys such as the *Binet* (24) and *Wechsler* (26) intelligence scales are being supplemented by *The Blacky Pictures* (1), the *Vineland Social Maturity Scale* (5), and other individual or projective devices to be used by the more sophisticated guidance specialist.

A real danger inherent in the individual analysis procedure is that the novice, or even a veteran with limited psychometric background, will depend too much upon the results of these special instruments. A guidance specialist with an adequate foundation in clinical or counseling psychology will select an appropriate instrument for use at an appropriate time. He will also use the results cautiously and in conjunction with other relevant information.

Group Analysis

The child study procedures described thus far have been largely oriented toward correction or remediation of pupil behavior. A vital function of the guidance specialist is to describe the characteristics of groups of pupils that will enable the specialist, the teacher, and other professional personnel to provide appropriate programs addressed to the prevention of pupil problems. As the child development consultant on the school staff, the guidance specialist must help all personnel to understand children and to recognize the conditions that may precipitate poor pupil behavior or adjustment.

Certainly the organization and interpretation of standardized test data can contribute to the effectiveness of teacher planning and instruction. One of the most vital services the guidance specialist can provide for pupils is that of assisting the teacher in the establishment of reasonable goals for each child. Research suggests that the individualization of instruction can have a real influence on the self concepts and mental health of children. An analysis of achievement and mental test data by frequency distributions and scattergrams often identifies both group and individual instructional needs. Test manuals and measurement texts suggest simple, but effective, methods of treating test data to make them more meaningful and descriptive.

One of the major weaknesses of the way test scores are reported is that they are not related to pupil behavior or expectancies. The research oriented guidance specialist can develop tables for the purpose of predicting pupil success in specific programs, with various materials, in special groupings, or using different instructional methods. With the mounting pressures bearing upon pupil achievement, it is necessary to have dependable descriptions of pupil populations both for instruction and guidance.

But, the analysis of test data represents only one group study procedure. Before the guidance specialist can plan appropriate programs of orientation or adjustment it is necessary to be thoroughly familiar with the pupil population. Some group analysis data that may suggest special emphases in the total preventive program are: class sociograms, pupil mobility ratios, pupil attendance records, socioeconomic conditions of the school attendance area, environmental pressure upon children, pupil retentions, pupil grading practices, delinquency or vandalism rates, racial characteristics of the neighborhood, and numerous other factors that affect pupil adjustment. Both group and individual procedures for improving the mental health and learning climate are suggested in the section dealing with child adjustment procedures.

Child Adjustment Procedures

Although this article is focused upon the techniques and procedures employed by the guidance specialist in direct work with the pupil, it is not practical to engage in child adjustment activities without considering the influence of parents, teachers, and other school personnel. In addition to his function of providing direct services to pupils the guidance specialist serves as a child development consultant to the entire school staff. To work with the child alone would imply that the purpose of the guidance specialist is to adjust the child to his environment—whether good or bad—and never be concerned about modifying environmental conditions to meet the needs of the child. This approach would also imply that the guidance specialist is the only person that can improve the mental health of a pupil.

Child adjustment procedures must be predicated upon an understanding of the child and his problems as he perceives them and an understanding of all of the conditions that impinge upon his personality. It has been suggested that it is possible to differentiate between symptoms and causes of problems, but in practice the symptom often is the problem (23). This is not to say that some personality problems do not need depth diagnosis and therapy. However, it is impractical and unwise to assume that all, or even a large proportion, of the pupils referred are psychiatric cases. Many times a pupil merely needs a confidant or an adult that is not an authoritarian figure who will help him to regain his own self-confidence.

Adjustment procedures are much more difficult to discuss than study procedures. Just as in practicing medicine by mail, it is difficult to prescribe cures without a complete understanding of the problem. Further, readers are prone to assume that medication recommended for one patient is appropriate for other patients with similar symptoms. While the function of child study may be demanding of solid psychological foundations, child adjustment procedures require a sound philosophical base on the part of the therapist. Before applying certain adjustive procedures it may be necessary for the guidance specialist to evaluate his own philosophical concepts: must every child realize his full academic potential? what is the "good life?" is there a conflict between freedom and responsibility? or should every child be socially gregarious?

If a guidance specialist waited for fully acceptable answers to all of these questions, he would likely retire without having worked on a single case. Recognizing the imperfect nature of adjustive procedures—the guidance specialist does not naïvely assume their validity—there are but two alternatives: do nothing or proceed with caution. Many pupil problems require immediate attention, so the following procedures are suggested for the guidance specialist to be used with caution.

Counseling Therapy

Only rarely is there a sharp distinction between child study counseling and child adjustment counseling. The techniques for pupil appraisal and pupil adjustment counseling are essentially the same, but therapeutic counseling is more sophisticated and demanding of counseling skills. The purpose of adjustive counseling can range all the way from mere information giving to very subtle therapy. Hahn and McLean (14) suggest the following outline of purposes for the counseling interview:

(1) To establish rapport between the counselor and counselee. While it is not always necessary to capture a child's liking or admiration, the counselor must win his respect and establish a helping relationship.

(2) To collect new information and amplify or interpret information already gathered. Many times the counselee needs someone to help him restate or understand what he already knows about himself.

(3) To permit the counselee to "think aloud" in the presence of a sympathetic listener. This technique, discovered by Socrates and exploited by Rogers, is not only appreciated by almost all counselees, but proves itself daily to veteran counselors.

(4) To convey necessary information to the counselee. One reason the counselee often seeks help is that he lacks some pertinent information. However, one fault of using too many informational materials, such as test profiles, is that the counselor may tend to become an instructor.

(5) To find socially acceptable and personally satisfying alternatives with and for the counselee. Good counselors spend much of their time opening new doors to realistic solutions and gently closing doors that are likely to lead to dead ends.

One of the most significant contributions that a guidance specialist can make for most children with problems is to help the child develop an adequate self concept. While this may not be altogether possible through the counseling procedure alone, it should be one of the uppermost motives of the counselor at all times.

Group Guidance

Guidance specialists may be accused of infringing upon the teacher's domain when group procedures are used. However, optimum personal and social development of a pupil cannot take place in isolation from the group. Further, many routine guidance activities can be performed more efficiently and effectively using group procedures. Good examples of such activities are programs of: orientation, general test interpretation, human relations, and group motivation.

For most children to be personally adjusted requires that they first be socially adjusted. Willey and Andrews (27) suggest four social needs of children: the need to belong, the need to be approved, the need for adequacy or self-assurance, and the need for ambivalence. This latter need often confuses the classroom teacher. The seeming inconsistency between the need for independence and the need for group security may manifest itself in mysterious ways. When his actions are understood, it is often apparent that the most flagrant non-conformist is trying the hardest to conform to some notion or concept.

A rewarding experience for any adult would be to observe groups of children discussing common problems in a symposium. With very little adult participation, especially older children will identify significant issues and appropriate solutions. The leaders of the Boy Scouts and other youth organizations have discovered and exploited the "gang" or "club" tendency of children. Even "bad apples" have been mellowed by the actions of their peers. Groups are basically democratic and require respect for individuals. What better vehicle could be used to promote democratic ideals and concepts?

Among the most promising of group guidance techniques is the open-ended story. Here the group leader begins the discussion by telling a story that poses a problem but does not provide a solution. By suggesting appropriate story endings, children show remarkable insight with respect to problems of: integrity, respect for authority, vandalism, human relations, study habits, moral values, and physical development. The technique appears to be most therapeutic when employed with small groups and keyed to familiar experiences. Ojemann (21) has prepared materials to assist the guidance specialist in using this technique, and Jones (18) reports very gratifying results. Dinkmeyer and Dreikurs (4) have suggested some simple but effective group procedures for teachers in their book, *Encouraging Children to Learn*, that the guidance specialist can profitably employ.

Therapeutic Activities

Just as it is sometimes good therapy for a business man to whack a golf ball or for a housewife to buy a new hat, children can relieve tensions and reorient themselves through certain planned activities. Some of the most popular and promising procedures are suggested by Willey and Andrews (27): play therapy, art therapy, bibliotherapy, and recreational therapy. Although these procedures tend to be clinical in nature, the sophisticated guidance specialist should be familiar with the techniques and use them when appropriate. Bibliotherapy, for example, can be employed to help a child develop a system of values and discover that seemingly serious handicaps can be overcome or even used to an advantage. Proper use of these therapeutic techniques requires extensive study of both the procedure and the child.

Placement

While the placement of children appears to be more administrative than guidance oriented, it can be a valuable adjustive tool. Ilg (17) contends that approximately seventy percent of the elementary pupils are "overplaced." This contention certainly has many implications for those who develop the curriculum, but until appropriate revisions are made it is evident that placement within the school program requires considerable attention of the guidance specialist. It is doubtful that any retention, acceleration, grouping, or sectioning should be accomplished without the involvement of guidance personnel. One vital role of the guidance specialist in the placement of pupils is to interpret the action to the child and his parents. Especially in cases of retention or placement in special programs, the understanding and cooperation of the home are paramount. No doubt school personnel will encounter resistance to certain placement decisions, but when it has been established that a certain action is in the best interests of the pupil a tactful job of selling may be required. The adjustment of pupil problems through the procedure of placement places a premium on child study, teamwork, and communication.

Referral

It may be argued that referral of cases is not an adjustive procedure in itself. Nevertheless, the guidance specialist must recognize when it is necessary to seek more sophisticated professional help for a pupil. He must also be able to suggest the kind of help needed and the appropriate sources. But his job is not complete until he has provided the referral agency all available information, and he has coordinated the efforts of the clinician and school personnel. In general, the school guidance specialist should not attempt therapy wih a child when he is receiving help from a clinician. An exception to this rule is when the clinician and the guidance specialist plan a coordinated program of therapy and have the approval of the parents.

It is evident that there can be no fine lines of distinction drawn between working with parents, working with teachers, or working with children; between child study and child adjustment procedures; or between corrective and preventive programs. The guidance approach starts with the child and his needs, and utilizes every person and every technique that might provide a solution to his problem and result in proper adjustment.

Personnel

In many school systems guidance services will continue to be provided by the classroom teacher and the principal. In other school systems elaborate pupil service programs involving counselors, nurses, psychologists, social workers, and other special personnel will be available. It is the opinion of the writer that the most effective pupil service program is developed around a school based, multi-disciplinary, guidance specialist supported by a more highly specialized clinical team. Most important is the establishment of a balanced, total school staffing plan. To maintain excessively high teacher-pupil ratios, in order to employ a staff of specialists, will defeat the purpose of the program. It would be possible to develop a program wherein overloaded, overtaxed, anxious teachers create more problems than even an extensive clinical program can resolve.

An optimum staffing formula, requiring approximately forty-five school based professional personnel per thousand pupils, would provide: class sizes of approximately twenty-five pupils per teacher, a full-time administrator per six hundred to one thousand pupils, three or four special teachers (art, music, physical education, library) per six hundred to one thousand pupils, a full-time guidance specialist per six hundred to one thousand pupils, and a clinically based staff (psychological, educational, and medical specialists) of three to four full-time equivalents per five or six thousand pupils. Naturally, other considerations will require certain modifications in these ratios. It is conceded at the outset that such staffing will require sympathetic financing; but a formula should be developed for each school system to assure a reasonable balance between instructional, administrative, and pupil service functions.

Descriptions of the competencies and training of the school based, multi-disciplinary, guidance specialist will vary greatly. However, common characteristics will include: an excellent teacher, good personal adjustment, good psychological background, ability to work with children and adults, a comprehensive understanding of the total school program, and an overwhelming desire to help children develop sound personalities, and knowledge and skills commensurate with their abilities.

Bibliography

1. Blum, G. S. *The Blacky Pictures.* New York: Psychological Corporation, 1950.
2. Bower, Eli M. "A Process for Early Identification of Emotionally Disturbed Children," *Bulletin of the California State Department of Education.* Vol. XXVII, No. 6, August 1958.
3. DeHaan, Robert F., and Kough, Jack. *Helping Children with Special Needs.* Chicago: Science Research Associates, 1956.
4. Dinkmeyer, Don and Dreikurs, Rudolf. *Encouraging Children to Learn: The Encouragement Process.* Englewood Cliffs, New Jersey: Prentice-Hall, Inc., 1963.
5. Doll, Edgar. *Vineland Social Maturity Scale,* Revised. New York: Psychological Corporation, 1947.

6. Felix, R. H. "Forward," Basic Approaches to Mental Health in the Schools, reprinted from *The Personnel and Guidance Journal.*
7. Flanagan, John C. *The Personal and Social Development Program.* Chicago: Science Research Associates, 1956.
8. Froehlick, Clifford P., and Darley, John G. *Studying Students—Guidance Methods of Individual Analysis.* Chicago: Science Research Associates, 1952.
9. Gesell, Arnold, Halverson, Henry M., Thompson, Helen, Ilg, Frances L., Castner, Burton M., Ames, Louise Bates, and Amatruda, Catherine S. *The First Five Years of Life—A Guide to the Study of the Preschool Child.* New York: Harper & Brothers Publishers, 1940.
10. Gesell, Arnold, and Ilg, Frances L. *Child Development.* New York: Harper & Brothers Publishers, 1949.
11. Gesell, Arnold, and Ilg, Frances L. *Developmental Diagnosis,* Second Edition. New York: Psychological Corporation, 1947.
12. Gesell, Arnold, and Ilg, Frances L. *The Child from Five to Ten.* New York: Harper & Brothers Publishers, 1946.
13. Gesell, Arnold, Ilg, Frances L., and Ames, Louise Bates. *Youth—The Years from Ten to Sixteen.* New York: Harper & Brothers Publishers, 1956.
14. Hahn, Milton E., and MacLean, Malcolm S. *Counseling Psychology.* New York: McGraw-Hill Book Company, Inc., 1955, pp. 83–84.
15. Hatch, Raymond N., and Costar, James W. *Guidance Services in the Elementary School.* Dubuque, Iowa: Wm. C. Brown Company, Publishers, 1961.
16. Hymes, James L., Jr. *Understanding Your Child.* Englewood Cliffs, New Jersey: Prentice-Hall, Inc., 1952.
17. Ilg, Frances L. "Developmental Guidance in the Elementary Grades," a paper presented at the National Conference on Elementary Guidance, Washington, D.C., 1965.
18. Jones, Pauline. "Open-Ended Stories: A Study in Group Guidance," *Teacher's Notebook.* Wichita, Kansas: Division of Pupil Services, 1963.
19. Kough, Jack, and DeHaan, Robert F. *Identifying Children with Special Needs.* Chicago: Science Research Associates, 1955.
20. Lundberg, Horace W. *School Social Work—A Service of Schools.* Washington, D.C.: U.S. Department of Health, Education and Welfare, 1964.
21. Ojemann, Ralph H. *Handbook for Fifth Grade Teachers,* Book V. State University of Iowa.
22. Richards, E. A. *Proceedings of the Mid-Century White House Conference on Children and Youth,* Health Publications Institute, 1951.
23. Russo, Salvatore. "Clinical Psychology as the Treatment of Symptoms," *ETC.: A Review of General Semantics.* Vol. XIV, No. 2, Winter 1956–57, pp. 265–271.
24. Terman, Lewis M., and Merrill, Maud. *Revised Stanford-Binet Intelligence Scale,* Third Edition. Boston: Houghton Mifflin Company, 1960.
25. Torgerson, Theodore L. *Studying Children—Diagnostic and Remedial Procedures in Teaching.* New York: The Dryden Press, 1947.
26. Wechsler, David. *Wechsler Intelligence Scale for Children.* New York: Psychological Corporation, 1949.
27. Willey, Roy DeVerl, and Andrew, Dean C. *Modern Methods and Techniques in Guidance.* New York: Harper & Brothers Publishers, 1955. pp. 426, 448.

Elementary School Counseling

Anna R. Meeks

Significant developments in the decade from 1950 to 1960 brought a recognition that organized guidance programs are as important on the elementary level as on the secondary level.

An increasing awareness that people are the most basic resource for a nation's continued progress and development focused attention upon the academically able student and, more especially, upon the underachieving able youth. Concern mounted for the conservation of human resources as it relates to the secondary youth in matters of "school dropouts," juvenile delinquency and general underachievement of able youth.

Belatedly there came a conviction that we must find means of preventing, rather than trying to remedy such situations after they occur. This conviction has brought an awareness that any attempt to solve these problems must begin with a strengthened program of counseling and guidance services in the elementary school, for in the early years of the school experience children develop self-concepts and values that determine the motivation for learning and personal development in the secondary school as well as in the adult years of an individual's life.

Research studies in the area of learning have strengthened the school's conviction that any adequate program for the conservation of human resources must be concerned with the development of good emotional, social and educational adjustment. Efforts to enhance the learning opportunities for every child have emphasized the need to individualize instruction through more effective ways of recognizing and meeting children's needs. An increasing awareness that individual differences not only are great, but that they involve much more than intellectual differences, continues to emphasize the need for elementary guidance programs.

A concept of what this program should be has been slowly emerging in recent years.

"Elementary School Counseling," *The School Counselor,* 10, 3 (March 1963) 108–111, has been reprinted with the permission of the author and of the publisher, the American Personnel and Guidance Association, © 1963 by the American Personnel and Guidance Association.

Too often elementary guidance has been identified as a process insep-arable from teaching. Efforts to meet the needs of children have relied on grouping procedures and curriculum revision with little or no use of special services to the individual. Such a point of view fails to see that the guidance process is concerned with the unique needs of the individual while curriculum is concerned with the common needs of a group of children.

A somewhat later point of view accepts guidance as a specialized service for children with severe problems, but not essential for every child unless it might be through the standardized test program.

More recently guidance is accepted as a process through which we can identify the needs of children and help them and their parents in developing realistic goals in order that they may have an opportunity for optimal development. Research studies are showing that a low self-image at school entrance can create barriers to intellectual accomplishment. It follows, then, that the earlier the school identifies the needs of a child and provides for a realistic atmosphere of success and acceptance, the greater will be the chance that the child's self-concept can grow as a basis for progress.

Organized Programs

The recognition of a need to provide earlier guidance services has resulted in a developing wave of organized programs of elementary school guidance. The number of schools offering such programs has steadily increased since 1950. In general these programs have been limited to indi-vidual school districts or large city and county units. The year 1962 saw the beginnings of statewide programs in at least two states, with the devel-opment of certification requirements and of programs for professional preparation especially designed to meet the needs of the elementary school counselor.

There is a general acceptance of the importance of the guidance func-tion in the elementary school, but there is not equal agreement on how this function may best be performed nor on who should be responsible for this function. There is a need to better define and clarify the guidance role and function as a basis for determining which personnel must be assigned responsibility for the development of adequate guidance services.

No one seriously believes that elementary guidance is solely a point of view but we have not completely emerged from a "crisis" concept of guidance that serves only those children whose problems become too great to allow them to function in a classroom. A more positive approach is centered in efforts to enhance the learning climate for *all* children. Interest in the development of learning situations that produce creativity and develop leadership is creating a demand for systematic and in-service edu-cation for teachers in today's most complex educational program.

Questions

A number of questions have emerged, and these must be resolved if maximum benefits are to be derived from organized guidance services.

(1) What personnel is needed to meet the needs of the child as a learner?

(2) When there is a specialist, how shall the guidance functions be delineated?

(3) What is the relationship of the guidance specialist to the administrator, teacher and other members of the school staff?

(4) What professional preparation does an elementary school counselor need?

(5) How can school counseling be made an integral part of the total educational program?

Guidance in elementary schools is emerging as a process primarily concerned with assisting the child as a learner. Essentially it is the process of helping the child to understand and accept himself in relation to his own needs and to those of his environment. Early identification of each child's needs and interests, interpretation of these to parents and teachers and counseling for every child would seem to be the chief goals for developing adequate guidance services.

Counseling is a significant aspect of the elementary program. Early counseling helps the child to make adjustments to new and difficult situations and thus strengthens the child's ability to apply his self-understanding to the solution of problems in later years.

Guidance, then, is an integral part of the total educational program, and to be most effective the guidance process in the elementary school must be a part of a continuous guidance process from the child's first contact with school until he has been placed in a "job" or in post-secondary education.

Emphases will change to meet the needs of a developing youth, but essentially guidance will be a process of helping him develop and accept a realistic self-concept as a basis for optimal development.

Techniques and procedures must fit the child's level of development, and it is here that the uniqueness of elementary guidance can be found. The use of toys, of open-end stories and of role playing so characteristic of elementary school counseling offers a different approach.

But the purpose of counseling—a more realistic self-concept and changed behavior—is just as pertinent in elementary guidance as in secondary guidance. Many children will receive individual counseling, but many will work in some form of group activity in order that the dynamics of an interacting group may help the child in his self-evaluation and self-acceptance.

Teacher's Role

The emphasis upon specialized assistance in no way indicates a lesser guidance role for the teacher. In fact, schools providing effective guidance services consistently report an enhanced role for teachers that recognizes guidance as that part of the teacher's responsibility directly related to the provision of conditions necessary for effective learning.

Every attempt to improve the learning climate in a classroom has made new and heavier demands upon the teacher's time and ingenuity. Gradually we are accepting the idea that the teacher has a *right* to expect specialized assistance in meeting the varying needs of children in her class. Administrators and teachers accept this concept and urge a clarification of the role and function of guidance in the elementary school, so that the development of organized programs can proceed at a faster rate.

While there is some evidence that universities are developing programs for the professional preparation of elementary counselors, there is a need for many more programs that give attention to the unique needs of various developmental levels of elementary children. Practicums in counseling must allow for experience with elementary school children. Play therapy and courses in human development and in the psychology of learning are musts for potential elementary counselors.

Prospects

The decade from 1950 to 1960 has seen remarkable growth in interest, understanding and in know-how in elementary guidance and has provided a readiness for professional leadership for the future development of organized programs.

The American School Counselor Association has had a committee working to clarify some of the issues mentioned above. A tentative report in 1959 at the APGA Convention in Cleveland aroused considerable interest. The response to meetings on elementary guidance in subsequent conventions gave evidence of the genuine interest and concern for the development of effective programs of elementary school guidance.

The work of the ASCA Committee is continuing as a part of the APGA project for the study of elementary school guidance. An initial survey of existing guidance programs is providing the basis for further study of the direction and trends evident in the expansion and development of these services. ASCA will be responsible for the preparation of a statement designed to suggest a desirable approach to the development of effective elementary school guidance. Such a statement will be developed after a larger committee has had an opportunity to study existing programs.

This statement will be followed with a period of research to determine the effectiveness of suggested organizations and techniques. Then APGA will release a statement of basic principles which can guide the development of the emerging and rapidly expanding program of elementary school guidance.

The decade of the sixties challenges us to bring vision, creativity and unceasing effort to the development of effective elementary school guidance in order that all children may find an opportunity for optimal development in a climate that minimizes barriers to learning through genuine individualization of instruction.

Developmental Counseling
in the Elementary School

Don Dinkmeyer

With the greatly increased extension of counseling and guidance serv-ices to the elementary school level, counseling theorists have become aware of a greater need for a theory of developmental counseling with children. This theory must take account of such basic factors as the nature of the child, the elementary school setting, and the goals, techniques, and process of the counseling. Furthermore, those who would counsel in the elementary school must become aware of the research in the broad area of child development and child psychiatry.

Nature of the Child

The most obvious difference between secondary school and elemen-tary school counseling stems from the nature of the child. The elementary school child is still in the process of becoming—physically, socially, emo-tionally, and as a total personality. He is in a process of unfolding and there are still certain developmental changes that will come about as the result of this growth process.

Research in child development points to the importance of consider-ing developmental changes. Thus, the counselor would need to be aware of "normal developmental problems" as contrasted with serious adjust-ment difficulties. He should know that there are wide individual differences in developmental patterns that are due to basic differences in rate of development. These developmental differences create adjustment problems for the child both in the tasks of school and social life.

"Developmental Counseling in the Elementary School," *Personnel and Guidance Journal* (November 1966), 262–266, has been reprinted with the permission of the author and of the publisher, the American Personnel and Guidance Association, © 1966 by the American Personnel and Guidance Asso-ciation. Don Dinkmeyer is Associate Professor of Counseling and Guidance at DePaul University. He also edits the *Journal of Elementary School Guidance and Counseling.*

The counselor, therefore, should have available developmental data that tell him about individual rates of development and enable him to infer something about the child's feelings about himself in the peer group.

Mussen and Jones (1958), in their study of the self-concept in late and early maturing boys, have indicated a variance in the self-concepts and motivation of these two groups.

It is important that each counselor be familiar with the basic needs of the child. The child has specific needs that relate to the guidance process. He needs to mature in self-acceptance, in his understanding of self, and in his comprehension of his assets and liabilities. The child needs to develop a more realistic self-evaluation and the counselor can help in this process. The counselor can also assist the child to develop, to mature in social relationships, to belong, and to identify. The child needs to develop independence, to take on responsibility, to make choices, and to be responsible for these choices. He needs to mature in his ability to plan. The counselor provides an environment in which the child is independent, makes choices, and becomes responsible for his decision. The child also needs to mature in understanding the role of work in life as it first appears in educational achievement and then as it appears in the environment as related to jobs and employment opportunities. The child needs to develop a realistic self-appraisal of his capacities, interests, and attitudes as they relate to the work tasks.

The counselor, at the elementary school level, will recognize that he needs to work with the significant adults in the child's life. This includes the teacher and the parents. With the teacher he will encourage intensive child study that takes into account developmental information and the developmental factors significant in comprehending the way in which the child approaches the developmental tasks of living. He will help the teacher to have available cumulative records that provide information about rate instead of status, dynamics of behavior instead of descriptions of the past. The cumulative record should show the pattern of development both physically and psychologically.

Behavior is purposive, and acquires its meaning in the social setting. Beyond the understanding of need, the counselor must understand the purposes of behavior in specific children. Purposes are the directive forces in the child's life, even though the child may not be aware of these goals and purposes. We need to look at the purposes of misbehavior as they are illustrated in attention-getting, the seeking to be powerful, to get even, or to demonstrate inadequacy (Dreikurs, 1957). As we become cognizant of the individual's purposes, we are able to deal with the child's private logic, and become aware of the basic style of life and concept of self and others. Psychological growth is patterned, and we must focus on the unity of behavior and the style of life, avoiding the collection of fragmentary data and instead looking at the direction of psychological movement.

Recent research tends to indicate that the early elementary years are much more significant than any of us have been truly able to determine prior to now. The research of Bloom (1964) indicates the significance of the first three grades in predicting the total pattern of achievement. Kagan and Moss (1962) at the Fels Research Institute recently released a study indicating that many of the behaviors exhibited by the child during the period from six to ten years of age, and a few during the period from three to six, were moderately good predictors of theoretically related behavior during early adulthood. This study indicated that the child who was achieving well early in school will generally continue to achieve well. There is a need to provide early encouragement for the academic achiever, and to identify those who are not meeting the academic tasks at this stage of life.

The elementary counselor should also be aware of the developmental task concept as first formulated by Havighurst. He needs to recognize that the pertinent tasks of middle childhood involve learning to get along with age-mates, and participating in the give and take of social exchange.

Most human problems are interpersonal problems and these problems increase as the child moves into a peer society. The research of Piaget (1929), which has increasingly attracted the attention of American psychologists, shows that during preadolescence the child begins to develop a concept of self quite distinguishable from the outer world. This is the time when the clarification of feelings, concepts, attitudes, goals, and an understanding of self would be most significant.

The development of conscience, morality, and values begins early in the elementary school. The child is in the process of developing this internal moral control and set of values. The child learns that rules are necessary and thus develops what Piaget calls the morality of cooperation. Piaget believes that middle childhood is a crucial period for the development of this cooperation. The counselor could be available to help the child through this stage as an awareness of values and goals emerges. The child will frequently need help in reconciling his values, his ideal self, and his actual performance. However, the child needs to learn to make plans, and to act in the present and immediate future independent of other parents and other adults. Counseling can provide the opportunity to assist in the making of choices, planning, and deciding.

Caroline Tryon and Jesse Lilienthal (1950) have provided an interesting presentation of the developmental tasks and their importance for the counselor. They indicate that these might be used as guideposts that permit us to assess the rate at which the child is developing in regard to the tasks of life. They suggest that the counselor might be aware of some of the following pertinent tasks:

(a) achieving an appropriate dependent-independence pattern;
(b) achieving an appropriate giving-receiving pattern of affection, learning to accept self as worthwhile, learning to belong;

(c) relating to changing groups, establishing a peer group, and learning to belong and behave according to the shifting peer code.

Counseling in the Elementary School Setting

The counselor cannot counsel without an awareness of the elementary school setting, and the fact that he is part of an educational team. He should be aware of the philosophy, objectives, and practices of the school. He should be familiar with the curriculum and the opportunities within the curriculum for the student's development. He must be cognizant of the teacher's crucial role in classroom guidance. The teacher should be encouraged to provide regular guidance activities, to identify problems, and to provide guidance through the teacher-counselor role.

Developmental counseling, which can be contrasted with adjustment, or crisis counseling, is not always problem-oriented in terms of assuming that the child has some difficult problem. Instead, the goals are the development of self-understanding, awareness of one's potentialities, and methods of utilizing one's capacity. Developmental counseling truly focuses on helping the individual know, understand, and accept himself. This type of counseling, then, becomes personalized learning, not individualized teaching. The child learns not only to understand himself but to become ultimately responsible for his choices and actions.

Unique Factors

The type of counseling we are considering Hummel (1962) has referred to as ego counseling. This implies that it may be a short-term service in which the relationship is basically collaborative and the child works on problems that are of concern to him. The counselor helps the child investigate, analyze, and deliberate to solve more effectively certain developmental problems. Thus, exploration, examination, and resolution are basic techniques. There is mutual survey of the facts, clarification of feelings, consideration of alternatives, development of problem-solving techniques, and arrival at decisions.

The counselor provides a non-evaluative relationship and offers his collaboration. His job is to clarify, to reflect, to restate as precisely as possible the meanings he perceives to be implied in the counselee's statements. However, the counselor, at times, will interpret, confront, question, and thus facilitate the child's capacity to solve his own problems.

The elementary school child is in the process of formulating a style of life and self-concept. There is a considerable body of evidence that indicates that the child with a poor self-concept, compared with those who have more positive self-concepts, will be more anxious, less well-adjusted, less popular, less effective, less honest, and more defensive (McCandless, 1961). One of the tasks of the school counselor is to assist each child to feel accepted as he is. The counselor seeks to help the child discover his potentialities, to acquire a realistic appreciation of his assets and limitations, and to set certain goals. This should enable the child to accept himself rather than seek to conform to standards that are out of harmony with what he is or would hope to be.

Principles in Child Counseling

What, then, are the fundamentals we need to be aware of in child counseling?

1. Counseling is a learning-oriented process carried on in a one-to-one social environment. It must utilize the best that we have available from learning theory.

2. The relationship is crucial in the counseling process. It should be one in which there is mutual trust and mutual respect, enabling the counselee to become more open to communication and more motivated to change. Change is always more possible in a non-evaluative, non-judgmental atmosphere.

3. The counselor helps the client to understand and accept what he is, and to use his newly acquired knowledge about self to realize his potential, to change in attitude, behavior, and, eventually, style of life.

4. The child is frequently not a volunteer. There is a real need for common purpose and a motivation for counseling. It is important that the goals of counseling be mutually aligned between counselor and counselee. It is important to understand the individual's objective viewpoint, to be emphatic, to recognize his private logic.

5. We need to listen not only for the words, but what is behind the words. We need to become skilled in guessing the child's psychological direction. Behavior is purposive and has social implications. We need to make the child more aware of his purposes, goals, convictions, and attitudes. As the child becomes aware of his faulty assumptions, he can "catch" himself.

6. There are certain dependency factors that will restrict the child from changing certain things in his environment. His choices may be limited in terms of restrictions placed upon him by adults such as parents and teachers.

7. There is a necessity for working intensively both with parents and teachers if we are to change the child's environment. Contact with the significant adults is directed at changing the adult's behavior and thus the child's perception of self and human relationships. The counselor most of all must become aware of the goals and the unity in the pattern of the counselee's behavior. Maladjustment is characterized by increased inferiority feelings, underdeveloped social interest, and uncooperative methods of striving for significance (Dreikurs, 1950). These dynamics help the counselor to explain and understand the child's behavior.

8. Because the child may not be as verbal as the adult, there is need for sharper sensitivity on the part of the counselor in working with non-verbal cues and non-verbal factors. We need to listen with the child's ears and observe to determine what is behind the total psychological movement. Our observation of a recognition reflex in his facial expressions sometimes enables us to comprehend his goal. Disclosure of the child's goals and purposes when given in appropriate fashion can be a most significant technique.

9. The counselor provides encouragement as a major therapeutic technique. He enables the client to accept himself so that he has the courage to function (Dinkmeyer & Dreikurs, 1963).

10. Some children have a minimal ability to relate their feelings. They may not always be sensitive to reflection, and they need a tentative statement in regard to feelings such as: "Could it be you feel the children are against you?"

11. The individual's perceptions are more important than the objective reality of the situation.

12. People will move in positive directions when they are really free to choose. We need to provide the atmosphere that permits them to make these choices.

13. The feeling of basic trust between counselor and counselee opens the channels of communication. The mutual alignment of goals also assists this development.

14. Counseling is looked upon as a re-educative process directed towards the development of self-understanding, the changing of convictions, and the development of increased social interest. It is not heavily oriented toward vocational guidance; instead it deals with the developmental tasks, problems, and needs of the child. Through self-understanding, self-acceptance, and clarification of feeling the greatest growth can occur.

15. The cognitive and conceptual development of the child is not always as advanced as we might hope and, hence, the counselor must be certain communication is meaningful. Children have limited experiences and, hence, will have a limited ability to comprehend certain concepts.

16. The counselor becomes aware that he needs to empathize so closely that he can guess what it is that the client is thinking, and that he can put this into the client's words. The effective counselor is one who understands the way in which the individual strives to be significant and helps the individual to accept himself. He sees the developmental problems as interpersonal problems. His communication with the client helps the client to understand new ways of relating to others.

Developmental counseling provides the child with an opportunity to explore his feelings, his attitudes, convictions. The counselor starts with the problems that the child perceives and helps him to solve them. The counselor in this situation provides a relationship that accepts, understands, and does not judge. It provides the counselee with constant clarification of his basic perception of life. This relationship enables the counselee to become increasingly self-directed so that the goal is one of enabling the counselee to deal with both the developmental tasks and the general problems of living. This type of developmental counseling suggests that counselors would not only be problem-oriented, but would be concerned about all students in the school population.

The goal is to take certain grade levels and to offer assistance to each student by providing an opportunity for some four or five contacts devoted to the specific objectives as they have been presented. When we can provide this form of counseling at the elementary school level, we can probably insure a greater productivity academically and hopefully much more effective social relationships between children and also between children and the significant adults in their atmosphere. Thus, we can see that elementary school counseling may need a new theory and a new set of practices. Developmental counseling might provide a direction quite different from that of typical secondary school counseling.

References

Bloom, B. *Stability and change in human characteristics,* New York: John Wiley, 1964.

Dinkmeyer, D., & Dreikurs, R. *Encouraging children to learn: the encouragement process.* Englewood Cliffs, N.J.: Prentice-Hall, 1963.

Dreikurs, R. *Fundamentals of Adlerian psychology.* New York: Greenberg, 1950.

Dreikurs, R. *Psychology in the classroom.* New York: Harper, 1957.

Hummel, R. Ego-counseling in guidance: concept and method. *Harvard Educational Review,* 1962, *32,* 463–482.

Kagan, J., & Moss, H. *Birth to maturity.* New York: John Wiley, 1962.

McCandless, B. R. *Children and adolescents: behavior and development.* New York: Holt, Rinehart and Winston, 1961.

Mussen, P., & Jones, M. The behavior inferred motivation of late and early maturing boys. *Child Development,* 1958, *29,* 61–67.

Piaget, J. *The child's conception of the world.* New York: Harcourt, Brace, 1929.

Tryon, C., & Lilienthal, J. Developmental tasks: the concept and its importance. *Fostering mental health in our schools.* 1950 Yearbook, Association for Supervision and Curriculum Development. Washington, D.C.: The Association, 1950.

ABC's of Counseling in the Elementary School

Henry R. Kaczkowski

A few years ago Hadley Cantril (1950) remarked that "a crucial question in education is to devise a method for teaching people how to improve value judgments which in turn will better guarantee a higher quality of experience." Although Cantril's challenge has not been ignored, no all-embracing solution has been found. The purpose of this paper is to suggest one possible way in which an elementary school counselor can assist some students in their quest for a more meaningful educational experience.

The literature is replete with a variety of ideas about what an elementary school counselor should do. Unfortunately, most of the verbalizations are in the form of free associations. The paper does not purport to cover the entire scope of the work of the elementary school counselor. It does review how counseling can help pupils have a meaningful educational experience.

Concepts of Personality

A counselor's effectiveness in a counseling relationship is directly related to his formulation of a concept of personality. The counselor's understanding of personality enables him to set boundary lines for the interaction so that the assistance given the child will have some direction. Personality is best viewed as a system of interacting characteristics in a state of mutual dependence. A child appraises a stimulus configuration (social or nonsocial) from three reference points: ideas or beliefs (cognition); expressive symbols (cathexis); or value orientation (evaluation).

"ABC's of Counseling in the Elementary School," *Elementary School Guidance and Counseling*, 3, 4 (Summer 1969), has been reprinted with the permission of the author and of the publisher, the American Personnel and Guidance Association, © 1969 by the American Personnel and Guidance Association. Henry R. Kaczkowski is Associate Professor of Education, University of Illinois, Urbana.

Cognition determines "what is seen," the cathetic mode determines the positive or negative reactions, and the consequences of reaction are forecast by the child's evaluative orientation. The traits of a personality system are so structured that each has an expected function in interpersonal relations. The counseling process helps the child examine his structure-function-expectancy system so that gross inconsistencies can be changed in order to facilitate the assimilation of new experiences.

Lecky's (1951, p. 214) self-consistency theory further substantiates the above view.

> According to self-consistency, the mind is a unit, an organized system of ideas. All of the ideas which belong to the system must seem consistent with one another. The center or nucleus of the mind is the individual's idea or conception of himself. If a new idea seems consistent with the ideas already present in the system, and particularly with the individual's conception of himself, it is accepted and assimilated easily. If it seems inconsistent, however, it meets with resistance and is likely to be rejected. This resistance is a natural phenomenon; it is essential for the maintenance of individuality. . . . If the pupil shows resistance toward certain types of material, this means that from his point of view it would be inconsistent for him to learn it. If we were able to change the self-conception which underlies this viewpoint, however, his attitude toward the material will change accordingly. With resistance eliminated, he learns so rapidly that tutoring is often unnecessary.

A counselor who accepts Lecky's thesis will establish a counseling relationship for the purpose of altering the student's attitudes. The student is not learning in the classroom because of a lack of ability but because of the standards he has set for himself. The counseling situation focuses on how the student feels and thinks about life matters and how this frame of reference impedes him from having a meaningful educational experience.

Theoretical Parts of the Counseling Relationship

The ABC notion of counseling is not a reference to the simplicity of the process but a mnemonic device to help the reader recall some of the important theoretical parts of the counseling relationship. ABC refers to the three dimensions in which the counseling process can take place: Affect, Behavior, Cognition. The letters D and E structure the role that the counselor and counselee play in the relationship. The counselor can either establish a *didactic* (teaching) relationship or an *experiencing* relationship. The counselee, on the other hand, should be able to *disclose* and to be *expressive*. Both the counselor and the counselee should communicate with *feeling* (emotion) and be *genuine* (honest, no facades). The counseling relationship is characterized as being warm, accepting, and permissive; both parties (counselor and counselee) actively participate in some form of communication interchange and they share their convictions, suspicions, inferences, and conclusions.

During the communication interchange the counselee declares, debates, demands, reflects, reasons, soliloquizes, and tests. The process is designed to bring about some kind of modification in the crystalized aspects of the self-structure so that the counselee may achieve some degree of congruence between his *humanity* (interpersonal relations, culturally determined ideas, external demands, etc.) and *identity* (interpersonal concerns, self-structure, frame of reference, etc.). The end goal of counseling is not to reconstruct the child but to make him more assertive in respect to his own being and the external pressures that bear on him.

If the counseling relationship can be construed as a socialization process then certain behavior experiences regarding the participants can be generated. In order to guide the counselor in his role as a socializer, Lennard and Berstein (1960) suggest that the counselor should answer the following set of questions: Who shall speak? How much? About what? When? How long? "Under what circumstances" shall "who speak," "how much," "about what?" These questions are designed to help the counselor structure the counseling relationship.

The first two questions, "Who shall speak?" and "How much?" delineate the degree of activeness of the participants in the counseling relationship. Many counselees enter counseling with the expectation that it is their task to state their problem and the counselor's to resolve it. If the counselor is viewed as an expert, then the counselee sees himself as a passive partner in the counseling relationship. The counselor must communicate the notion that he expects the counselee to play an active part during the counseling relationship.

The third question, "About what?" is concerned with two things. First, the counselee must "unlearn what he thought he was supposed to talk about, and become sensitive to the expectational terms to the requirements of the situation in which he finds himself" (Lennard & Berstein, 1960). For example, the child should not continue to hold to the idea that the counselor is another (listening) teacher but a person who is genuinely interested in him as a person. Secondly, although the counselee is selective in what he talks about during the interview, he should become aware that a high degree of selectivity will limit the amount of gain he obtains from the counseling relationship.

The fourth question, "When?" is directly related to the principle of behavior reciprocity. The counselee must be aware of the fact that the counselor and counselee will behave "differently" as counseling progresses. "In learning about differentiation while in therapy, the patient becomes more sensitive to the unfolding patterns in relationships in general, and he learns that movement toward a goal in interpersonal relationships requires different actions at different times" (Lennard & Berstein, 1960). By the same token the counselor should become sensitive to the counselee's adroitness in meeting the various demands of the counseling relationship.

The last question, "How long?" is concerned with the duration of the counseling relationship. Many of the counselees (and their teachers) expect an immediate change in the client. Consequently, the teachers expect the counselee to miss only a few classes. Although there is no set rule for estimating the length of the counseling process, the counselor should be able to sense the "pace" at which to proceed with the counselee. This will enable him to arrange for advance scheduling of students who have been referred to him.

The Therapeutic Process

The concept of pacing may also have another meaning. Since the counseling relationship is sequential in nature, it suggests that the process is made up of a series of parts. Kelman (1963) has suggested that any therapeutic process consists of three stages: compliance, identification, and internalization. In the compliance phase of the counseling relationship, the student learns the basic aspects of being a client. Because the student's need for approval is high, he engages in the verbal interchange on a superficial level. The counselor plays the role of a trainer (teacher). In the second phase, the counselee comes to realize that the situation is not only pleasant but safe and can in the long run become beneficial to him. He makes his commitment to counseling known to the counselor by disclosing more of his self-structure. The counselor plays the role of an accepting, permissive, expert listener. In the third phase the counselee begins to internalize some ideas, values, and attitudes that have been generated in the counseling relationship.

In addition, some of the interpersonal encounters he has made outside the counseling setting have been used to test the temporary modifications in the self-structure. The permanent change comes about through what Kelman (1963) calls "corrective emotional experience." During this phase the counselor encourages the counselee to make a self-examination. Although some theorists disagree with the stage concept, Kelman's views do help explain why some counseling relationships do not result in any positive change in the student. They rarely get past the first stage.

Kelman raises the issue of whether a counselor should be concerned only with what goes on within therapy or also with behaviors outside therapy. Does the counselor want the client just to commit himself to interacting within the counseling setting or should the counselor prepare the counselee for real life? Some children are very apt at verbal interchange during the interview but do not change their behavior pattern outside the counseling room. The counseling relationship must generate an interaction pattern within the process so that the counselee can generalize to settings outside the interview. This generalization is facilitated if the counselee has internalized the concepts of role versatility and role adequacy. The counselor should not assume that there will be an automatic transferring of new behavior patterns.

It should also be brought out that for some counselees the "corrective emotional experience" can only be gained outside the counseling relationship. Some children can be helped only if a "significant other" (a person whose opinion they value) changes his attitude toward the child. In this type of situation the counselor should consult with the "significant other" to secure the needed behavior modification. Without their cooperation the relationship should be ended.

Glad (1959), after analyzing a variety of therapeutic conceptions, reached the following conclusions about what is helpful in promoting gain in clients:

(1) Start working with concrete concerns and expand the relationships from there.

(2) Work with assets rather than with debits.

(3) Create a positive and rewarding atmosphere.

(4) The counselor should be aware that during the counseling relationship he communicates a set of values that provide the counselee cultural acceptability and personal effectiveness.

(5) Successful psychotherapy may be conceptualized simply in the proposition that under favorable conditions of learning, one is most likely to adopt those values and skills that are available in the learning situation.

From an examination of the above list it becomes apparent that the counselor should have some idea of the direction he hopes the counseling process will take. He should not, however, become so wedded to a theoretical orientation that he cannot shift his style to meet the demands of the counselee. He should keep in mind that his personality structure is a system. If a counselor is to have meaningful interpersonal relations, he too must have role versatility and role adequacy. He should be willing to deviate from his theoretical orientation if he senses that this step will be beneficial to the counselee.

It should be remembered that the above delineation of counselor activity is predicated on the premise that the counselor is a socializer. If the premise is accepted, then the goals of counseling complement the goals of the school. Each is concerned with the enhancement of self so that the child in succeeding years not only realizes his own being but at the same time becomes a contributor to the general welfare of others. The counselor should be able to relate the process of socialization to the personality development of the child. The context of counseling interviews therefore centers on developmental tasks and how the child is meeting the demands of society. They serve as guidelines for the selection of topics to be discussed and prevent the child from wandering about during the course of the interview.

The socialization process essentially consists of the internalization of an array of culturally determined ideas. An individual acquires the cultural patterns by means of role behavior:

Role behavior, we argue, is social interaction brought about by the stereotyped expectations referring to the individual who plays the role and the latter's internalization of these expectations and resultant felt obligations. We do not assume that such expectations must be clearly recognized by the individual who plays the role to the extent that he can verbalize them as a list of musts and must nots. He may be rather sensitive toward them even though they are never expressed verbally. . . . The interaction with fellow beings thus becomes smooth and need-satisfying to the extent that one is sensitive to one's role prescriptions. The more general and generally accepted a given pattern of role expectations is, however, the earlier and more gradually is it internalized and the greater is the probability that even professional students of society fail to see. (Rommetveit, 1955, p. 35)

What the child learns or does not learn in school is dependent to a large degree upon his accepting the notion that roles structure his behavior. The initial awareness of this structuring is generated by pre-school play.

White suggests that early mastery in exploratory play, speech, and motor skills leads to competence in academic skills, and Kagan and Moss suggest that this intense striving for mastery at the primary school level (6–10-age level) is lasting (Raph, et al., 1966). Children learn that competence in skills is a source of satisfaction. A by-product of competence is that it helps formulate a base for intrinsic motivation on which much of school instruction depends. It has been suggested that mastery of intellectual skills is a cultural requirement and a source of satisfaction to a child (Raph, et al., 1966). The child who fails to assimilate this idea is doomed to failure in his school work. Early identification of this type of child is essential.

The school's typical reaction to the child who has failed to assimilate the idea that intellectual mastery is a cultural requirement is to place him in a remedial setting. The child's appraisal of the remedial process (stimulus configuration) will tend to follow these steps: (a) It's just like any other classroom: teacher, books, and homework. I will not be told how to behave (cognition); (b) I dislike being told what to do therefore I hate reading (cathexis); (c) Since I am my own boss, I won't pay any attention—therefore I can't learn to read (evaluation). The counselor working with this type of child centers his effort in the affective domain.

Many children have learning difficulties because their basic attitude in life is "Nobody is going to tell me what to do." The rejection of any rules and codes by the child precludes his learning how to read and spell because these skills are essentially rule-following activities. Dreikurs (1957) further characterizes this type of child as having low self-esteem, withdrawal tendencies, and as being easily discouraged. This observation is supported by Atkinson and Feather (1966) who feel that an achievement-oriented child is one who derives satisfaction from the exercise of his skills and avoids failure by means of striving. The failure-threatened child has low levels of aspiration, is anxious, and "resists activities in which his competence might be evaluated against a standard or competence of others" (Atkinson & Feather, 1966). The counseling process, as a modifier of the structure-function-expectancy system, focuses on changing the child's passive nature to active participation in the classroom by making him aware of his negative attitudes. During the counseling process the attitudes change from "can't" to "I can do" to "I am."

The child's failure to internalize appropriate social roles impedes his development of adequate interpersonal relations. Although many reasons have been advanced for why some children fail to accommodate certain external pressures, Buhler's (1962) observations on the problem have some bearing on why the school should be concerned with the acquisition of appropriate social roles. Buhler is of the opinion that up to age four the child's behavior is fundamentally task-determined. That is to say, the factors outside the child structure many of his activities. However, at age four the child slowly begins to free himself from task-determined activities so that by age eight he has a high degree of personal autonomy. This does not mean that he does anything he wants but that he is in a position to be selective of his behavior responses. The child is beginning to have a degree of inner control over his responses rather than acting in an impulsive manner. He selects responses in terms of culturally determined ideas and ego ideals (Buhler, 1962). In activities that demand interaction between individuals he knows the appropriate role patterns and acts accordingly. In this manner the child gains acceptance from adults and peers and from this is able to generate a sense of belongingness and worthwhileness.

The child who fails to gain a sense of autonomy by the end of the primary level will tend to be rejected by those with whom he comes into contact. His behavior pattern is characterized by impulsive actions, passivity (he waits for things to be done to him), and agitation rather than action when he encounters a block to his goal. Since he tends to be rejected, he tries to placate his social hunger by resorting to a variety of attention-getting procedures. To the teacher he is a nuisance and to the class he is a clown or a bully. The counseling process with this type of child centers on helping him become autonomous, gain a degree of self-control, and overcome social ignorance. Although the child's specific behaviors are discussed, the counselor should help the child become aware of his feelings toward learning appropriate social roles.

Poor interpersonal relations are generally due to social ignorance. Fundamentally, the child has failed to internalize the principle of behavioral reciprocity. In order to be competent in interpersonal relations an individual must have (Jourard, 1966) the "ability to fulfill a variety of roles (versatility) in socially acceptable ways (adequacy)." Cameron and Cameron (1951, p. 114) amplify this idea in the following manner:

> To gain social perspective a person must be able to put himself realistically in another person's place, to have the other's attitudes and so be

able to predict and understand what the other does. . . . The skilled role-taker, like the skilled motorist, is more likely than the unskilled to meet competently a sudden unlooked-for stress and continue operating effectively in the face of protracted strain. . . . To have many roles is to have many tools; but to have many tools in any trade and be unable to shift quickly under changing conditions from one tool to another is to be far below optimal adequacy. A person must be able to shift quickly in a critical moment from one pattern of role behavior to another—whether this be done in terms of manipulative, verbal, or imaginative operations. . . . Skill in shifting perspective is acquired just as other skills are.

The principle of behavioral reciprocity can also be expressed as "it takes two to tango." The child who learns to assimilate and to accommodate environmental pressures will have interpersonal relations that feature free verbal interchange and a sharing of inferences and conclusions. The child who is unable to share his ideas with others will have a restricted number of friends and will not participate in the classroom activities.

In essence, the counseling relationship represents a sustained sequential situation in which the counselee is helped to acquire the symbol system of the culture (Reiff, 1966). Modification is not brought about by edict— or remonstrance. It demands that the counselee verbalize his thoughts and feelings. During the process the counselee's attitudes toward culturally determined ideas are explored. Typically this type of examination of the counselee's role and functions brings about a change in behavior. The degree of change is directly proportional to the child's self-investment and participation in the counseling process. Thinking, like loving and dying, is something that each person has to do for himself.

Although the concept of a counselor as a socializer puts a stress on normative behavior, the idiosyncratic needs of a child are not necessarily ignored. If one assumes, as Parsons and others have, that all human action (individual and group) is goal-oriented, then the focus of the child's activity can be conceptualized as centering on pattern maintenance, goal attainment, adaptation, and integration (Frohock, 1967).

The concept of socialization suggests that the boundary lines of individual activity are set by societal interests and demands. In essence, society generates stereotyped expectations of what goals an individual *ought* to strive for, what his behavior repertoire ought to be, how he ought to face crises, and how his self structure ought to look. The manner in which the personal needs are satisfied is structured to a large degree by societal expectations. Deviations from the norm are punished.

The quality of the educational experience a child has is predicated on the degree to which he has accommodated and assimilated stereotyped expectations. Failure to accede to societal expectations forces the child to expend a considerable amount of energy defending his deviant behavior. He has little psychic energy to spend on learning classroom material. What is imposed may not necessarily be "good." However, the adult, not the child, has the prerogative to contemplate the nature of his existence. What is asked of the child is that he accept the imposition with the understanding that at some future date he will have a right to vary from the expected and in some instances to reject it. It is also understood that behaving like a student leads to a satisfactory state which is beneficial in meeting select personal needs. The work of the elementary school counselor should center on those children who have trouble in accommodating and assimilating culturally determined ideas. Once a child accepts societal impositions his self-control increases and so does the quality of his experiences. The counseling relationship explores the ideas that limitations not conformity, flexibility not rigidity, selectivity not impulsiveness, are the keystones to a meaningful educational experience.

References

Buhler, C. *Values in psychotherapy*. New York: The Free Press, 1962.

Cameron, N., & Cameron, M. A. *Behavior pathology*. New York: Houghton Mifflin, 1951.

Cantril, H. *The "why" of man's experience*. New York: Macmillan, 1950.

Cartwright, D. Achieving change in people: Some applications of group dynamics theory. *Human Relations*, 1951, *4*, 381–392.

Dreikurs, R. *Psychology in the classroom*. New York: Harper and Row, 1957.

Frohock, F. M. *The nature of political inquiry*. Homewood: The Dorsey Press, 1967.

Glad, D. *Operational values in psychotherapy*. New York: Oxford University Press, 1959.

Jourard, S. *Personal adjustment*. New York: Macmillan, 1966.

Kelman, H. C. The role of the group in the induction of therapeutic change. *International Journal of Group Psychotherapy*, 1963, *13*, 399–432.

Lecky, P. *Self-consistency: A theory of personality*. Long Island: Island Press, 1951.

Lennard, H. L., & Berstein, A. *The anatomy of psychotherapy*. New York: Columbia University Press, 1960.

Raph, J. B., Goldberg, M., & Passow, A. H. *Bright underachievers*. New York: Teachers College Press, 1966.

Reiff, P. *The triumph of the therapeutic*. New York: Harper and Row, 1966.

Rommetveit, R. *Social norms and roles*. Minneapolis: University of Minnesota Press, 1955.

Counseling Children in Groups

Merle M. Ohlsen

Counseling school children in groups has increased with recent developments in elementary school counseling. As consultants to teachers, elementary school counselors also have been encouraged to help teachers adapt group techniques for teachers' use. Though this paper is primarily concerned with introducing group counseling to children, with selection of clients, and with adapting group counseling methods for children, the writer will discuss briefly some of the possibilities for helping teachers use group techniques.

The writer assumes that the readers of this journal understand the counseling process, including the kinds of interaction that occur within a group of normal children as they talk about the problems that bother them and try to help each other learn to behave increasingly more effectively (Ohlsen, 1964, Chapter 5). Clients must learn to help others as well as obtain help for themselves. All of the competencies required of the counselor in individual counseling are required here and more, too. Besides trying to understand the client who is speaking, to capture his feelings, and to help him express his feelings and change his behavior, the counselor must help clients learn to help others and to observe how the speaker's comments, as well as the various members' nonverbal behavior, influence each of the other members. He also must select clients with care, taking account of their possible impact upon each other, and enlist their assistance in developing a therapeutic atmosphere.

The setting for group counseling meets the optimal conditions for learning described by Seeman (1963, p. 8): "It is a safe environment; it is an understanding environment; it is a caring environment; it is a participating environment; and it is an approving environment." Clients also perceive counseling as a place where it is safe to be open, honest, and frank —where it is safe to test their ideas and the solutions to their problems and where they can obtain frank evaluations of their efforts to change. As a consultant to teachers, the elementary school counselor also can use his knowledge of behavior within groups to help teachers develop Seeman's optimal conditions for learning within their classrooms.

Introducing Group Counseling

As a regular member of the school staff, rather than as a specialist functioning out of the central office, the elementary school counselor has many opportunities to get to know the pupils and the staff and to describe his services for them. When, therefore, he wishes to introduce group counseling, he will be able to describe (to teachers either in informal contacts or at a faculty meeting and to pupils in their classrooms) group counseling, to explain how pupils may be helped in groups, and to answer their questions on what will be expected of clients in groups. Such presentations encourage self referrals and help teachers to understand the nature of the treatment process.

When pupils ask to join a counseling group or are referred by their teachers they are scheduled for an individual interview. The purposes of the individual interview are: to answer any questions a prospective client has about group counseling; to help the counselor get to know the child better in order to determine how he can best be helped and with whom he would best fit in a counseling group; to give the child a chance to discuss the problems with which he hopes to obtain assistance in the group and thereby increase his readiness to discuss these problems in the group; and to assess his readiness for group counseling and commitment to change his behavior. The counselor often supplements the information obtained in the individual interview with a teacher conference, a parent conference, and a careful examination of the child's cumulative record.

Since only a few individual sessions are required to help many school children, not all children who refer themselves or are referred by their teachers will be assigned to groups. Thus, the intake interview may become the first in a series of several individual counseling sessions. Sometimes a counselor will decide to work with a child on an individual basis and later decide to assign him to a group.

Selecting Clients for Groups

Children who seem to profit most from group counseling include shy children, children who have difficulty participating in class discussion, children who want to make friends, and children who have better ability than their performance indicates. Usually the last type needs help in accepting their ability before they actually improve their performance. Rarely is it advisable to include in a single group only one type of client, e.g., gifted underachievers. Usually such children can best be treated along with some other children who can accept their ability and are concerned about why they are not doing better than they are. Ohlsen (1964) reported that best results were obtained when, after describing group counseling to children, more children volunteered than could be included in the next group to be begun. Under these circumstances prospective clients tried harder to convince the counselor in the intake interview that they were ready for counseling and that they really had something to talk about in the group. As they tried to convince the counselor that they should be included in the next group, they increased their own readiness for counseling.

A counselor must select clients carefully for every group. He must be permitted to accept only those clients whom he feels reasonably certain he can help and preferably only those who want to join a group after they have learned what will be expected of them and what they can expect from others in the group. Even after a group is organized the counselor must feel free to take an unproductive member from the group or reassign anyone who does not seem to fit into the group. Both Fiedler (1949) and Broedel, Ohlsen, Proff, and Southard (1960) found that even a single blocking client can sometimes take such an anti-therapeutic stance that its members never establish a therapeutic climate.

Ohlsen and Gazda (1965) concluded that for group counseling to be effective with even upper grade elementary school children, both pupils and their parents must understand what will be expected in the counseling groups and accept these conditions. Sonstegard (1961) obtained significant results with similar clients, but he also provided group counseling for the pupil's parents and teachers. Where this is not feasible, or possibly not even necessary, Ohlsen and Gazda suggested that at least regular consultations with parents and teachers are essential. Their underachieving fifth graders discussed many situations in which they felt they had been treated unfairly and felt there was nothing that they could do about it. A fifth grade boy described his feelings as follows: "We're just kids and don't count for much; even our dogs are treated nicer than we are." Whereas adolescents are able to help a peer convey to the person who has hurt him *how* he has been hurt and can help him do something about his situation to improve it, fifth-graders feel trapped. They lack the independence and the adolescent's repertoire of social skills to cope with life's problems. Hence the important adults in their lives must accept considerable responsibility for helping them cope with problems and improve their environment [Ohlsen and Gazda, 1965, p. 81].

Adapting Group Counseling Methods for Children

The writer's counseling experiences and research with groups indicate that though the same basic principles of counseling apply to all ages, the counselor must adapt his techniques to his clients' social and emotional maturity, their previous experiences in groups, and the development of their communication skills. Work with fifth, sixth, seventh, and eighth graders clearly suggests that the discussion type of counseling that is effective with high school and college students also works well with seventh and eighth graders, but certain changes are recommended for fifth and sixth graders which probably also apply to fourth graders:

1. These younger children need more structure and more carefully defined limits. Even when they are carefully selected for a group, they have difficulty defining limits and enforcing them as the committed older children do. They must understand what is expected in group counseling and how this differs from what is expected in their classrooms.

2. Associated with the need for more structure, Ohlsen and Gazda (1965) concluded that there seemed to be a need for more active participation on the counselor's part than was required in the adolescent group. These younger children did not seem to be able to detect and reach beyond mere talk to respond to significant therapeutic material as Ackerman (1955) indicated that his adolescents were able to do. Though their ability to do this increased over the treatment period and they were able gradually to accept more responsibility for helping develop a therapeutic climate, fifth and sixth graders required more time to learn to do this than did adolescents. Furthermore, when the counselor failed to participate enough, especially during the early sessions, the clients became restless, were easily distracted, and often competed for the counselor's attention.

3. Though these children do have some ability to empathize with peers, as Lerner (1937) reported, they have difficulty maintaining a sustained interest in another's problem. Consequently, Ohlsen and Gazda (1965) concluded that these children should be treated in smaller groups (perhaps five or six instead of seven or eight) and for shorter periods of time (perhaps forty to forty-five minutes instead of an hour). They also recommended three meetings a week instead of two.

4. Ginott (1961) reported that prevailing practice in clinics is to separate boys and girls for treatment during the latency period. Ohlsen and Gazda noted that in their group girls were more mature, exhibited more interest in boys than boys did in girls, tended to threaten boys with the discussion of topics related to sex, were more verbal, and tended to dominate discussions. Hence, though they generally favor the treatment of mixed groups, they conceded that it may be wise to treat girls and boys of this age in separate groups. On the other hand, they had some strong reservations concerning this recommendation: the counseling group may be the best place for boys and girls to deal with these antagonistic feelings and to learn to relate to each other.

5. Within the group clients often need to act out as well as talk out their problems. Role playing is effective whenever a client has difficulty describing a situation or conveying to others how he feels about it; or he wants to obtain others' reactions to his way of meeting a situation; or he

feels that he needs practice in meeting a situation (Ohlsen, 1964, pp. 174–178). Puppets also may be used with them effectively, especially when the group develops the skits to be portrayed by the puppets. Other play materials such as family dolls, finger paints, and sketching paper may be used with these children, but care must be taken in selecting the materials lest the children perceive use of these materials as "kid stuff."

Finally, the writer would like to consider briefly how a counselor may work with primary school age children in groups. Though this writer believes that the normal children with whom he has worked can put their feelings in words better than many authors have indicated, special attention must be given to communicating with these children. Since this is discussed in another paper it will not be discussed again here (Ohlsen, 1965). Suffice it to say that more use should be made of play materials than was suggested above for fourth, fifth, and sixth grade children. A short description of a counselor working with five first- and second-graders illustrates how children who had difficulty talking to each other can be helped in groups. All of them tended to be shy and two were having difficulty learning to read. Before they entered the rooms, the counselor had laid out sheets of brown wrapping paper, finger paints, modeling clay, and various sizes of dolls—some dressed as adults and others as children. When they came into the room, each selected the materials of his choice and sat down to play. Provision was made for the children to sit around a long table in a large office which was used as a playroom. One of the girls and two of the boys chose to play with finger paints. The third boy played with clay and the remaining girl played with dolls. As the children played, the counselor moved about, responding first to one child, then to another. As he watched a child play, he would try to determine what the child was trying to express and respond to him in the child's medium, e.g., if the child was playing with finger paints, he would respond to him with finger paints. The children were also encouraged to interact with each other. Occasionally, one would speak to the entire group—a sort of show and tell. When necessary, the counselor helped such a client get the attention of the entire group. He also tried to convey to his clients that not everyone was expected to speak to the entire group just because one wanted to do so. Although normal children do seem to express themselves verbally better than disturbed children, counselors are urged to take note of Ginott's (1958, p. 413) warning: "Many serious mistakes in child therapy are committed by adults who try to give verbal insight to children whose language is play. Forcing them to verbalize is like compelling them to converse in a foreign language."

Teacher's Use of Group Techniques

Most elementary school teachers are interested in their pupils as individuals, and many are already using group discussion techniques. They exhibit this interest in their pupils by listening to them when they bring problems to school, by encouraging them to talk about their interesting experiences in show and tell sessions, and by giving them a chance to role play situations that trouble them.

The teacher's guidance responsibility is to listen and to try to under-stand—to let his pupils know that he cares about them and that he will set aside time to give them a chance to discuss special topics that concern them. When his pupils begin to discuss topics that the teacher feels should not be shared with the entire group, he arranges private conferences with individuals or small groups. On the other hand, the teacher should not be expected to do counseling. It should be reserved for persons who are qualified to do it. With the help of a counselor, however, the teacher can encourage normal social, emotional, and intellectual development of chil-dren with effective use of group techniques.

Rogge (1965) did an excellent demonstration to illustrate how a teacher can use group methods to motivate learning. He set aside a time when pupils were given a chance to ask any questions they wished. Rather than to merely answer their questions, he helped them explore where they could find the answers to their questions and helped them talk about how they felt about each other's questions. In order to excite learning further when one pupil has answered a question, the teacher may ask them still further questions.

Since some teachers doubt their ability to field such questions and to deal with the embarrassment associated with some questions, they often need help in learning to apply Rogge's methods. He usually begins with a demonstration in the teacher's classroom. After they have discussed it and sometimes even critiqued his tape recording of it, he encourages the teacher to make a recording of the discussion so that he will have specific responses to discuss in helping the teacher critique his own session. Teachers also can help each other critique tape recorded sessions of such discussions.

Role playing (some call it sociodrama) is another group technique that the classroom teacher can use. It differs from "playing house" or "playing school" in that it is an organized effort to teach pupils to cope with specific problems. It provides the pupil who requests assistance with an opportunity to relive a specific problem, to express his feelings about it within a safe emotional climate, to test his ideas for coping with the prob-lem, to obtain his classmates' and teacher's ideas for solving his problems, and to practice these solutions interacting with people whose reactions he values. In fact, when a child describes a situation and the people involved in it, tells how he feels and how he thinks they feel, directs and partici-pates in the scene role played, and answers his classmates' many and varied questions before playing the scene, he usually understands himself and the whole situation better even before he role plays the scene.

> For example, Robert, a second grader, was beaten up by Mike, a fifth grader, during the lunch period. After helping Robert clean up, Miss Pickens suggested that perhaps the class could help Robert figure out

how to cope with Mike. Since Mike had been picking on several of the small boys in the neighborhood, this idea appealed to the pupils. They set the stage for the sociodrama by having Robert describe what happened during the incident. Then members of the class volunteered for the various roles; several children volunteered for their own roles. The others in the scene were briefed by Robert. Finally, Miss Pickens pointed out that though they should try to re-enact what happened, they should not worry about saying precisely what was said before—instead they should try to say and act as they felt their characters would. When Miss Pickens thought they had gone far enough into the scene to help Robert, she interrupted and asked Robert to tell what he would have done differently and suggested that he ask questions about the issues which concerned him. Then she gave the other players a chance to comment on how they felt about what happened and to make suggestions to Robert. Finally, she gave the rest of the group a chance to express their feelings about the scene and to offer Robert suggestions. Not only did Robert get many good suggestions but all of them obtained ideas for coping with bullies [Ohlsen, 1959, pp. 640–641].

Thus, group techniques can be used effectively by teachers, too. Though there are many questions for which no one has answers at this time, much can be done to help children in groups. Lack of qualified personnel is probably the most serious problem facing school counselors who want to initiate group counseling programs. These personnel are needed to counsel pupils and to help teachers improve their competencies in working with groups.

References

Ackerman, N. W. Group psychotherapy with a mixed group of adolescents. *International Journal of Group Psychotherapy*, 1955, *5*, 249–260.

Broedel, J., Ohlsen, M., Proff, F., & Southard, C. The effects of group counseling on gifted underachieving adolescents. *Journal of Counseling Psychology*, 1960, *7*, 163–170.

Fiedler, F. E. An experimental approach to preventative psychotherapy. *Journal of Abnormal and Social Psychology*, 1949, *44*, 386–393.

Ginott, H. G. *Group psychotherapy with children.* New York: McGraw-Hill, 1961.

Ginott, H. G. Play group therapy: A theoretical framework. *International Journal of Group Psychotherapy*, 1958, *8*, 410–418.

Lerner, E. The problem of perspective in moral reasoning. *Journal of Sociology*, 1937, *43*, 294–299.

Ohlsen, M. M. *Guidance services in the modern school.* New York: Harcourt, Brace, and World, 1964.

Ohlsen, M. M. (Ed.). *Modern methods in elementary education.* New York: Henry Holt, 1959.

Ohlsen, M. M. The elementary school counselor. A mimeographed paper, College of Education, University of Illinois, 1965.

Ohlsen, M. M. & Gazda, G. M. Counseling underachieving bright pupils. *Education*, 1965, *86*, 78–81.

Rogge, W. M. A demonstration on elementary school teachers' use of group discussion methods to motivate learning. Mt. Zion Conference, June 10, 1965.

Seeman, J. Motivations to high achievement. Guidance Summer Lecture at University of Colorado, 1963.

Sonstegard, M. Group counseling methods with parents of elementary school children as related to pupil growth and development. Mimeographed report, State College of Iowa, 1961.

The Elementary School Counselor and the Gifted Underachiever

In a large midwestern city, the elementary school counselors were asked late in the school year to identify and refer youngsters to rooms for the gifted by following these instructions.

(1) List all who qualify by means of one or more mental maturity tests.

(2) Get the teachers' recommendations.

(3) Because of lack of time do not try to give individual intelligence tests; refer those who show an IQ of 130 or better.

The following children were referred from one school, in the order chosen by the teacher, and using results of California Mental Maturity Tests, Short Form:

Name	Choice	Language	Non-Language	Total IQ
Donna	First	140	141	140
Yolanda	First	140	131	136
Ray	Second	140	138	139
Clarence	Second	140	143	142
Janet	Third	158	122	141
Cindy	Not Considered	148	114	137
Tommy	Not Considered	136	131	134
Douglas	Not Considered	123	138	131

"The Elementary School Counselor and the Gifted Underachiever," *Personnel and Guidance Journal* (April 1963), 716–719, has been reprinted with the permission of the author and of the publisher, the American Personnel and Guidance Association, © 1963 by the American Personnel and Guidance Association. Edna L. Harrison is a school psychologist at the Special Education Diagnostic and Resource Center, Wichita, Kansas.

The teacher's comments follow: "Donna and Yolanda are the top ones in my room. Their vocabulary and speaking ability are excellent. So are their research and reports. Ray is slow, deliberate, a perfectionist. Became enthusiastic over his *llama* report, outgrowth of President's visit to South America. Good vocabulary and speaking ability. Clarence fails to do his best. Had knowledge of his high ability. Sitting down on the job. Probably finds school boring. Can do good research and report work. Needs much experience in it. Janet does not seem as capable. Cindy is disorganized. Not as capable. Tommy won't listen, dig in. Rattlebrained. Jumps from here to there. Douglas is a perfectionist. Too slow at thinking. Not a voluble reporter."

Three were accepted in Special Education: Donna, Yolanda and Clarence. Donna did not take advantage of the offer: her parents were dissuaded by Donna's teacher. Clarence and Yolanda were placed in the "Gifted Room" the following fall. Clarence was the only one to have had a Binet before referral.

Subsequently, the others were given individual Stanford-Binets by their counselors; scores were as follows:

Donna, 142; Yolanda, 134; Clarence, 135; Ray, 135; Janet, 111; Tommy, 99; Douglas, 113; Cindy, 151.

On the Iowa Test of Basic Skills and on all achievement tests given, the three accepted for the gifted room scored about two years above their grade level. Ray, Janet, Tommy, and Douglas scored approximately one year above grade expectancy and Cindy only eight months, on more tests, to a year and eight months on a single test. The counselor, however, gave her the California Achievement Test subsequent to the Binet, with a resulting score of two years, nine months above her grade level. The following fall, in beginning fifth grade, she reached a total of seven years, with a percentile of 87, on the Iowa Test of Basic Skills.

Working with the Teacher to Identify Gifted Children

Placement in the special room for the gifted now requires (1) the results of all tests given through the years, (2) the counselor's diagnosis, (3) health data, and (4) the teacher's remarks concerning the child's strengths and weaknesses, all entered in a referral form of six pages. The teacher of the gifted room then confers with the teacher of the sending school. It is upon her estimate that the final decision is based. The teacher's estimate, as shown above, often leaves something to be desired. In recognition of that fact, it becomes the counselor's responsibility to work with the teacher to help identify gifted children. Such identification should begin in kindergarten.

There is a number of procedures that can be used as the child advances in school. It is especially necessary that the counselor work with the third grade teachers since referral begins at that level. He can read through thirty folders in an hour or less, set aside those which show no promise, separate those of children with whom he has already worked, and put the new ones that reflect promise into a pile by themselves. The latter he will read carefully, watching for clues in notes and reports that might indicate exceptional performance in some area.

Second, he can interview the teacher concerning each child whose records show potential. In so doing, he should use some type of checklist, such as that given by French (1), or any composite list of the characteristics, any of which might apply to a gifted child. If the teacher can be persuaded to use a roster such as that made up by DeHaan and Kough (2), so much the better.

Third, the counselor can interview the child's past teachers in the same way, except that he would not ask them to use the roster.

Lastly, he would interview parents and others outside the school who may have worked with the child in some children's organizations. (One teacher was surprised to find that a child she had considered slow was a member of a "rock hound" club, had a rather noteworthy collection of his own, and could tell the names of his rocks and their derivation. His Binet revealed an IQ of 148.)

Confirming or Refuting the Teacher's Judgment on Giftedness

Teacher-administered tests, as in the case of Janet, Tommy, and Douglas, may fall short of adequacy. The counselor can confirm or refute the teacher's judgment by testing the group under observation in the mental maturity and achievement areas. Correctly given, the California Short Form Test of Mental Maturity will, in general, compare favorably with the Binet. Rather than spend hours of the counselor's time on individual testing, the results of the California tests should eliminate some of the subjects from further consideration. If official requirements must be met, the Stanford-Binet may then be given to the rest.

Reconciling Counselor and Teacher Judgments

In cases where judgments conflict, the counselor and teacher will meet, review findings, and decide upon those to be referred. It is well to place their findings before the principal, both for his information and for his judgment concerning the cases involved. It is in such team atmosphere that much can be done in the way of in-service training which could involve (1) the use of folder information, (2) objective observation practices, (3) testing methods, and (4) an explanation of the differences in children who are high achievers in the work of the average classroom and those who fall in the gifted range.

The counselor can also demonstrate an interview with a child whom the teacher does not recommend to the program, using a checksheet in the hands of principal and teacher by which to measure the results of the interview. A child's interests in various types of collections, his ability to use vocabulary fluently, and his capacity to generalize in certain situations might well be a part of the scheme.

The final decision for placement in the gifted room should be made only when the "team" from each school, consisting of the principal, the sending and receiving teachers, and the two counselors involved meet to go over the history of each child. Such a history might well be assembled in writing so that each participant may have a copy to which he can refer. Accompanied by oral observations and anecdotes, the approach should be most valuable to parties from both schools.

Responsibility for the Underachievers

Most teachers are really searching for help from the counselor in the matter of identifying and planning for gifted children. It is in the area of underachievement that counselor-teacher opinions differ more often and most widely. Conciliatory efforts must be of long-term duration. An intensive, long-term plan must involve (1) gaining *rapport* with the teacher, (2) accepting her need for elevating the children of lesser ability to the top, (3) tactfully pointing out differences between giftedness and high average achievement, (4) placing before her articles and books as needed, and (5) helping solve the problems she encounters with the underachieving child of high capacity.

Rinsley (4), in a fine article on "Basic Fears," Passow (3), in his report for 1961 on the Talented Youth Project, and French (1), in the section on "Underachievement" in his book of readings, all offer excellent help for teachers and counselors in this area. But, in the last analysis, it is the counselor who must study the child, diagnose his weaknesses, build upon his successes, and help the teacher to do the same.

Working with Pupils and Parents to Encourage
Underachievers of High Capacity

Parents must accept some of the responsibility for certain underlying factors that cause underachievement in their gifted children. Their attitudes toward the school situation, toward educational achievement, and toward the importance of "an education" in general have an effect upon the child's progress in school. It has been shown that underachieving children often come from homes where the parents are too busy to read to or play with their children, who somehow do not infuse them with pride in success, with confidence, with personal security, with educational aspirations, and with a feeling of parental support and interest (1).

Cindy's parents are taking a second look at her lack of achievement in past years and are striving to make up for the years when she was, in a sense, deprived of their support and interest. It is the counselor's responsibility to help parents discover needs that affect their child's performance and ways in which those needs can be met. Cindy's parents grasped at the opportunity to make up for lost time. They made plans for significant choices for summer interests and explorations. They included in their plans more time and attention, and taking into account Cindy's ability to plan for herself.

Cindy is beginning to respond to her parents' efforts. Since both are school people, they could apply their knowledge and experience toward the educational rehabilitation of their own child. But working with parents in deprived areas is not an easy task. The greater part of the burden may fall upon the school. However, where the parents are themselves of good, average, or high capacity, they can be motivated toward the desire for more and better education for their children. Like one such parent, they can discover that "the best things in life are free" and instill in their children desire for a better life educationally. It is the counselor's responsibility to help find the way.

Just to have the respect and attention of the counselor and the teacher will oftentimes bring alive the latent ambition of a gifted child to succeed. The counselor may suggest ways in which the teacher can help him surmount his difficulties in the classroom and at the same time encourage the child to strike out on his own. When a child who has not been achieving to capacity at last substitutes the feeling of success for failure, he is already halfway up the hill. Getting to that point of self-realization is the hardest part of the battle. Sometimes helping parents, teachers, and peers to see him as a success rather than a failure is equally hard.

The counselor must follow up on his findings concerning the child, see him regularly, reinforce in every way possible his new feelings or security in his own ability, and help the teacher to find ways in which he can do the same. One teacher has been seeing such a child a few minutes after school each day to talk with him on subjects of special interest to which he was exposed during the day. The companionship thus formed will help him to see himself as a person of worth.

Parents who enjoy their children are off to a good start, but sometimes it becomes necessary for the counselor to help both parents and children understand their responsibility in handling their gift in a manner that is inoffensive to others. One of the counselor's first obligations is to consider with them the idea that such a gift is not *earned* by them but has been *given* them for one purpose only: for productive use. All gifted children can be told that theirs is a gift from their Creator. All can listen, regardless of religious convictions, to the story of the ten talents and of the foolish man who buried his. All can understand what happens to the talent of a violinist or singer if he neglects to use it to the best of his ability. Bright people are quite willing to take the reference to themselves. Handled carefully, this story is the best means known to this counselor to prevent the destructive effects on a gifted person of extravagant boasting and self-aggrandizement.

References

1. French, Joseph L. *Educating the gifted: a book of readings.* New York: Henry Holt, 1959.
2. Kough, Jack, and DeHaan, Robert. *Teacher's guidance handbook,* Vol. I and *Roster,* Elementary Edition. Chicago: Science Research Associates, 1955.
3. Passow, A. H., and Goldberg, Miriam L. The talented youth project: A progress report. New York: Horace Mann-Lincoln Institute of School Experimentation, Teachers College, Columbia University, 1961. Mimeographed.
4. Rinsley, Donald B. The basic fears a child brings to the classroom. *NEA Journal,* March, 1962.

Occupational Information in
the Elementary School

Dugald S. Arbuckle

At first sight, this appears to be a rather dull and pointless topic; a topic about which a person could write little. I could, of course, indicate that we must integrate occupational information into the elementary school curriculum, that teachers must be less occupationally naive, that textbooks should be more occupationally realistic, and that we need to have work experiences at the elementary level so that children may learn that it is just as honorable to be a garbage man as it is to be a teacher, even though no teachers want to be garbage men, and don't even associate with garbage men. But everyone seems to know this, for this is about all that is found in guidance and counseling literature.

The *Review of Educational Research* for April, 1960, contains 73 references to occupational and educational information with only one referring to the elementary school. Perhaps the author of the chapter was guilty of inner frame of reference reading, or perhaps there wasn't really much to report. In the last eight years of the *Vocational Guidance Quarterly,* there were only four articles dealing with vocational guidance in the elementary school. There was an equal paucity of material in ten years of *The Personnel and Guidance Journal,* where only two articles dealing with vocational guidance in the elementary school were found.

Nor is there much to be found in representative textbooks. In 84 articles in a book of readings by Farwell and Peters (6), there were five articles dealing with elementary school guidance, but nothing on the place of occupational information in the elementary school. This was also true of a book by Johnson, Buford, and Steffire (13). Gilbert Wrenn's (30) recent opus paid little attention to the elementary school counselor in a

"Occupational Information in the Elementary School," *Vocational Guidance Quarterly,* 12, 2 (Winter 1963–1964), 63–64, has been reprinted with the permission of the author and of the publisher, the National Vocational Guidance Association. Dugald S. Arbuckle is Professor of Guidance and Counseling at Boston University.

changing world. In Willey's (29) book there were no references whatsoever, and a blank was also drawn in a book by Bernard, James, and
Zeran (2). Cottingham (3), Barry (1), and Crow and Crow (4) made
only the most fleeting of references to the place of occupational
information in elementary school guidance in their books. All of these,
it should be noted, are books dealing specifically with guidance in the
elementary school.

At this point, one might wonder if this indicates that all these writers
were missing something, or is it just that there is not much to write about
when it comes to the place of occupational information in a program of
elementary school guidance? From my reading, however, I did get
some impressions.

Specifics Are Easy

Specific answers to specific questions about the place of occupational
information at the elementary level seem to be answered fairly briefly and
fairly easily. One of the two best examples I found occurred in
Mathewson's book (19, p. 229) where he described the stages of a child's
development, beginning in the early grades. He stressed identification of
aptitudes and potentialities as:

> . . . Fundamental appreciations of conditions of social living, including
> common occupational pursuits being followed in the community and
> their meaning in fulfilling social needs.

More specifically, Norris, Zeran, and Hatch (20) indicate a need for
information in early elementary grades to develop wholesome attitudes
toward all fields of work, to make children aware of the wide variety of
workers, to help children answer questions about occupations, and to bring
out the varying rewards of work. They suggest that in upper elementary
levels, occupational information will help a child learn about workers at
the state, national and international level, it will aid him in seeing the
interdependence of workers, and it will acquaint him with the abilities and
qualities needed for successful performance on the job. In addition, they
suggest occupational information will help him to know the areas of
information important in making vocational choice, it will acquaint him
with the problems of choosing and holding a job, and it will acquaint him
with the fact that it is necessary to give careful study to making a choice of
a future career.

Suggestions Are Debatable

The specific suggestions of "what to do" are more debatable than they
appear to be, however, particularly in light of current personality theory,
learning theory, and theories of vocational development. The "how-to-

do-it" cookbook suggestions are easy to understand, and worthwhile, to a point. The only trouble is that the cookbook often only makes sense to the person who wrote it. When someone else tries a recipe, it just isn't the same. In fact, the cake often comes out quite flat, even though the cookbook was followed to the letter.

A good example of this is a reference by Hoppock (12, pp. 351–352) to a social studies program built around occupations where stress was on the study of man rather than the study of environment. It sounds wonderful, but it can probably serve only as a springboard for other creative teachers and counselors who will develop something of their own. Those less creative individuals who try to copy it will have a rather pallid version of what Hoppock describes, since the vital ingredient, the people who worked out the original plan, are not there.

Theories Are Challenging

More vague, but much more challenging, is the question of the place of such a seemingly drab subject as occupational information in the elementary school, when considered in the light of various theories of vocational development. Webster gives plenty of leeway in the various definitions of a "theory." One definition states a theory as being "a more or less plausible or scientifically acceptable general principle offered to explain phenomena" while another, "a hypothesis; a guess." Too frequently, however, theories become viewed almost as facts. They develop a sort of halo that enables one to excuse almost any act, as long as he is following some theory.

Even better, of course, is developing your own theory of vocational development or choice. The pages of the *Journal of Counseling Psychology* abound with such theories. Often the educated people who develop these educated guesses are the first to agree that this is all they are. Unfortunately, however, sometimes theories become viewed as cause rather than effect, and studies are undertaken to show that what is true is true.

Empirically and existentially, one might question a situation where a theory becomes an acceptable reason for a certain action or movement that one human makes toward another. At least it seems reasonable to question those counselors who determine the future direction *of others* on the basis of someone else's guess as to where they should go and what they should do. Theories should not be viewed as determiners of human action.

One might assume that theories relating to vocational development should show some relationship to the actions proposed by some writers regarding what might be done about occupational information at the elementary school level. Unfortunately, they are often contradictory. With nearly all theories, at least in the area of human behavior, there is usually much evidence gathered on both sides. Theories which are more specific are more vulnerable, while generalized statements or guesses are more subject to modification according to the direction of the wind.

Roe (22), for example, comes forth with a fairly definitive statement when she theorizes that certain kinds of family atmospheres create a psychological climate depending upon whether they satisfy or frustrate the early needs of a child. On this basis, she predicts particular and specific career groups toward which a child will move. The specific hypothesis, however, is not supported in such reported studies as those by Grigg (7), Hagen (9), Switzer, Grigg, Miller, and Young (27), and Utton (28). On the other hand, a study by Kinnane and Pable (15) confirms the general hypothesis that family influences are critical in the development of work values.

We find a somewhat similar contradiction of a more specific hypothesis when we note a study by Davis, Hagen, and Strout (5). This study tends to support the more specific aspect of the Ginsberg theory that tentative choices are made between ages 11 and 17, rather than the fantasy choices of earlier years. Small (24) reports a study in which no evidence was found to support the theory of fantasy choice prior to eleven, or a movement toward tentative choices from 11 to 17. On the other hand, O'Hara's study tends to indicate that the normal upper limit of fantasy choice should be 8 or 9 rather than 11.

We also note that in 1962, sociologist Lipsett (18) commented that "If the thesis is accepted that social factors are of great importance in the vocational development and career planning of an individual, it follows that a counselor needs to understand these social factors and their influence upon an individual." It is interesting to find that Super (26) anticipated him by some six years when he said, ". . . although social action is important in understanding the development of the self, it does not satisfactorily explain the selection and synthesizing process which leads to the development of a self picture."

Most of what might be called the rather broad and general, and thereby safer, theories of vocational development tend to reflect the generally acceptable behavioral science, middle class views and values of the authors.

Holland (11), for example, discusses his theory, which ". . . assumes that at the time of vocational choice the person is the product of the interaction of his particular heredity with a variety of cultural and personal forces including peers, parents, and significant adults, social class, American culture, and the physical environment. Out of this experience the person develops a hierarchy of habitual or preferred methods for dealing with environmental tasks."

Segal (23) reports on an attempt ". . . to demonstrate that psychoanalytic theory can be utilized to predict personality differences in individuals choosing one of two vocational outlets . . . These hypotheses were derived from information about the kinds of activities each of the professions required of an individual, and the interaction of such activities with the satisfaction of the individual's needs.

Hadley and Levy (8) refer to a "reference group theory"—the influence of groups on an individual's attitudes and behavior, and under what circumstances this influence is most effective, and the manner in which the influence is exercised.

All of these statements tend to point in a similar direction, in that they all reflect . . . a somewhat . . . deterministic, behavioral science view of man as being a creature *of* destiny, rather than the creator *of* his destiny. And while, at this point, one might say: what in the world has this got to do with the question of occupational information at the elementary school level, I would think it has a good deal to do with it, since much of the current writing and thinking on the "what to do" regarding this question tends to reflect the various theoretical postulates. Let us now take a questioning look at some of the thoughts and ideas that have been reflected in these past few pages.

Environment Reflects Man

Current occupational literature tends to operate on the assumption of a determined man living in an outside-of-him determined world, and in this sense accepts the general view of empirical science. Super (25, p. 2) voices this as well as anyone when, in defining his concept of vocational counseling, he refers to it as ". . . the process of helping the individual to ascertain, accept, understand, and apply the relevant facts about himself to the pertinent facts about the occupational world, which are ascertained through incidental and planned exploratory activities."

While we talk "freedom" and "development" and "choice," Super's statement, and others like it, carry a strong implication of understanding in the sense of accepting and adjusting to what is. The environment becomes the center of life rather than the individual. The "world-of-work" becomes some vague outside-of-the-person force to which man must learn to adjust. It becomes a sort of fixed field without people: It would seem, actually, to differ very little from the fitting of a certain shaped human to a similarly shaped occupational hole.

There is, however, another existential view of man which is somewhat different. Man is not seen as the determined victim of a determined world outside of him, but rather as the creator of that world. "Environment" is not something outside of me to which I must, in order to get along, learn to adjust, but it is, rather, a reflection of me. I have a responsibility, not to adjust to a fixed environment, but as a result of my living, to do something to modify and change both it and me. Indeed, one may question whether one could actually say "it" and "me," since they are both entwined with each other.

However, in this case the *me* is the essential ingredient, and the *it* something which is the product of the *me*. The reality of the Mississippi environment of James Meredith is not the same as that of another Mississippi Negro who humbly accepts his fate as a member of an inferior race. The James Merediths are the creators and the movers of their culture, not the passive victims of it.

To the child the occupational world, the much talked about world of work, does not become a dark outside bogey man to which he must adjust some sad day. Rather, it is a world of people, just as work is people. In this sense, it is no different than the world of work which is currently a part of him, whether he is 8 or 80.

The stress on prognosis, prediction, and the matching of a child's abilities to someone else's plans, implies a high level of the imposition of one human on another. It is restrictive. The implication is that one is bound by one's boundaries, and that the taking of a chance, the risking of possible failure in doing something to challenge those boundaries, is to be avoided at all costs.

Failure is only deadening when an individual feels and believes that there is nothing he can do about it. However, failure need not be traumatic if an individual feels that there is a chance for movement, that there is another direction where he may go. I do not accept the concept that it is always better to move a child away from a venture where the odds are that he will fail, as long as the direction he is going is the direction where he wishes to take a chance, to take a plunge.

In our culture, color of skin, religion, level of intelligence, physical deformity, may, of course, be restrictions to movement. However, they only chain an individual when he confuses his inner freedom-to-be with the restrictions on his outside freedom. One always has an inner freedom. It cannot be taken away. One can use this inner freedom to widen gaps and cracks in those outside forces which restrict outer freedom. Socrates was a freer man than those who offered him the cup. Christ was a freer man than those who nailed him to the cross. James Meredith is freer than the white students who spit at him.

These men have always been with us, and without them there would be no forward movement. The child can learn that this is the way he can be too, that actually, this is the way he *is*. Surely the elementary school teacher and counselor can help the child to move in the direction of being what he is, to live in a world of his making, unless they too, of course, have accepted the numb, secure, and deadening comfort of the world of Mr. Orwell, which is not unlike that of Mr. Skinner.

Information Is Unreal

If we at least consider the possibility that people and work are irrevocably related; that one does not learn how to best fit into the other; that to a high degree, one is the other; then we may raise the question of the part occupational information plays in the life of a young child. Certainly we can assume that occupational information, per se, has as little personal meaning as the vast majority of information which is poured, shoved, and ground into a child during his years of formal education.

Talk about the dignity of all jobs, including that of garbage man, probably means as little to a child as the suggestion that there is a relationship between that strange ingredient we call intelligence and successful performance as a surgeon. Both are quite unreal in the living world of a child. The garbage man, incidentally, must be getting a bit sick of being used as the occupational example of a fellow who is really doing an honorable job, usually by teachers or writers who would rather be dead than be a garbage man!

We might wonder if most occupational information must continue to be somewhat unreal to children and to all of us in a personal meaning sense. I agree with Hatch (10, p. 69) on the need for stress on occupational exploration in the elementary school, as indeed there should be the element of exploration in all learning and education. However, we should emphasize the use of information only as a vehicle and a means for exploration. What children remember specifically and didactically about a trip to a glue factory seems to me to be of no point whatsoever. What is important is the process and the involvement of the individual in the glue factory.

I question what seems to be a general assumption that an increase in the amount of information about anything will somehow result in a broader learning by the student. Learning, after all, is a process. It does not come with an automatic piling on of more and more information. Also, I agree with Lifton (17) when he says ". . . from both their teachers and their texts youngsters were receiving a distorted picture of the importance and types of job activities," and with Kowitz and Kowitz (16, p. 154) who say "On the elementary level the selection is too often limited to about a dozen service occupations such as the milkman, postman, and policeman."

Only, however, when this distorted picture is assimilated as a part of the person will it have a negative effect. We might assume that meaningless, distorted pictures are as hard to digest as meaningful, undistorted pictures. I would have a hunch too, that real distortion . . . depends on . . . the attitude and the value system of the teacher as she presents the information, valid or not, to the children. I applaud Kaye (14) when she says, in describing the results of an occupational unit in Grade 4, that it ". . . helped the children to work toward the goals of all good teaching; critical thinking, respect, and understanding." If this happens, it is more likely to be because of the teacher and her ability to get children involved in an exciting and exploratory journey of learning, rather than because of the information she used.

Words Are Restrictive

There also seems to be some unfortunate implications in the use of the words *fantasy* and *choice*. Choice is very much like freedom in that it is a relative, changing, moving, concept. Restrictions to choice, like those to freedom, may be from the outside as well as from the inside. Outside restrictions regarding choice that continually face the child are bad enough. Even worse, however, is the implication that choice, like freedom, is an outer decided matter, rather than an inner determination. The child may grow to believe that he has no choice. Unfortunately teachers and counselors often teach him this lesson.

Choosing is not finding the "right" thing, but rather the ability to move within restrictions, modifying and changing them. The real lack of choice that faces many adults today is not an overt condition, but rather their acceptance of the concept that the extent of their choice depends on something else. It is a belief in their inability to have any choice that makes the lack of choice real.

The word fantasy as it is related to choice usually carries a negative connotation and is considered to be something which is not really real. In the field of occupations, fantasy choices are usually defined as translations of simple needs and impulses into occupational goals. Tentative choices on the other hand, are decisions based upon capacities, interests, and values.

This again, however, suggests outer determination of individual movement, and implies that unless we move in an occupational direction, where, according to the data, we "fit," we are being unreal and guilty of fantasy. This, I assume, is why Ginzberg would consider early occupational choices as fantasy, since the child has not yet had time to discover what his shape might be, and thus cannot fit himself into an appropriate niche.

The life which a young child in the elementary school is living, however, is very real to him. For him, his current life is his world of work. Because he is involved in it day by day, I sometimes wonder if the so-called fantasy of his occupational dreams is possibly a good deal less fantastic than the occupational future that certain concerned adults are planning for him. While we consider fantasy to be akin to the discrepancy between the ideal self and the operating self, they are both a real part of real living. If we aim at reducing them to nothing, we may reach that unhappy stage of complete adjustment when we no longer will be alive.

This real world of children was illustrated in a recent conversation I overheard between four 8 and 9 year olds. They were talking about religions, and one of them said, "Well, I don't think I'd want to be a Jew," to which another replied, "Of course, if you were a Jew you'd feel different about being a Jew." The others all agreed. It might be better if we were to stop talking about preparing a child for the world to come, and help him to do the best he can in living the life he is living. The only real life that he can know is the life he lives. In all the rest there must be an element of fantasy and dreaming.

In occupational literature, the terms fantasy and choice are usually used in a behavioral science sense. They both smack of a concept where one spends a part of his life preparing to fit into something which will be best for him, and then after he is cozily fitted, that is that. However, since the life of a child differs only in degree from the life of an adult, the only way a child can "prepare" for the years ahead is to live the present years, which we might hope would include an element of what the more prosaic adult might consider fantasy.

Occupational information, then, has a claim to a place in the elementary school curriculum just as any other information and knowledge. Like any other information however, it is important only to the extent that a teacher or counselor is able to use it to help a child become involved in the learning process. I know of no evidence to indicate that memorizing the fact that the salary of a mailman is less than that of a high school principal will have any bearing on the vocational development of a child.

We might hope, too, that teachers and counselors, using information which is representative, valid, and accurate will help children to see that they may always have freedom of choice, no matter what the restrictions placed upon them may be. This freedom of choice implies that there will be no guarantee of success and happiness; that the choice they make may turn out to be wrong. They may even feel more certain about being uncertain and fantasize about the adult world of tomorrow, because it is simply an extension of their very real world of today.

References

1. Barry, John A. *The Elementary Teacher and Guidance.* New York: Henry Holt, 1958.
2. Bernard, Harold W., James, C. Evans, and Zeran, Franklin R. *Guidance Services in Elementary Schools.* New York: Chartwell House, 1956.
3. Cottingham, Harold F. *Guidance in Elementary Schools.* New York: McKnight & McKnight, 1956.
4. Crow, Lester D., and Crow, Alice. *Readings in Guidance.* New York: David McKay, 1962.
5. Davis, Donald A., Hagen, Nellie, and Strouf, Judie, "Occupational Choice of Twelve-Year Olds," *The Personnel & Guidance Journal* 40: 628–629; March, 1962.
6. Farwell, Gail F., and Peters, Herman J. *Guidance Readings for Counselors.* Chicago: Rand McNally, 1960.
7. Grigg, A. E., "Childhood Experiences with Parental Attitude: A Test of Roe's Hypothesis," *Journal of Counseling Psychology* 6:153–155; Summer, 1959.
8. Hadley, Robert B., and Levy, William V. "Vocational Development and Reference Groups," *Journal of Counseling Psychology* 9:110–114; Summer, 1962.
9. Hagen, Douglas, "Careers and Family Atmospheres: An Empirical Test of Roe's Theory," *Journal of Counseling Psychology* 7:251–256; Winter, 1960.
10. Hatch, Raymond N. *Guidance Services in Elementary Schools.* Dubuque: W. C. Brown, 1951.

11. Holland, John L., "A Theory of Vocational Choice," *Journal of Counseling Psychology* 6:35–45; Spring, 1959.
12. Hoppock, Robert. *Occupational Information.* New York: McGraw-Hill, 1957.
13. Johnson, Walter F., Steffire, Buford, and Edelfelt, Roy A. *Pupil Personnel and Guidance Services.* New York: McGraw-Hill, 1961.
14. Kaye, Janet, "Fourth Graders Meet Up with Occupations, *"The Vocational Guidance Quarterly"* 8:150–152; Spring, 1960.
15. Kinnane, John F., and Pable, Martin W., "Family Background and Work Value Orientation," *Journal of Counseling Psychology* 9:320–325; Winter, 1962.
16. Kowitz, Gerald T., and Kowitz, Norma. *Guidance in the Elementary Classroom.* New York: McGraw-Hill, 1959.
17. Lifton, Walter M., "Vocational Guidance in the Elementary School," *The Vocational Guidance Quarterly* 8:79–81; Winter, 1959–60.
18. Lipsett, Laurence, "Social Factors in Vocational Development," *The Personnel & Guidance Journal* 40:432–437; January, 1962.
19. Mathewson, Robert H. *Guidance Policy and Practice.* New York: Harper, 1962.
20. Norris, Willa, Zeran, Franklin, and Hatch, Raymond. *The Information Service in Guidance.* Chicago: Rand McNally, 1960.
21. O'Hara, Robert P., "Talk About Self," *Harvard Studies in Career Development,* No. 19, October, 1959. (Unpublished)
22. Roe, Anne, "Early Determinants of Vocational Choice," *Journal of Counseling Psychology* 4:212–217; Fall, 1957.
23. Segal, Stanley J., "A Psychoanalytic Analysis of Personality Factors in Vocational Choice," *Journal of Counseling Psychology* 8:202–212; Fall, 1961.
24. Small, L., "Personality Determinants of Vocational Choice, *"Psychological Monograph,* No. 1, 1953, p. 67.
25. Super, Donald E., and Crites, John O. *Appraising Vocational Fitness.* New York: Harper, 1962.
26. Super, Donald E., "Vocational Development: The Process of Compromise or Synthesis," *Journal of Counseling Psychology* 3:249–253; Winter, 1956.
27. Switzer, David K., Grigg, Austin E., Miller, Jerome S., and Young, Robert K., "Early Experiences and Occupational Choice: A Test of Roe's Hypothesis," *Journal of Counseling Psychology* 9:45–48; Spring, 1962.
28. Utton, Alden C., "Recalled Parent-Child Relations as Determinants of Vocational Choice," *Journal of Counseling Psychology* 9:49–53; Spring, 1962.
29. Willey, Roy D. *Guidance in Elementary Education.* New York: Harper, 1960.
30. Wrenn, C. Gilbert. *The Counselor in a Changing World.* Washington, D.C.: APGA, 1962.

Occupational Information for Groups of Elementary School Children

Goldie Ruth Kaback

Two basic assumptions are usually taken for granted when a child enters school. First, it is assumed that he is now old enough to profit from well-defined learning experiences even though he may differ from others with respect to intellectual endowment, motivational aspects, and general living experiences. Second, it is assumed that he is now ready to learn how to get along with teachers and classmates, and to derive feelings of personal satisfaction from successful group experiences. It is not generally conceded, however, that the average child might also be ready to learn to relate what he perceives about him, through everyday living, to his future vocational development. Yet, observant teachers note almost daily that most children continue to offer clues, through various activities, of interests related to the work of the policeman, the teacher, the fireman, the doctor, and the airplane pilot.

In his play, the average child demonstrates that all occupations are of equal importance to him, for he has not yet learned about the "social status" of occupations. So far as he is concerned, he can be and do anything. He can wear a particular uniform, and he becomes what he wears; he can drive a tractor, a spaceship or an automobile without any special training; he can jump, hammer, lift imaginary weights, and climb the highest peaks with the greatest of ease. His natural curiosity, excitement, and enthusiastic acceptance of various vocational roles provide the basis for a dynamic relationship with the occupational life that surrounds him.

The following group experiences involving occupational information

"Occupational Information for Groups of Elementary School Children," *Vocational Guidance Quarterly*, 14, 3 (Spring 1966) 163–168, has been reprinted with the permission of the author and of the publisher, the National Vocational Guidance Association. Goldie Ruth Kaback is Professor of Education at The City College of the City University of New York.

have been tried out by various teachers in my classes who are preparing themselves for elementary school counselor positions.

Early Elementary Projects

As a group assignment, one kindergarten teacher had suggested that the children in her class draw pictures of "People Who Work in Our School." When the majority of pictures turned out to be pictures of teachers or teachers and principals, the children began to examine the duties of the other school personnel whom they later visited. They soon discovered that the maintenance people, the lunchroom attendants, the nurse, the policeman on the corner, the persons who delivered food and books and supplies also contributed to the welfare of the school community.

Another kindergarten teacher asked the children in her class to draw pictures of "What I Would Like to be When I Grow Up." As the children help up their pictures of spacemen, baseball players, nurses, doctors, teachers, firemen, and cowboys, the teacher proposed a game wherein each child was to imagine living in a community where all the adults would be employed only in the occupations which their pictures represented. After a lengthy discussion the children concluded that there were many workers whom they had not considered before who were also very important members of the community. In particular, they mentioned the shoe repairman, the barber, the milkman, the workers in the supermarkets, the gardeners, the men who collected ashes and refuse, the taxi drivers, the dentists, and those who delivered daily newspapers and supplies.

Throughout the year the children brought in pictures from newspapers and magazines to supplement their own portfolio of drawings about "Men and Women in Jobs." Each child was also encouraged to tell what he knew about the various jobs in his particular portfolio. A construction worker from a nearby housing development project was delighted at the idea of coming to the school to tell the children what he did, after they had observed him at work one afternoon. He invited them to come again and showed them how to keep a record, in picture form, of the different floors added as the housing development neared completion.

A first grade teacher asked the children in her class to note the various types of business on their way to school and to discuss the jobs of the different people who worked there. Children who had formerly passed by groceries, florist shops, drug stores, vegetable stores, laundries, and clothing shops suddenly became aware of the dozens of different occupations represented within a few blocks of the school building.

In order to show the interdependence of workers, one second grade teacher had her children role-play a typical family that paid for a doctor's visit; another scene showed where the same money was later paid to the doctor's nurse who used the money to pay for groceries; the grocer in turn paid the delivery man for delivering supplies to his store, and the delivery man's wife used the money to buy shoes for their children. Sometime later, this teacher asked the children to act out the vocational roles suggested by their surnames. Thus, Eddy Taylor, Marian Baker, Tommy Stone, Alice Tanner, and Margaret Smith soon found themselves engaged in a variety of suitable occupations; the other children whose surnames did not lend themselves readily to occupations adopted what they felt were congruent activities. For example, Henry Goldstein began to make jewelry, Emily Robinson decided that she should own a pet shop, and Mike McGregor played the role of a golf pro. The excitement of the group as they vied with each other in thinking through suitable occupations in connection with their names led to a discussion of where surnames originally came from and how names were sometimes changed by newcomers to this country so that they could be written and pronounced more readily.

In another second grade class, after the children had reported on the occupations of their mothers—office workers, secretaries, nurses, teachers, and machine operators—one little girl remarked, "My mother does nothing; she just stays home." That week the teacher suggested that the children in class observe the work of their mothers at home and then come to class ready to describe what they had observed. As each pupil made his contribution, the teacher listed on the blackboard: nurse, chauffeur, cook, dressmaker, bedmaker, window washer, baker, cleaning maid, homework helper, letter writer, cashier, buyer of food and clothing, waitress, laundress, gardener, general manager, and beautician. The mother's role that had formerly been taken for granted now took on new proportions as the class began to discuss the skills involved in each of these occupations and what it would cost to hire a different person for each occupation mentioned.

3rd and 4th Grade Activities

A detailed examination of the kind of work that children perform in their classrooms frequently provides the basis for stimulating discussion on occupations. Thus, in one third grade where one child had served as the class librarian by checking books in and out and arranging them on shelves, another had cared for the plants, another had been responsible for collecting papers, and still another had passed out milk and cookies, the class began to discuss what these class assignments meant in the real world of work: what they would have to know in order to become a librarian, a botanist, a baker of cookies, or a worker in a dairy. The relationship between what they had formerly taken for granted as classroom assignments took on major importance as they began to realize that adults in the community also were performing similar kinds of work on a daily basis.

In preparation for a visit to the neighborhood bank, one third grade class, divided into several committees, gathered pertinent information from their parents and friends about people who work in banks: the bank clerks, the bank tellers, the assistant managers, the guards, the men in charge of the safety vaults, and the maintenance persons. During the visit the bank personnel were pleasantly surprised at the type of questions that the children asked and the degree of interest in the variety of jobs performed. The highlight of the visit came when each of the children was permitted to punch a card on a newly installed computing machine for the recording of interest and deposits. Discussion on their return now included new information about computing machines and key-punch operations. Their vocational horizons had really been widened as a result of the one visit to include occupations which they and their teacher had personnally not known about before.

One fourth grade teacher asked each child to interview an adult who was engaged in the kind of work that the child himself was interested in. As a result, one girl interviewed a teacher and made notes regarding the work of the teacher, the preparation involved, the satisfactions as well as the disadvantages of teaching; another girl interviewed the school nurse and made notes accordingly. One boy spoke to a junior high school shop teacher about woodworking; another boy interviewed a neighbor who happened to have been a baseball player some years ago. The pupils later reported on their interviews in class. The interview notes themselves were mimeographed and distributed as "Junior Occupational Handbooklets" so that the children could discuss the numerous experiences cited with their parents.

For a Christmas week assignment, one teacher suggested to a fourth grade class that they use their newly acquired cameras to take pictures of people engaged in different occupations in their neighborhoods and then to bring the pictures to class for discussion. Hundreds of slides and snapshots were passed around in class as the pupils finally classified the pictures into groups of occupations and job families. Each child was then asked to select the one occupation that he liked and the one that he did not favor and to find out all that he could about these two occupations. As the children presented their findings in class, there were many different opinions as to the relative merits of each occupation. They talked about abilities, opportunities, training, and the nature of the work involved, the advantages and disadvantages of each, as well as vacations, pay, and other fringe benefits.

5th and 6th Grade Projects

In one school, two fifth grade children accompanied each working parent who was a member of the PTA on a visit to his respective job. On their return, the children exchanged experiences regarding the work and the workers they had observed. One pupil told about his day in a law office, another described how he had helped sell vegetables in a neighborhood store, a third indicated that while driving a bus might be exciting for a while, he for one would be bored, "because one must drive through the same streets every day." The children learned about occupations from actually having been involved in the daily job experiences of real people.

After several visits to neighboring business establishments, a fifth grade teacher asked the children to discuss the relationship of the subjects they were studying (arithmetic, spelling, social studies, reading, writing, and art work) to the visits. Many of the children realized, perhaps for the first time, that what they were learning in their classrooms was actually useful in the everyday life of the community.

Another fifth grade became involved in a unit on shelter as a social studies and science assignment. As the children talked about different kinds of houses, how they were built of wood, brick, glass, steel and cement, plumbing, electricity, gas, oil, and water, one pupil decided to bring in a picture of a carpenter whom he placed next to a picture of wood; another pupil followed suit and brought in a picture of a person who worked as a landscape architect because his uncle was engaged in landscaping. One pupil supplied a picture of his father as superintendent because his father happened to be the superintendent of the apartment house in which he lived. The teacher's report on this project revealed that she herself had found it to be one of the most exciting and interesting lessons that she had ever participated in. "The feeling of involvement and enthusiasm on the part of the children," she stated, "has been something that I have never experienced before when the class had merely discussed the type of shelters that people lived in."

A sixth grade teacher recently reported the following experience about providing occupational information to a group of socially disadvantaged children. Acting on impulse, she called the Urban League in her city and asked whether they could send several people to talk to her pupils about the hardships they had encountered before they entered their present occupations. Six men, representing the professions and the trades, responded eagerly. As she told it, some of the teachers were moved to tears as the children sat enraptured at the personal and occupational information spread out before them. The men too were so enthusiastic about the response from the children and the type of questions asked of them that they have since called the school to ask when they might come again and for the school not to forget that they were always available for discussions of this kind.

Utilizing the lives of famous people as their birthdays are celebrated (Columbus, Washington, Lincoln), as well as names of people who appear in the newspapers or on TV, served as a basis for discussion in another sixth grade not long ago. The pupils traced the many occupations that each person had been involved in before he had settled on his final vocational choice. Comparing different types of occupations and how the nature of the work had changed over time led to intensive research and provoked rather heated debates as to whether people were happier and more satisfied with present day or with former jobs. The topic of leisure also came in for examination and the need to prepare for leisure through the development of hobbies and extra-curricular activities aroused a great deal of interest and speculation.

One sixth grade class, located in a very low socio-economically deprived area, invited former pupils now in junior and senior high school to return to the class and to discuss their educational experiences and what they hoped to do later on. A former elementary pupil, now a Peace Corps Member, also visited the school one day and fired the imagination of the pupils as he told about his work in one of the underdeveloped countries. One of the members of the city government, who had attended this elementary school many years before, also returned to talk about his days at the school and about his educational and vocational experiences which finally culminated in his present position.

Presenting Information

In addition to the occupational information projects mentioned here that teachers have worked out with their elementary school pupils, there are of course the usual films, slides, visits, interviews, and preparation of career booklets that every well-trained guidance counselor knows about. However, the mere imparting of occupational information is not enough. If occupational information is to have dynamic appeal to pupils, it must be related to their interests and to the subject matter under consideration in the classroom. Inviting individuals to discuss their occupations without giving pupils an opportunity to select the occupations they want to hear about or ignoring pupils' votes as to the number of occupations that should be represented merely means that teachers are carrying out syllabus assignments without taking into consideration the needs and the aspirations of the pupils in their classes.

The younger the child the greater the interest in the actual job performance itself. Most children are natural born actors; they want to act out in order to understand what it feels like to be a carpenter or a ball player. Elementary school children are less likely to be interested in the cost of preparing for a particular kind of work, how to apply for a job, or changes in the labor market over a period of time. They are more interested in the actual nature of the work than in the relationship of personal abilities to vocational demands. It is only later, as they mature and prepare to enter the labor force, that they become concerned about being interviewed for a job and the more practical aspects related to job information.

Many of our elementary school children need discussion about occupations because many of them come from homes where unemployment has now been the pattern for one or more generations and where future goals with respect to vocational choice are unspoken and unknown. The school then must become the link between education and eventual employment.

While younger children may continue to identify themselves with public figures and TV personalities, it is not too early for them to begin to identify themselves with attainable vocations represented in their immediate neighborhoods.

Scores of children in our elementary schools come from families where high school and college education are the exception rather than the rule. These children need to be made aware that there are high school and college opportunities available for all even when one's parents and siblings did not attend. Many of the underprivileged children must be motivated to think and plan for the same kind of vocational levels that we take for granted among middle and upper class children. Their "poverty of experience" must be replaced by "multi-experiences." And many parents, and teachers too, must come to realize that their own attitudes toward work, whether these be attitudes of respect for all kinds of work, or attitudes that place a premium only on certain kinds of work, affect the attitudes of the growing, developing, inquiring children with whom they come in contact.

References

1. Arbuckle, D. S., "Occupational Information in the Elementary School," *Vocational Guidance Quarterly,* 1963–64, *12,* 77–84.
2. Bennett, Margaret, E., "Strategies of Vocational Guidance in Groups," in Borow, H. (Ed.), *Man in a World at Work,* Boston: Houghton Mifflin Company, 1964, 460–486.
3. Grell, L. A., "How Much Occupational Information in the Elementary School?" *Vocational Guidance Quarterly,* 1960, *9,* 48–55.
4. Gunn, Barbara, "Children's Conception of Occupational Prestige," *Personnel and Guidance Journal,* 1964, *42,* 558–563.
5. Hill, G. E., and Nitzschke, D. F., "Preparation Programs in Elementary School Guidance," *Personnel and Guidance Journal,* 1961, *40,* 155–159.
6. Kaback, Goldie R., "Occupational Information in Elementary Education," *Vocational Guidance Quarterly,* 1960, *9,* 55–59.
7. Kaback, Goldie R., "Using Occupational Information with the Culturally Deprived," *Academy of Teachers of Occupations Journal,* 1964, *1,* 23–31.
8. Kaback, Goldie R., "Automation, Work, and Leisure: Implications for Elementary Education," *Vocational Guidance Quarterly,* 1965, *13,* 202–206.
9. Kaye, Janet, "Fourth Graders Meet up with Occupations," *Vocational Guidance Quarterly,* 1960, *8,* 150–152.
10. Lifton, W. M., "Vocational Guidance in the Elementary School," *Vocational Guidance Quarterly,* 1959–60, *8,* 79–82.
11. Lifton, W. M., "Social Forces and Guidance in the Elementary School," *Vocational Guidance Quarterly,* 1963–64, *12,* 89–92.
12. National Society for the Study of Education, *Personnel Services in Education.* The Fifty-Eighth Yearbook of the National Society for the Study of Education. Part II. Chicago: University of Chicago Press, 1959.
13. Norris, Willa, *Occupational Information in the Elementary School.* Chicago: Science Research Associates, 1963.
14. Roe, Anne, and Siegelman, M., *The Origin of Interests,* American Personnel and Guidance Association Inquiry Studies, 1, 1964.
15. Simmons, D. D., "Children's Rankings of Occupational Prestige," *Personnel and Guidance Journal,* 1962, *41,* 332–336.

16. Stewart, L., "Occupational Level Scale of Children's Interest," *Educational and Psychological Measurement,* 1959, *19,* 401–409.
17. Tennyson, W. W., and Monnens, L. P., "The World of Work through Elementary Readers," *Vocational Guidance Quarterly,* 1963–64, *12,* 85–88.
18. Tyler, Leona E., "The Relationships of Interests to Abilities and Reputation among First-Grade Children," *Educational and Psychological Measurement,* 1951, *11,* 255–264.

Depth Consultation
with Parents

Eleanor Cartwright Crocker

One evening recently, while I was trying to keep up with the appetites of my family and the world situation at the same time, I heard the news commentator announce that the station was about to broadcast a message of general interest to parents of young school children. My interest and amazement grew, as the president of the National Education Association (NEA) delivered a short talk, the purpose of which was to promote better home-school relations. She was alerting parents, especially of children of kindergarten age, to some of the crises that could be expected. Her general advice in meeting these was to keep a cool head and find out the facts before jumping to the conclusion that Sammy's trousers really were muddy because that horrible little Kevin had pushed him into a puddle on the way home, or that the teacher had yanked the missing button off his coat in rough haste because he wasn't dressing fast enough for outside play.

This set me to reflecting, somewhat nostalgically, about how things have changed since the days when children were sent to school with a lunch pail and a warning: "Mind teacher and don't let me hear of any back-talk from you." At about that same time teaching was considered a calling and teachers dedicated people who were almost shy about accepting pay for the privilege of molding young minds. Although there have been many changes in our world, and so necessarily in the field of education, teaching requires no less sensitive dedication than it did in the little red school house, and some of you might hasten to add that the salaries also are comparable. But, because of our expanding knowledge about human beings, and particularly about how they grow into adults, there are some new areas of which the community, as well as alert educators, are requiring teachers to take notice.

With the growing influence of psychoanalytical thought, particularly its imprint on current theories of child development, our society has come increasingly to take upon itself the burden of health or illness. No longer is deviation (on either side of the norm) thought to be solely the result of genetics, which is to say, beyond our control. If who and what children are does indeed develop mainly through the parent-child relationship and if, as Anna Freud (4) suggests, a child transfers to his teachers feelings and behavior from this relationship, then, willingly or not, the school often finds itself involved in what our elders jealously considered "family affairs." This is particularly clear with the preschool child, whose main needs and ratifications are still being met or frustrated through his parents. How often, for instance, teachers are faced with the situation of a new baby arriving in the home of one of their three- or four-year-olds and one of the following consequences: Mother is so delighted that Jimmy "just adores his baby sister" and has had none of the naughty reactions all the books had prepared her for; however, the child is quite destructive with materials at nursery school, angry with children and especially the teacher, until she, along with Jimmy, wishes he'd never had a baby sister. Or, on the other hand, Andrea's mother is desperate because her lovable daughter has become an absolute brat since the baby arrived. Besides being openly rebellious, she has tried to punch the baby several times; to add insult to injury, she refuses to go home at noon and insists that she is now going to live with the teacher. In either situation the teacher must do *something*—either because of professional concern for the child or out of personal desperation.

Although many types of social work agencies offer a range of services to help people with their problems, the preschool setting is by definition child-centered. Its purposes, which are defined in the literature and recognized by the community, are to provide, as an adjunct to the family, a growth-stimulating experience by means of program and materials, peer and adult relationships, so that the child may develop, as far as he is able, socially, intellectually, physically and emotionally. Another recognized function of some preschool settings includes providing care for children who must be away from home all day. While these have been the traditional areas of responsibility, the field of preschool education is receiving increasing pressure both from the community and from within some branches of the profession to do more earlier in preparing children to cope with the many demands of our complex society. "Modern trends in our society have forced the school to do more of the child's training and guidance that was formerly the task of the home," observes Edith Leonard. (7) It therefore becomes increasingly necessary to interpret the function of preschool education both to ourselves and the public.

Certainly it is not within the defined purpose, skills or knowledge of education to attempt to "treat" a disturbed child or family situation, even though this is affecting a child's ability to progress in school. Although there may sometimes be a fine line of decision as to where and how much the school could help, it should be kept in mind that psychiatric treatment implies a change in over-all behavior resulting from the rechanneling of emotional energies and, like marriage, is not to be entered into unadvisedly. Stated more clearly, psychotherapy is the systematic utilization by a trained therapist of personality dynamics, with the goal of mitigating emotional difficulties. On the other hand, and especially with the preschool child, it is often difficult to assess whether what appears to be disturbed behavior on the part of a child is the result of a normal life crisis, such as the anticipated birth of a sibling, or from a deeply disturbed mother-child relationship or, perhaps, an effect of severe marital conflict. To decide where the teacher and the school stand in relation to the problem, she must usually discuss the situation with the parent.

Although the ensuing discussion may be generally helpful in all contacts with parents, it is specifically aimed at those situations in which a child is in trouble, the school has exhausted its resources within the program, and the parent must be involved if the child is to be helped. Two methods are suggested for dealing with this situation, both a synthesis of thinking from the field of social work. They are intended to aid in learning ways of relating to people, to facilitate working together on a problem.

The rather imposing adjective suggested for this discussion is "depth" consultation with parents. I am rather puzzled as to what to offer as a concise definition for this term. To avoid the old trap of semantics, I suggest for consideration the following definition of what a parent-teacher conference should be: *a focused discussion between teacher and parent, the scope of which is determined by the preschool setting, in which information relative to the nursery situation is shared with the aim of helping the child integrate the preschool experience to the maximum of his capacities.* While it is desirable in such an interview to use some of the same techniques used in an interview to get acquainted with parents, one must conduct oneself in specific ways with a parent when discussing a more "touchy" or feeling-laden subject. Let me now treat these specific ways: (1) the teacher's preparation for such a conference, (2) two methods for consultation, the exploratory and the supportive, (3) techniques for both of these and, in conclusion, (4) some general comments on how conferences can be improved.

Preparation

In preparing for talking with parents, it is helpful to recognize and think through several factors. First, take note of the difference between the classroom setting and a conference, which usually consists of two or, at the most, three persons. Teachers customarily work with a group instead of one person, talk with the children instead of about them, and are in relative control of the group. Consultation with parents, therefore, calls upon the least exercised aspects of a teacher's total professional role. Such a shift in role often makes us uncomfortable and unsure of ourselves. It is important to recognize the source of these usually vague but bothersome feelings. Parents are frequently also unsure of what to expect, and the teacher can do much to put them at their ease at the beginning of a conference by defining her role in relationship to them as well as making clear what this particular conference is for.

As professional people dealing with parents, we need continual self-examination to increase our self-awareness, for our own attitudes and experiences color what we see or hear, how we feel toward parents and what we say to them. People are teachers because they love children; good teachers because they are able to empathize with the child. Therefore, if a teacher senses that a difficult child is constantly angry or resentful toward his parent, it is not surprising that she soon finds herself vaguely irritated and impatient with that mother, even though the latter has been only pleasant and co-operative with the school. We therefore conclude, often against the better judgment of previous experience, that the child has been in the wrong hands and that the right person and educational regime will put him on the road to progress. Although Erik Erikson is a child psychiatrist, he made a point important for all professions who work with children: "Our occupational prejudice is the rejecting mother." (3)

Kathrine D'Evelyn makes the following point:

> One last consideration, but not least in importance, is the sound mental health of the teacher. If he is to confer with the parents and help them to do constructive thinking, he must be reasonably well adjusted emotionally. This does not mean that the teacher must be superhuman. No one ever reaches a state of complete adjustment. It does mean, however, that he should have insight into his own motivations, needs and desires. He should know wherein lie his greatest satisfactions and his faults. (2)

Step one, then, is to take account of yourself, your abilities and your limitations, and how these can be utilized toward the ultimate goal of helping the child.

Next, go over all available material on the child and from this set basic goals for the conference. This includes family background, your summary of the child's experience at nursery, his use of materials, his social relationships, your estimate of his strengths and the areas in which there is difficulty. Again quoting from D'Evelyn:

> The teacher who understands child behavior will find it easier to win the parent's confidence and cooperation, as well as to lead the discussion into constructive planning. At this point the age of the child enters into the picture; the teacher must know what to expect of a given age; he must know whether a child is deviating from the norm enough to cause concern, and must be able to help the parent to understand what to expect of the child. (2)

What is implicit in this statement should be explicated—conferences are not a substitute for creative programming aimed at individualized needs of children. They are an ancillary effort that is indicated when, after skillful and consistent effort on the part of a teacher, the child's problem still persists.

It is necessary to elaborate on setting goals. There are at least two kinds: studied, or those you take with you to the conference; and evolved, or those developed as you talk with the parent and gain new information and impressions. It is enough to say, set your goals but stay flexible—just as you do in the classroom. First impressions may be lasting, but they aren't necessarily accurate. Understanding your goals, an integral part of consultation, is a dynamic process, a combination of what you already know about a child and his parents plus what you are learning during the session.

Third, along with your knowledge about the individual parent, it is important to know something about the typical feelings and attitudes parents bring to a conference, particularly if the child is having difficulty. The basis of this knowledge comes from personality and role theory.

Think for a moment of your own experience as a mother or what you have observed of other mothers as they react when someone else, however loved or trusted, makes an evaluative comment about their child. Nursery is frequently the parents' first continued experience in presenting to the world outside the family what they, as parents, have done for the child. Obviously preschoolers do not yet have the abilities to develop a strong identity separate from the parents. Because this age group is still so dependent and requires so much of the mother's time and energy, it is no wonder that she takes every comment about her child personally.

A certain amount of this identification of mother and child is not only normal but necessary, yet nursery teachers often see this in its exaggerated form. To use a term from psychoanalytic theory, mothers who are aware that their child is having difficulty come to the conference with their "defenses up." A *defense* is the characteristic way of dealing with anxiety; it involves unconscious measures adopted by an individual to protect himself against painful feelings or occurrences. These may be constructive or destructive to a person's total functioning.

It has been my observation that the two defenses most frequently encountered in anxious mothers of young children are *projection* and *denial*. In projection, the person attributes his own feelings and attitudes to other persons or situations because he is unable to admit them to himself. Have you ever tried to discuss your concerns with a mother who kept insisting that if James was resistant to routines it was because the teacher wasn't handling him right? Denial, another defense, is the refusal to acknowledge intellectually or emotionally feelings and events because they are highly threatening in some way. For example: It is obvious from a mother's description that Susie is keeping the household in a turmoil with her tantrums, by her demands for her father's attention and by refusing to stay in bed at night. The mother will say all this and in the next breath con-clude, in a very calm tone, that she really doesn't have any difficulties with Susie big enough to worry about, and she guesses her daughter is just an active child.

In both instances the mothers are defending themselves from the knowledge that somewhere along the line they haven't done the best possible job as parents; or, equally often, that they do not know what to do now. There may be many reasons, some of them unavoidable, for the child's behavior. But it still boils down to the fact that the mother feels criticized.

It is not necessary for a teacher to deal with all the intricacies of defense mechanisms and certainly not within her role to comment on them directly to the parent. It is important that she be able to recognize the reasons for certain kinds of behavior in parents and understand the causes, so that she does not respond in what would otherwise be a natural argu-mentative manner, thereby limiting her usefulness to the child. If a parent finds it emotionally necessary to deny that her child has difficulty, then all the earnest and often angry teacher will do with a more detailed descrip-tion of atrocities is to make the mother even more anxious, thereby increas-ing her need to deny. There are ways of handling these defenses.

It is important to remember that from their own past parents bring with them to the conference experiences, often consciously forgotten, with schools and teachers. That is to say, they transfer to the relationship with their child's teacher certain expectations, causes for which are not always to be found in the current situation. Again, it will be helpful to borrow two terms from psychoanalytic theory. The first is *transference,* the displacement into the current situation of emotions, behavior and attitudes whose origins are in earlier experiences and relatively independent of current reality. The now classic example of this is the man who chooses a wife because she reminds him of his mother, thereby transferring a parent-child relationship to marriage. Parents usually see teachers as persons of authority and the ways in which they relate are influenced by whether their past experiences with authority figures were constructive or unpleasant. Parents transfer many mixed feelings to a conference. The important thing is for teachers to learn to recognize the roots of these feelings, while at the same time accept-ing the parent's sincere desire to co-operate and help his child.

Some knowledge of what parents are like inside, and why, is cer-tainly a necessary aspect of planning. Such understanding helps to make decisions on how to say what more easily, to bring about the desired results. Keep in mind that teachers also have defenses and make transfer-ences. Have you ever heard a teacher come out of a conference saying, "Mrs. Smith just makes me so mad—I tried to tell her how she could make mealtime pleasanter for Sam and the whole family, but she just seems to have a chip on her shoulder." In this case, the understandably frustrated teacher has gone beyond the point of relating to Mrs. Smith as a confused and worried person who needs help and is simply angry at the mother's antagonism. That is, the teacher is responding to the way in which the mother responds to her.

This phenomenon is known as *countertransference,* that is, responses determined by the type of transference from another person, which occur in the form of emotions, behavior and attitudes whose origins are in earlier experience relatively independent of current reality. It is helpful to keep in mind that, just as parents bring to us their past experiences with teachers, we teachers carry within ourselves responses to past experiences with our own parents and families, and that these influence our current relationships.

The first step to successful consultation with parents is to organize what you know about the child and to take account of yourself and your abilities and limitations, as well as those of the parent you are to see.

Methods

What is it that actually happens when you interview? Why does a parent listen to you, accept or reject what you have to say, argue or cooperate? The way in which parents and teachers are able to work together depends on the nature of their *relationship.* This word indicates a mutual experience resulting from direct interaction of two or more people in which feelings, attitudes and ideas are shared and in which, to some extent, each person influences the other in these matters. All the points so far discussed are major ingredients of any relationship. It is the aim of the teacher to build a positive relationship with a parent, to achieve specific goals for the child. There are ways to facilitate this. First, if a conference is a mutual exchange of information, then the teacher is a collaborator, not a questioner. The expectation of parent participation and responsibility, so far as is reasonable, should be set from the beginning. It is important to learn to be a creative listener. In so doing we can hear what the parent is telling us explicitly, as well as what may be behind what he is saying, that is, the implicit content—how he is feeling, which is conveyed by gestures, mannerisms and general appearances. One approach is to ask parents to tell you, rather than your telling them or beginning by giving advice. Comments should be designed to help parents think through situations for themselves. For instance, instead of beginning by saying that you asked to see the parent because Johnny's hitting presents a problem, you might say, "I wonder if you have any idea why I asked to talk with you." Often if the difficulty is immediately reiterated to the parent, the latter begins to feel criticized—that she is a bad mother or has failed her child—and the defenses go up.

There are two methods, *exploration* and *support* that seem appropriate and helpful for parent-teacher conferences. Having a method suggests a systematic and deliberate way of doing something. These two are separated only for the purpose of presentation; certainly they are often used in the same interview if the teacher feels that this is indicated.

Exploration is defined as "a process by which the teacher, using various techniques, obtains information relative to the child's developmental, medical, emotional history and his current family situation as it affects the preschool experience." Louis Lehrman has made the helpful distinction between *horizontal* and *vertical* investigation. The former aims at establishing behavior patterns and total aspects of the life situation. The latter implies a deeper understanding of the causal dynamics behind these. It is the horizontal type of exploration that lies within the realm of parent-teacher conferences. While it is important for teachers to understand the nature of the feelings parents bring, it is not always necessary to comment on them. Exploration should help to give some idea as to what the parent sees as the problem, for comparison with how the teacher sees the situation. This helps you assess the degree of the parent's understanding and gives clues as to your next goals.

The supportive method differs from exploration. It is "a process in which the teacher, by means of various techniques, lends her strength and knowledge to reinforce and encourage the parent's existing strengths so that abilities of the latter are mobilized and further breakdown is prevented." No matter how disturbed a parent-child relationship, the parent somewhere within himself always wants very much to help the child and is angry with herself because she does not seem able to do so. The teacher looks for and attempts to encourage this strength. It may be done simply by verifying a mother's knowledge, thereby giving her the needed courage to act on her convictions. In talking with the parent, the teacher can perhaps help her to accept the things her child does well and thereby give balance to the parent's perception of the bothersome child. As with exploration, the teacher must proceed with sensitive discrimination, assessing when a mother can tolerate further questions, how much support is realistic in this particular situation, and how able the parent is at this time to recognize the better qualities of her child.

There are other helpful factors. It is important not to do too much too fast. The first conference should help parent and teacher get acquainted and establish a relationship of mutual confidence. Whatever information a parent presents at whatever time must be treated with confidence. It is often difficult for a parent to relax until the teacher has defined her role, explained the purpose of the conference and assured the mother that whatever she says will be for their use only. If it is necessary to pass on any information given in confidence, one must be sure to get the parent's permission.

Everyone who has ever interviewed, particularly the novice, is eager to know "just how." Techniques often elude definition because they are so much the result of the opportunities of the situation, combined with sensitivity, skill and knowledge. Most people who interview soon develop their own style, a by-product not only of knowledge but also of individual personality. One of the most important aspects of technique is the interviewer's attitude toward the parent as a person, as well as toward what is said. As a professional, one should aim to be objective, neutral and uncritical. Facial expressions and manners often belie our thoughts and feelings as well as those of the parent.

It is most important to try always to begin where the parent is. For example, one parent may be warm and giving but really lacking in knowledge about child development, making the inconsistent behavior of her four-year-old quite distressing to her. Another parent may know exactly what to expect but be totally unable to integrate this knowledge constructively in the actual handling of her child.

Techniques

We have already mentioned the technique of *enlisting the parents' help* and getting them to tell you rather than your telling them. In general, this is best accomplished by such nondirective questions as, "I wonder if you could tell me just a little more about that." Another technique that is often necessary in exploration and that can help keep a conference within its defined scope is *focusing*. This means simply to select a point for attention. It is usually achieved by more directive questions, comments or suggestions, such as, "You said something earlier that I was interested in—I wonder if we could go back to that for a minute." One technique especially helpful in building a positive relationship is that of *relating your comments to the feelings inherent in what the mother is saying,* rather than to the facts. For example, when a mother is telling you about the havoc of putting Joan to bed, this is no time to lecture on techniques of discipline. A comment on the mother's feelings such as, "You might get pretty exasperated at times," will let her know that you understand her as well as the child. One word of caution about this technique: It is best to be pretty sure that your reflection is accurate—when in doubt, don't comment. *Universalization* is a technique that can be quite supportive. This is a way of indicating to the parent that she is not the only one who has ever had this problem. You might say, "This is a difficulty parents traditionally have with their three-year-olds." *Suggestion* is a technique that should be used sparingly. Experience proves that it is almost always useless to give advice when it is not requested. The most successful way by far is to help the parents, through encouraging their thinking, to discover the solution themselves. The need for *clarification* is indicated when a parent is distorting reality or obviously confused on some point. For instance, I recently saw a mother whose little girl had had two temper tantrums at school. The teacher mentioned this and no more to the mother, who immediately assumed that Mazie was a behavior problem and I had asked to see her because the child was going to be terminated. A parent may need *reassur-*

ance, if he seems unrealistically concerned about something that is quite normal. Finally, one should *be prepared to give information in such a way that the parent can accept and use it.* These eight techniques of enlisting parents' help, focusing, relating to the parents' feelings, universalization, suggestion, clarification, reassurance and giving information are intended as guides to help you develop your own style of consultation. They should be used only when you are fairly sure that to do so is realistic.

Comments

In summary, I should like to suggest how conferences can be improved. First, see your director or supervisor for help in preparation, whenever possible. The objectivity of a third person not directly involved with either child or parent can be most helpful in clarifying and correcting one's thinking. Second, record your conferences. Choice of style depends upon your school's requirements and individual preferences, but write something down. It is always surprising how much one forgets. There is also a growing tendency to use consultants from other professions, both for evaluating children's disturbances and for help with interviewing. Third, survey the available literature and take a course if your training has been sparse in the area of consultation. Don't be shy about saying No if you honestly feel that at this time you could not be helpful to a parent in a conference. If a parent requires help that the school cannot offer, limit your contacts with the parent and help refer him or her to an appropriate agency. A familiarity with community resources is essential.

Bibliography

1. *Conference Time for Teachers and Parents: Teacher's Guide to Successful Conference Reporting.* Washington: Joint Committee for Conference Time, National School Public Relations Assn., 1961.
2. D'Evelyn, Kathrine. *Individual Parent-Teacher Conferences.* New York: Bureau of Publications, Teacher's College, Columbia University, 1945.
3. Erikson, Erik. *Childhood and Society.* New York: W. W. Norton & Co., 1950.
4. Freud, Anna. *Psychoanalysis for Parents and Teachers.* New York: Emerson Books, 1947.
5. Hefferman, Helen, ed. *Guiding the Young Child.* Boston: D. C. Heath & Co., 1951.
6. Langdon, Grace, and Stout, Irvin. *Parent-Teacher Interviews.* New York: Prentice-Hall, 1954.
7. Leonard, Edith, Van Deman, Dorothy, and Miles, Lillian. *Counseling with Parents in Early Childhood Education.* New York: The Macmillan Co., 1959.
8. Menninger, William C. *Self-Understanding—a First Step to Understanding Children.* Chicago: Science Research Associates, 1951.
9. Wills, Clarice, and Stegeman, William. *Living in the Kindergarten.* Chicago: Follett, 1956.

Improving Home-School Relations

Gerald T. Kowitz and Norma G. Kowitz

Our country is experiencing a series of significant social changes which mandate changes in our schools. The current status of our nation, as a world leader and as the most affluent society history has known, may not have been a direct result of excellence in our schools; certainly, there were other forces. However, there can be no doubt that our ability to sustain progress is directly related to the quality of education provided our youth. Unless they are prepared to begin at the apex of our achievements, the trend of social progress will become one of social deterioration.

It is no longer enough to insure a child a basic, minimum education. Programs are needed which will support the maximum development of individual talents. Academic achievement will, of course, be one major goal, but we will also need a high level of personal development—the ability to live with the anxieties of the times and to strive toward a future which often is frightening.

The school cannot do the job alone. It must have the support and, at times, the active cooperation of the home. Communications between the school and the home, while an integral part of the educative process, are also often seen as a source of problems. The long and embarrassing history of problems between the school and the home makes it evident that there is no easy solution. On the other hand, as a school moves toward a quality program, there are some things which can be done to improve the relationship.

Many of the problems between the home and the school can be studied in terms of four types of communications:

"Improving Home-School Relations," *The National Elementary Principal*, 43, 5 (April 1964), 22–25, has been reprinted with the permission of the authors and the publisher. Copyright 1964, Department of Elementary School Principals, National Education Association. All rights reserved. Gerald T. Kowitz is Professor of Education at the University of Oklahoma, Morman. His wife, Norma, contributes frequently to educational literature.

(1) Flow of information about the child to the school

(2) Flow of information about the school, its policies and operations, to the home

(3) Periodic reports

(4) Special problems.

As we shall see, each of these types of communication is requiring more specialized techniques. Guidance workers have a growing responsibility in each.

Information About the Child

If the school is to do a job of quality education, it must have information about the child. In fact, quality in education can be defined in terms of providing opportunities for the child to develop his talents. Among other things, this means that the home must help the school to understand the child and also the aspirations his parents have for him. When parents are expected to provide the school with information, much of it of a personal nature, they have a right to know how it will be used to advance the education of their child.

As in the past, parents will continue to provide information for administrative and legal purposes. Additional information will be needed for guidance purposes. The frustration of parents who are asked to provide the same information over and over again or to provide data that seem irrelevant is rivaled only by the dilemma of the school: What is to be done with the growing heaps of information? There is little point to collecting large amounts of data on a routine basis with only a vague hope that some day it may be helpful. Studies of data processing indicate that excessive data usually confuse the issue and always overburden the processing system, whether human or electronic. The identification of information that is pertinent to the educative process is a difficult task. Just what must the school know about the child to serve him best? Specification of information that will be useful and its collection and efficient handling will be a major guidance problem for elementary education in the next decade.

As the role of information expands from that of a simple administrative requirement to a necessity for proper educational guidance, the procedures for handling it must change. The importance of good relations with the home suggests that the guidance worker may devote a major part of his time to visiting homes with the dual goal of securing information about the child and giving information about the school and its program.

But what about the teacher who has carried this responsibility? It is probably impossible, and certainly unrealistic, to expect teachers to develop a high level of competence in the many content areas and also be trained guidance workers. Already, many elementary schools have teachers who specialize in reading, art, science, music, mathematics, and foreign languages. There are also specialists in personal development—the nurse, the psychologist, and the guidance worker. The growing number of specialists denies a continuation of present practice: communication with the home only through the teacher. The report card has been obsolete for some years, and it is not realistic to expect parents to confer periodically with three or four teachers and as many specialists. As specialization increases, the classroom teacher will see less of the child, and each teacher will see different aspects of his development. The specialists will have still other views. The guidance worker who is trained in personality development and in educational theory and who is familiar with school practice appears to be the logical person to carry the responsibility for gathering the pertinent information and communicating with the home.

Information About the School

Many of the problems in home-school relationships emerge from the fact that the school is a social institution. As such, it functions with an institutional value system. At the same time, the goal of the school is to serve the individual child as he matures. This requires a very personal, individualized set of values. It is inadequate to assume that what is good for the group will be good for each individual in the group. Nor is it reasonable to verbalize the doctrine of individual differences but to expect all children and their parents to respond alike or to assume that a rule will be equally applicable to all.

Since the school is a large and complex institution, it must have rules and regulations in order to operate. Very few of these rules have ever been evaluated or even thoroughly studied, especially in terms of their educational implications. Many guidance problems arise because of the incompatibility of several policies. For example, while the school may recognize that the development of each child is unique and continuous, decisions on his promotion are traditionally made only once a year. Furthermore, if the child is judged inadequate for promotion, he must repeat the entire year, even though he may lack only a few specifics. In fact, he may have made remarkable progress if we accept the notion of judging his achievement in terms of his own developmental pattern.

Policies on homework are also a source of recurrent problems between the home and the school. An important goal of education is to train the child to work on his own. However, busy work is no more profitable at home than at school. On the other hand, if assignments are so difficult that the child must be tutored by his parents, they may soon begin to wonder why the teacher is employed. With the trend toward introducing new materials and new methods into the curriculum—a trend which must continue if we are to have quality education—parents are finding themselves increasingly inadequate as teachers. The goals of homework and the policies for achieving these goals require careful planning and continual study.

Adequate communication with the home is a vital element in the program of homework.

A related policy, the expectation of parental participation, is a frequent source of problems which usually need not exist. If the school expects parents to participate, parents must know and understand what is expected of them. If, on the other hand, the school has a "hands-off" policy for parents, this should be made clear. Only conflict can be expected if school policy requires the child to work alone, but the evaluation of that work assumes extensive parental help. Similarly, if the parent-teacher organization exists solely as a fund-raising corporation, this should be made clear. If its purpose is better communication between teachers and parents, a different structure is needed.

Where the goals of the school are not clear or where the preservation of traditions or defense of arbitrary policy is more important than the development of the child, the problem is not communication with parents but manipulation of them. In the case of attempted manipulation, the process of parent-school relationships is no longer one of solving mutual problems but rather one of coercion, conflict, and cold war.

Periodic Reports

Education is unique among the professions in that it is a continuing activity and not dependent upon a special problem or project. Because it is continuous, periodic reports will be expected by those who support it.

Many problems can be avoided by communicating expectations at the beginning of the year. It is usually inadequate to inform only the child. In fact, parents will expect more information and explanation than the child.

While in the past some believed that children could be frightened into working harder, there is no place in the quality school for a psychology of fear. A climate of fear in the classroom is as unreasonable academically as it is mentally unhealthy. An attitude of enthusiasm, or at least expectation, is far more useful than one of fear or apprehension.

Any time of evaluation may be a time of anxiety. Evaluation—that is, a judgment on the progress a child has made—is an important function. Without assessment, effective guidance and sound planning for the future are impossible. The school occasionally reneges on the matter of judgments. It seems easier to say, "Teachers do not give grades; pupils earn them," or, "The school did not make the decision." Of course, teachers give grades and schools make decisions, and both of these are judgments upon the child which will affect his future. Furthermore, all children cannot receive favorable reports. No teacher or school can guarantee this. However, a minimum requirement of an unfavorable report is that it must be a judgment of the child's work, not a condemnation of the child. It must, in the case of an inadequacy or deficiency, report how the situation can be corrected. It is not enough to say that the child must work harder or that he is careless. These are innocuous statements that neither clarify the problem nor suggest how the child may be helped.

When parents are kept informed of the progress of their child in relation to the expectations of the school, and when they know that the school has made a concentrated effort to help the child, the likelihood of conflict is lessened. Nevertheless, even with newer innovations such as the ungraded unit, there will be moments of truth—a time when some parents must be told that their child is not able to move ahead with his peers. Here is a growing role for the elementary guidance worker. The decisions which must be made require data from many sources. Unification of data, like counseling with parents, requires special skills.

Periodic reports suggest report cards. Although simple grading schemes are known to be inadequate, some parents continue to demand them. One reason for this persistence is that most adults were taught when they were pupils, perhaps unintentionally, that grades are the most important thing about school. What they learned to feel about grades is far more important to their present attitudes than what the school may have attempted to convey by the grades. Along with attitudes about grades, some parents also acquired strong negative feelings about teachers and school. There can be no doubt that an important part of establishing good relations with the home is planning a generation ahead. Unless children gain a reasonable perspective of the school as pupils, they will not have one as parents.

Semantic confusion—that is, a failure to establish common meanings —is fatal. Adequate definitions cannot be found in dictionaries nor can a school write enough specifications to define the terms used in reporting. Since the school works with children in human relationships, the emotional connotations of terms are usually more important than specific denotations. As we learn more about the process of communication, it becomes increasingly clear that the goal of purging terms of their emotional loadings is a foolish one; communications with parents about their children will always carry an emotional cargo. The goal cannot be to remove it, only to insure an appropriate loading.

Special Problems

No area of guidance shows the need for special training more than counseling with special problems.[1]

A fundamental principle in solving problems is to establish communications early and maintain them constantly. While this is easy to say, is it reasonable to expect a teacher to establish and maintain a close relationship with thirty or forty sets of parents? Perhaps a more pertinent question is whether we should expect a teacher to provide quality education to such a large class.

Actually, each year will bring only a few serious situations in which a counseling relationship will be needed. When such problems arise, it is often too late for the teacher to begin to develop the relationship of trust and confidence which is needed. Involving another person, such as a guidance worker, who is not in an administrative position, can sometimes provide a neutral and accepting situation.

In any decision-making conference the goals must be made clear to all parties. To the extent that one party is coerced or forced to accept the goals of the other, the decision will be unacceptable and the subsequent actions will fail for lack of wholehearted support.

In any relationship that approaches the complexity of the education of the child, it is inevitable that there will be problems. Regardless of the nature of the problem, there are some general rules which can be used.

A first step is to define the position of the child and his parents. This should be done without apology or negative implications. Such phrases as, "I know you may not agree, but . . ." or "Well, I suppose you think . . ." set the stage for conflict and failure. A first goal is to demonstrate an open mind and place the school in the role of an ally rather than an antagonist.

A second step is to develop mutual agreement on the problem. This flows quite naturally from the first. Where the school and the parent can agree on what the problem is, the stage is set for a solution. In fact, until this is done, any progress toward a solution is an illusion.

A common obstacle to defining the problem, one that is usually disposed of easily, is school policy. In some cases, the policy is such that an exception can be made to support the well-being of the child. In others, where the policy is so important that it must be inflexible, the goal is understanding and eventual agreement, not just enforcement.

Another obstacle, not so easily overcome, is the concept of the child held by the parent. This concept too often corresponds more closely to the idealized image the parent has of himself than to a real image of the child. When this is the case, it is essential to have the best possible working relationship with the parent before attempting to solve the problem. Again, an accepting relationship, established and maintained in the past, will be far more useful than a few rapport building moments at the beginning of the conference.

Where the concept the parent holds of the child is at variance with the one held by the school, a useful approach is to point out that a child may play a rather different role in school than he does at home. After all, the requirements and expectations are very different, and the child adjusts by developing alternate roles. Somewhere in the maturational process, usually in adolescence, the child tends to unify his roles. Integration is never complete; all of us play somewhat different roles in various situations. By recognizing the need for different roles, and the requirements of each, both the home and the school can gain a better understanding of the child. The goal is not to blame or condemn the child but to understand his position in the educative process and help him cope with the educational encounter. With the parents allied behind the school, chances for success are increased.

Guidance is an essential component of quality education. Like other innovations in elementary education, it requires specialized training.

A major function of guidance in the elementary school is communicating with parents. The goal is neither a grudging compliance nor an armed truce. The goal is to provide guidance for the child so that he may receive maximum benefit from his education.

Note

1. For an extended discussion of techniques for counseling with parents, see: Kowitz, Gerald T., and Kowitz, Norma G. *Guidance in the Elementary Classroom*. New York: McGraw-Hill, 1959, pp. 293–307.

Play as a Counselor's Tool

George W. Murphy

The intent of this article is to summarize psychological literature in an attempt to determine the value of play as a technique for understanding the child, and as a tool for the elementary and junior high school counselor.

The study of play as a means of understanding the child is a comparatively new approach in the field of psychology. It is a technique whereby the child can express his feelings and emotions with something he is familiar.

Rousseau was the first to advocate that the child be educated through play. He offered the suggestion that the teacher himself enter into the play activity (10). Although Freud used play as a means of therapy, he only touched the surface of its possibilities. Only in the last thirty years have people become interested in play as a technique for better understanding the emotions of a child.

Prior to 1919 little work was done with children, because of the difficulty of utilizing free association as is achieved in adults. Prior to this time no work was done with children under six years of age (9). After 1919, Melanie Klein and Anna Freud began to employ the technique of play as a means of analyzing children. Melanie Klein feels that the super-ego is highly developed in the child under six years of age, and Anna Freud feels that the child at this age has not developed a complete super-ego (10).

Since the first use of play as a technique in understanding the child, much has been written about the use of toys, the type of toys, and techniques that should be used. The tools employed have broadened to include all types of toys, psychodrama, drawings, fingerpainting, clay, music, and almost everything that is known to the young child.

Before one can fully understand the use of play as a technique, it is important for him to understand the development of play in the child.

"Play as a Counselor's Tool," *The School Counselor*, 8, 2 (December 1960) 53–57, has been reprinted with the permission of the author and of the publisher, the American Personnel and Guidance Association, © 1960 by the American Personnel and Guidance Association.

Play involves all types of activity, beginning in the very young child. He passes through sequential developmental stages including motor activities of grabbing, picking up objects, and placing special meanings to things. As the child progresses in age, so do his play activities. He begins to incorporate what he has learned in the past to carry out present activities. As he matures his realm widens: first it includes friends in the neighborhood, and then those at school. With each new group of friends his scope of play activities increases.

Many types of play rooms have been described in the literature. In the beginning, Melanie Klein used play in the home of the child as a technique. She felt that the child would relate better in an environment with which he was most familiar. After experimentation she found that the child would relate much better outside the home in a setting which was geared for play. By this means the child was removed from the many threats the home offered to his security (9).

The play room should be kept as simple as possible. With the exception of the basic furniture, the only things which should be there are toys. There should be a sink, and the floor should be washable. The toys should be the type that would instill the child to use his imagination as much as possible to reveal his emotional needs.

It should be emphasized that the type of toy used in therapy is not really important. It is far more important that it be something that will motivate the child to structure as well as endow the materials with conceptional functional content (14). Toys used should be inexpensive, for during acts of aggression it is not uncommon for the child to break the toy. It has been suggested that the child's toys be kept locked, allowing only the same child to use the toys each time. This offers the child a sense of security, feeling they are his own and no one else's (9). Another suggestion is that the child be allowed relative freedom in selecting the toys with which he desires to play.

Studies have been made of the type of toys which are available for the use as tools in therapy with the child. The supply of such toys is practically unlimited, and new ones are coming on the market each day. The following toys are examples of those used to demonstrate motor activity, pattern activity, mechanical activity, and unstructured activity: guns, soldiers, farm animals, baby dolls, telephone, doll family, furniture, trucks, planes, balls, nok-out bench, goose, clay, scissors, paste, pencils, crayons, and paper. The child was then observed to see which toy he picked to best express his needs. It was found that the doll family was chosen most by the child. The conclusion was that he seemed to be able to best express his feelings through this medium (2).

There are two schools of thought with regard to the manner in which play therapy should be carried out. The first is unstructured play. The child is given complete freedom in his choice of toys, and in setting his own stage for play. In this approach, the therapist becomes an observer.

watching what the child does. He may enter into the play on the request of the child, taking whatever part the child desires. The second is the structured plan. The therapist sets the stage for play, gives the child the toys, and asks him to act out what would happen. The main advantage of this plan is that it enables the patient and the therapist to get to the root of the problem more quickly. It also enables the therapist and child to join forces in order to reach a common goal (8).

There are certain facts to be kept in mind in dealing with play as therapy. The person should have a genuine respect for the child as a person. At all times he should display patience and understanding. As in any work with a child, the therapist should first understand and accept himself. The therapist should allow himself sufficient objectivity and intellectual freedom in understanding the things the child is attempting to tell him. Sensitivity, empathy, and a good sense of humor are essential qualities demanded of the personality of the therapist (1).

The child should be helped to understand that he can do anything he likes in the room—that this is his play room. He should also understand that the therapist will not tolerate any physical violence to either himself or the child. Under no circumstances should the adult display any emotion when the child shows aggression and destroys a toy. At the same time, the therapist should not try to force the child to play with a certain toy. He will return to it when he is ready.

In periods of aggression, the child will often destroy the toy with which he is playing. The child will completely ignore the toy for a while, but eventually come back to play with it. Once the child has expressed his aggression and again plays with the toy, he shows the therapist that he has mastered the cause of the aggression and is accepting it in a new light. The child will often discuss how he feels using the doll family to show his emotions (13).

Often in play therapy the child takes the part of the adult and asks the therapist to take the part of the child. Transference takes place between the child and the therapist. Through his role-playing as a child, the therapist can feel with the child in his dealings with the world of adults. Through this medium the child is given an opportunity to learn about himself in relationship to the therapist (1).

The statement made by Lawrence K. Frank in his article *Play in Personality Development* sums up the theory behind this technique: "This approach to personality development emphasizes the process whereby the individual organism becomes a human being, learning to live in a social order and in a symbolic cultural world. Thereby we may observe the child from birth on, grownig, developing child play as a means to exploring the world around himself" (4).

One of the basic factors reported in the literature was that the toys used with each child should be within his realm of play. A child should not be exposed to toys that are too old for him because he would not be able to express his true emotions through them. By using toys he is used to playing with, the child will feel freer to play and enter into the world of make-believe. The adult observing him will also obtain a truer picture of what the child is experiencing.

In order to do any work with children it is necessary for the person (psychologist, analyst, or a school counselor) to understand children and have a desire to work with them. The qualities of acceptance and empathy are the most important qualities. It is essential that the person working with the child accept him as he finds him—advancing the child forward from that point toward mutual understanding of the problem. It is also necessary that the adult understand, as well as feel, what the child is experiencing if he is to be enabled to help the child.

In general all the authors were in agreement concerning the type of toys that can be used. The writer found two main differences of thought expressed in the literature. First, there is disagreement regarding the importance of the strength of the super-ego in the young child. Second, authors do not agree on the merits of using the structured techniques or the unstructured. In the case of the first, this writer feels, the therapist will be guided by his own psycho-analytical theories. This should not produce a disagreement. Basically it is a difference in ideals and training. The second difference involves the technique employed, and this will be determined by the amount of training of the therapist, as well as his ability to understand what the child is trying to say through play.

It was a general fact that the doll family was considered the best means of getting the child to express his true feelings about the home situation. When this device is used, it is important to keep the doll family limited to the size of the child's family. Quite often the child will destroy the person within the family that is causing the problem. This may be done by either breaking the doll, completely ignoring it, or stating that he is going to send him away. It is not uncommon for feelings of guilt to follow the removing of the threat to his security. Eventually, the child will again include the doll that had been left out of the play. When this happens the therapist knows that the child is showing acceptance of the problem, and is ready through the world of make-believe to attempt to cope with his personality conflicts.

Everyone agrees that it is extremely important for the person in therapy to be non-emotional. He should not show any display of emotion if a toy is destroyed. By keeping control, the therapist helps the child feel that the room is a place he can do as he pleases. Usually the first time the child destroys an object, he will look at the adult for rejection. When this is not forth coming, it will give the patient the security of acceptance. This is one of the basic factors in the use of play therapy. It helps the child understand his personality, and its relation to himself as well as the world around him.

Play therapy is a comparatively new and underdeveloped field. Its scope is wide—ranging from toys to art and music. This paper has dealt only with the use of toys employed to help the therapist better understand the child.

The three objectives of the study were to determine: (1) the value of play in understanding the child, (2) the possible use of play by the school counselor, (3) the extent to which it could be applied to the junior high school.

Due to the child's lack of ability to understand himself and the world around him, play therapy is an invaluable tool. It allows a trained person to observe the child in a certain setting. In adults this is done through talking and reasoning, using past experiences. Due to his limited experience, the child is not capable of doing this. Through the use of play, he can accomplish what the adult does by talking.

The use of this technique in our schools can be very helpful to the counselor in his efforts to aid the child to understand himself. However, it is important that the counselor *always* keep in mind that he is *not* a trained psychologist, or therapist. It should never be used to analyze a child, for that is not the counselor's job. With training, this technique could become a valuable tool to the school counselor as he endeavors to help the child achieve maturity and self realization.

The use of toys in the junior high school guidance program is not advisable. The main objection is that chronologically the majority of junior high school pupils have little interest in toys. At this age, the child has the power to reason. Play can be used in the junior high school through such techniques as music, draw a person, draw a house—a tree—a person, finger painting, scatter drawing, and psycho-drama.

References

1. Axline, Virginia M., *Play Therapy Procedures and Results, Amer. J. Orthopsychiat.*, 1955, **25**, 618–627.
2. Beiser, Helen R., *Play Equipment for Diagnosis and Therapy, Amer. J. Orthopsychiat.*, 1955, **25**, 761–771.
3. Conn, J. H., *Play Interview Therapy of Castration Fears, Amer. J. Orthopsychiat.*, 1955, **25**, 747–755.
4. Frank, L. K., *Play in Personality Development, Amer. J. Orthopsychiat.*, 1955, **25**, 576–591.
5. Frank, L. K., Goldenson, R. M. and Hartley, Ruth, *Understanding Children's Play*, Columbia University Press, New York, 1952.
6. Gessell, A., and Ilg, F., *The Child From Five to Ten*, Harper Brothers Publishers, New York, 1946, 359–374.
7. Graham, T. F., *Doll Play Phantasies of Negro and White Primary School Children, J. Clin. Psychol.*, 1955, **11**, 11–25.
8. Hambridge, G., *Structured Play Therapy, Amer. J. Orthopsychiat.*, 1955, **25**, 601–618.
9. Klein, Melanie, *The Psychoanalytic Play Technique, Amer. J. Orthopsychiat.*, 1955, **25**, 223–283.
10. Lebo, D., *The Development of Play as A Form of Therapy, Amer. J. Psychiat.*, 1955, **12**, 418–442.

11. Moustakas, C. E., and Schalock, H. D., *An Analysis of Therapist—Child Interaction In Play Therapy, Child. Develpm.,* 1955, **26,** 143–157.
12. Piaget, Jean, *Play, Dreams, and Imitation In Childhood,* W. W. Norton & Company, New York, 1951, 147–168.
13. Soloman, J. C., *Play Technique and The Integrative Process, Amer. J. Orthopsychiat.,* 1955, **25,** 591–601.
14. Woltman, A. G., *Concepts of Play Therapy Techniques, Amer. J. Orthopsychiat.,* 1955, **25,** 771–784.

A Theoretical Framework
for Group Play-Therapy

Haim G. Ginott

The tendency to regard group therapy as "superficial" has abated considerably during the last decade. On both a national and an international scale, group therapy has been gaining acceptance by individual clinicians and treatment agencies. Two factors account for the change in attitude toward group therapy: (1) group therapy has evolved a systematic theory with principles and processes that can be tested scientifically; (2) necessity, the mother of invention, has compelled many therapists to try group therapy in an effort to meet more realistically the growing demands for service. In the course of trial and error, many have found group therapy to be not just a watered-down individual therapy extended simultaneously to several participants but a qualitatively different experience with rich potentialities of its own. Hobbs expressed the thoughts of many group therapists when he wrote: "It is one thing to be understood and accepted by a therapist, it is considerably a more potent experience to be understood and accepted by several people who are also honestly sharing their feelings in a joint search for a more satisfying way of life" (37, p. 281).

The aim of all therapy, including group therapy, is to effect basic changes in the intrapsychic equilibrium of each patient. Through relationship, catharsis, insight, reality testing, and sublimation, therapy brings about a new balance in the structure of the personality, with a strengthened ego, modified superego, and improved self-image. The inner experience responsible for curative effects is the same in all therapies, just as the repair value of certain medications is the same, whether administered orally, intramuscularly, or intravenously. Every therapeutic system must explain and justify its effectiveness in terms of its impact on the identifiable variables of therapy. In evaluating a particular therapy approach, the following questions must be answered:

(1) Does the method facilitate or hinder the establishment of a therapeutic relationship?

(2) Does it accelerate or retard evocation of catharsis?

(3) Does it aid or obstruct attainment of insight?

(4) Does it augment or diminish opportunities for reality testing?

(5) Does it open or block channels for sublimation?

The variations in the intensity and richness of these five elements account largely for differences in treatment results attained in different therapies. The above five criteria will be used in evaluating group play-therapy.

Does Group Play-Therapy Facilitate or Hinder the Establishment of a Therapeutic Relationship?

The presence of several children seems to facilitate the establishment of a desired relationship between the therapist and each child. A group setting proves especially helpful during the initial meeting. The first encounter with the therapist is frequently frightening to the small child. He is reluctant to separate from his mother and to follow a strange person to an unfamiliar room. It is less threatening for him to enter the new situation in the company of two or three children of his own age. In individual therapy, it is not unusual for a child, at his first session, to feel ill at ease, withdraw completely, and spend the whole session without daring to utter a word or touch a toy. In group play-therapy the presence of other children seems to diminish tension and stimulate activity and participation. The group induces spontaneity in the children; they begin to relate to the therapist and to trust him more readily than they do in individual therapy. This is illustrated by the following play-therapy sequence:

Seven-year-old Edna refused to enter the playroom for her first session. She sat in the waiting room, her face buried in mother's lap and her arms around mother's waist. In an emphatic voice she proclaimed, "I ain't going in without my mother." In spite of her loud protests, the therapist led Edna to the playroom. She looked like a lamb going to the slaughter. She stood in the corner of the room crying bitterly, "I want my Mom." The two other girls observed Edna with curiosity. "Why is she crying?" asked Betty. Ruth, who only ten sessions ago had a similar experience, answered, "She's afraid of the doctor. That's why she's crying." Ruth turned to Edna and said sympathetically, "You're scared, aren't you?" Edna did not reply, but she stopped crying. "I know you're scared," Ruth went on. "I felt the same when I first came here." "You did?" said Edna, turning her face away from the wall. She took one step forward and said to Ruth, "You was afraid, too? I'm scared of doctors 'cause they hurt you." "Not this one," assured Ruth. A few minutes later, Edna and her newly acquired friends were busily digging in the sandbox.

Identification is the crucial process whereby the group experience can become therapeutic. The group provides opportunities for multilateral relationships unavailable in individual play-therapy. In addition to an accepting and respecting parent surrogate, the group also offers the patients other identification models. Children identify themselves not only with the therapist but with the other members of the group. An effeminate boy, for example, may derive ego strength from associating with an accepting masculine playmate, and an over-protected child may become more independent by identifying himself with more autonomous group members. The tendency to withdraw into fantasy, so characteristic of the schizoid, is likely to be dispelled by the reminders of reality provided by others in the group. On the other hand, hyperkinetic children may become less active and more introspective under the neutralizing influence of calmer group mates. The result is that both the withdrawn and the over-active achieve a healthier balance between the inner world of fantasy and the outer world of reality.

The focus of treatment in group play-therapy is always the individual child. No group goals are set and no group cohesion is looked for. Each child may engage in activities unrelated to other members. Subgroups form and disband spontaneously according to the ever-changing interests of the participants. Yet, interpatient relations are an important element in group treatment. The therapeutic process is enhanced by the fact that every group member can be a giver and not only a receiver of help. Hobbs summarizes it: "In group therapy a person may achieve mature balance between giving and receiving, between dependence of self and realistic self-sustaining dependence on others" (37, p. 293). This point is illustrated in the following group therapy excerpt:

Barbara, aged eight, had not seen her father in two years. She missed him keenly. During one of the therapy sessions, while handling a gun, she hurt her finger. It was a minor injury, but she reacted with much emotion. She cried bitterly and pleaded with the therapist.
BARBARA: Please let me go. My finger hurts, and I need my mother.
THERAPIST: It's not only your finger that hurts. Something hurts inside.
BARBARA: Yes.
THERAPIST: You miss your Daddy.
BARBARA: My Daddy went away and I don't have a Daddy. He never comes home, and I need my Daddy.
Barbara stood close to the therapist and cried.
Shirley, aged 9, came over, put her arm around Barbara and said: "I don't have a Daddy either. My parents are divorced, and my father is far away in California."
The two girls stood close to each other, sharing their common sorrow.

There are also risks in group play-therapy. For example, a child who is ostracized by the group may relive original trauma too vividly and with damaging results. However, such dangers are not inherent in group therapy; they are a result of faulty grouping. Just as in adult therapy, patients in play-therapy should be grouped for the therapeutic impact they have on each other.

Does Group Play-Therapy Accelerate or Retard Evocation of Catharsis?

Children differ greatly in their use of cathartic media and in their preferences for "playing out" or "saying out" their problems. The therapeutic medium best suited for young children is play. In therapy, the term "play" does not connote its usual recreational meaning, but it is equivalent to freedom to act and react, suppress and express, suspect and respect.

Group play-therapy provides two media for catharsis, play and verbalization, so that each child can utilize the symbolic means of expression which best meet his need. In individual therapy, catharsis is mostly free associative. It consists of the child's free movement from activity to activity and from play to play. Seemingly unrelated activities, like verbal free association, can lead to the emergence of themes related to the patient's core problems. Group play-therapy has an advantage over individual treatment in regard to catharsis. Besides "free associative" catharsis, it provides also "vicarious"* and "induced"* catharsis. Many children, especially the more fearful ones, participate covertly as spectators in activities that they crave but fear. The group accelerates the child's awareness of the permissiveness of the setting. When one child comes forth with a "daring" activity, others in the group frequently find it easier to do the same. Children who are afraid to initiate any activity on their own gain the courage to do so in the company of others. It is as though the children help each other to realize that the playroom is a safety zone amid life's heavy traffic, where they can rest or roam without fear of authority figures and careless drivers.

It is dramatic to observe a child who stands in the corner of the room, not daring to take a step and yet following with eager eyes the activities in which he would like to indulge. He is frightened and fascinated when another boy spanks the baby doll or shoots the mother doll. It is rewarding to see children moving from passive observation to occasional involvement, to initiation of activities, and finally to cooperation with others.

> Ten-year-old Jim held a rubber snake in his hand and said with great venom, "I like this snake better than my brother. I hate my brother. He's not just a nuisance; he's a pest." Nine-year-old Todd, who was standing in the corner of the room, withdrawn and quiet, came over to

* This term was coined by S. R. Slavson.

Jim and said, "My brother's a pest, too." The eyes of the two boys lit up with a strange glitter as they helped each other to express their hatred of siblings.

JIM: I can't stand my brother.
TODD: My brother is no good.
JIM: Mine is more no good.
TODD: Mine's the worst.
JIM: I wish I didn't have a brother.
TODD: I wish my brother would disappear.
JIM: I wish my brother was never born.
TODD: I wish my brother was never thought to be born.

This was Todd's third session. The first two sessions he spent in complete silence.

It must be stressed that catharsis is always grounded in relationship. It occurs only when there is trust between the child and the therapist. Only in a secure atmosphere do children feel free to regress and to relive early emotions in a constructive milieu.

Does Group Play-Therapy Aid or Obstruct Attainment of Insight?

There is no direct relationship between insight and adjustment. There are many psychotics who have an uncanny grasp of the dynamics of their personality, whereas the bulk of so-called "normal" people have relatively little insight into the motivation of their behavior. This remark is not made to devaluate insight but to point out its limitations as a catalyzer in therapy. Frequently, insight is a result rather than a cause of therapy, attained by persons who have grown emotionally ready to get acquainted with their unconscious. This pertains to both adults and children. Through growth in inner security, children acquire a keener awareness of themselves and of their relations to the significant persons in their lives. This insight is frequently derivative and non-verbal and attained without the aid of interpretations and explanations. As Slavson points out: "In activity groups in which no interpretation is given, children become aware of the change within themselves and of their former motives and reactions" (74, p. 192). In play-therapy, insight is both direct and derivative, both verbal and non-verbal.

Some leading therapists feel that with adults individual therapy provides a better setting for achievement of insight than group therapy. They believe that only the deep transference relationship of individual treatment can give patients the security and the courage to face their unconscious. This may possibly be true in adult therapy. However, experience with groups of young children has indicated that mutual stimulation of ideas and feelings brings to the surface profound insights. Self-knowledge is developed through experience with many different relationships. In group play-therapy children are forced to re-evaluate their behavior in the light of peer reactions. The following example from a group session will serve as an illustration.

> Horty, aged nine, is extremely domineering and critical. During the therapy hour, there is hardly a moment in which she does not boss, criticize, or belittle the other children. In this session her victim was Linda. When Linda wanted to paint, Horty said, "That's not how you paint. Let me show you how to do it." Without waiting for Linda's consent, Horty poured paint all over Linda's paper. When Linda wanted to use brown paint, Horty commanded, "Don't use brown; use purple." She grabbed the brown paint out of Linda's hand and gave her a jar of purple. When Linda wanted to put starch on her painting, Horty said, "Don't use starch; use water." Over Linda's protests, Horty poured water on the painting. Linda sighed.
>
> The therapist said, "You wish she did not boss you so much."
>
> LINDA: You boss too much.
>
> HORTY: No, I don't.
>
> LINDA: Yes, you do. Listen how you talk. You talk like a teacher. Do this! Do that! You better stop being so bossy!
>
> Horty had no answer. She retreated to a corner of the table, and painted in silence for a long time. Suddenly she turned to Linda and said, "Am I really so bossy?"

It seems that the group crystallized the situation for Horty. It made her aware of her problem, so that she could face it and reflect upon it in the very situation that ordinarily provoked the difficulty. In individual therapy it would have taken much longer for the child even to be confronted with the problem.

Does Group Play-Therapy Augment or Diminish Opportunities for Reality Testing?

Unlike individual treatment, group play-therapy provides a tangible social setting for discovering and experimenting with new and more satisfying modes of relating to peers. The group constitutes a milieu where new social techniques can be tested in terms of reality mastery and inter-individual relationships. The inhibited child learns that he can attain objectives by voicing his desires, and the driven child learns that they are also served who only stand and wait.

The presence of several children in the playroom serves to tie the therapy experience to the world of reality. Infantile feelings of omnipotence and magic that interfere with good adjustment are unmasked and modified by the group. The children help each other to become aware of their responsibilities in interpersonal relations. The following excerpt from a case record illustrates the group's ability to put pressure on an unsocialized member, much beyond what could be expected in individual therapy.

> The minute Pat, aged nine, gets into the playroom, she starts annoying the other children, and in spite of their protests, she keeps up her attacks.

Thus today she shot the airgun into the ears of the other girls, and threatened to put paint on their clothes. In defense, the girls teamed up against Pat with a verbal barrage:

JANET: I bet even your mother doesn't love you.
PAT: Yes, she does.
JANET: Nobody could love anybody like you.
PAT: My mother loves me.
JANET: I bet your mother would like to get rid of you.
PAT: I have the best mother in the world.
MARGIE: You're crazy. You're ready for the nut house.
PAT: I am not crazy.
MARGIE: Are you a tomboy?
PAT: No!
MARGIE: Do you want to be a tomboy?
PAT: NO!
JANET: Then why do you act like a tomboy?
  Pat was surprised by the intensity of the attack, and began to cry. She wanted to leave the playroom.
THERAPIST: You are very unhappy. It hurts you that they don't like you.
PAT: I am not coming back. They hate me.
THERAPIST: You want them to like you.
PAT: Yes.
JANET: How can we like you when you act like that? You don't accept any rules.
MARGIE: Don't fight so much and we'll like you better.

However, the usual circumstance is that the group allows children to experience external reality as satisfying and helpful. To many children, reality has become charged with massive negative expectations. They perceive the world as hostile and depriving, and they expect from it nothing but doom. These children find the conditioned reality of therapy an emotionally moving experience. They have had previous group experiences, but in those they had to be most unlike themselves and constantly on guard. In ordinary groups, they have had to conceal more than reveal, and the barrier between them and other persons was at its highest. The following excerpt from a group play-therapy session will serve as an illustration.

Garrulous Gracie, aged ten, was in therapy with two very quiet and withdrawn girls. For many sessions Gracie dominated the scene with her ceaseless jabber, and she could really talk a blue streak about everything and about nothing.

One day Linda, aged eleven, turned to Gracie and said in a very soft and sympathetic voice, "Why do you always talk so fast, Gracie?" The question caught Gracie by surprise. She mumbled unintelligibly for a moment and then blurted out, "Because nobody listens to me, that's why! The minute I open my mouth, my mother says, 'Here she goes again,' and my father yells, 'Shut up!'"

"Oh," said Linda, "that's too bad. But we're not your family. We'll listen to you."

In therapy groups, children are exposed to a new quality of intimate relationships. They learn that they can shed defenses and yet remain protected, that they can get close to contemporaries and an adult and not get hurt. In the security of the therapeutic atmosphere, the children can face each other squarely and honestly and experience emotional closeness to other people. The group as a miniature society offers motivation and support for change, as well as a safe arena for testing new modes of behavior. The children learn that the sharing of materials and ideas is acclaimed by society and that their own contributions are expected and welcomed.

Does Group Play-Therapy Open or Block Channels for Sublimation?

One of the aims of child psychotherapy is to help children to develop sublimations consistent with society's standards and expectations. The capacity to accept some, repress a few, and sublimate many primitive urges is the mark of maturity.

Group play-therapy provides children with a richer repertory of sublimatory activities than does individual play-therapy. In individual therapy, a young child may engage in the same activity session after session. For example, he may paint with water colors and never use finger paints, or he may sift sand and never make mud. This self-imposed play restriction may be due to lack of inventiveness or to lack of security on the part of the child. Group play-therapy reduces the child's propensity to repetition; in a group, children teach each other to employ a variety of materials and to engage in a variety of activities, thus increasing each child's stock of sublimatory outlets.

The presence of group mates enables children to engage in competitive games. In group games, children can vent hostility symbolically against substitute siblings. In the initial stage of therapy, children tend to displace hostility upon group mates and the therapist. They attack group members, grab their toys, and interfere with others' activities. As therapy progresses, sublimations replace displacements. Instead of squirting water at one another, children feed dolls; instead of splashing paint, they color pictures; instead of throwing blocks, they build houses; instead of attacking each other, they engage in target shooting and in other competitive games. Such competitive activities, experienced in the accepting atmosphere of the playroom, eventually result in reduced sibling rivalry at home.

Summary

The basic assumptions of this chapter are that the inner experiences responsible for the healing process are the same in all therapies and that every therapy system must explain its effectiveness in terms of its contribution to the identifiable variables common to all therapy. The unique contributions of group play-therapy to the establishment of a therapeutic relationship, to the evocation of catharsis, to the derivation of insight, to the testing of reality, and to the development of sublimations are pointed out and evaluated.

Selected References

37. Hobbs, N., "Group-Centered Therapy." In C. R. Rogers, *Client-centered therapy*. Boston: Houghton Mifflin, 1951.
74. Slavson, S. R., *Child Psychotherapy*. New York: Columbia University Press, 1952.

Selection of Children for Group Play-Therapy

Haim G. Ginott

Clinical experience indicates that no one method of psychotherapy is effective with all persons. Different patients require different treatment methods. A process akin to matchmaking is required for successful therapy —matchmaking between a suitable patient and a proper method of treatment. This statement pertains also to child psychotherapy. Children accepted for treatment in guidance clinics are usually assigned either to individual or to group play-therapy. The rationale for the differential assignment is not set forth clearly in the literature. In fact, Dorfman states: "Thus far, there are no clear criteria for deciding whether to offer group or individual therapy in a given case" (21, p. 262). In her classic book, Axline devotes only one paragraph to the problem of selection of children for group play-therapy: "In cases where the child's problems are centered around social adjustments, group therapy may be more helpful than individual treatment. . . . In cases where the problems are centered around a deep-seated emotional difficulty, individual therapy seems to be more helpful to the child" (2, p. 26).

Lippman's recent book contains a single paragraph on the indications for group therapy: "Group therapy is the method of choice to help the withdrawn child learn that other children are friendly and safe. The group should be small and include children who are not aggressive or destructive" (49, p. 140). The need for clear criteria for assignment of children to therapy groups is especially urgent because of the recent popularity of group methods. Slavson (71, 72, 73, 74, 77, 78) has provided the most original and articulate discussion of indications and counter-indications for various types of group therapy. However, his contributions apply mainly to activity- and interview-therapy rather than to play-therapy.

The writer believes that group play-therapy is the preferential treatment for many young children and that it should be used extensively in child guidance. This statement is not a blanket endorsement of group play-therapy. Group therapy is no substitute for individual treatment; it is beneficial only in specific cases, which must be carefully selected and grouped. When children are assigned to groups haphazardly, the method not only is ineffective but may actually be harmful.

It must be stated that there are few, if any, validated criteria for the selection or rejection of children for group play-therapy. The writer knows of no published experimental studies in this area. Personal communications with colleagues brought little clarification; for each therapist who asserted that certain children are unsuitable for treatment in groups, there was one who reported success with just such children. It seems that the selection of children for play groups is still uncharted territory in the field of psychotherapy.

This chapter aims to formulate criteria for the selection and rejection of children for therapeutic play groups. The suggestions are not based on research findings but on theoretical considerations, on informal study and experience, and on clear successes and conspicuous failures in treatment of children in group play-therapy.

The Basic Criterion: Social Hunger

A large number of children seen in guidance clinics do not suffer from gross disorganization of personality but evidence symptomatic reactions to stressful situations and emotional conflicts. Typically they are wanted children, reared by parents who are either too ambitious and overwhelming or too weak and over-indulgent. Though they may present a variety of emotional problems that require therapy, for the most part these children have had some satisfaction of primary needs; in their infancy they experienced maternal care adequate for the development of social hunger (Slavson). It is the presence of social hunger that makes these children eligible for group therapy. "Social hunger" can be defined as a person's desire to gain acceptance by his peers, to act, dress, and talk as they do, and to attain and maintain status in his group. In return for peer acceptance, a child is motivated to change his behavior. The desire for acceptance stems from satisfactory primary relationship with a mother or mother-substitute who not only fulfilled the child's needs but who created in him needs for the recognition and approval of other people. Such children can benefit from the corrective relationships and curative environment that group play-therapy provides.

Children who in their infancy and babyhood missed close contact with a mother figure cannot utilize group therapy. Because their primary relationships have failed them, they are suspicious of *all* relationships.

They find it difficult to delay gratifications or to modify impulses in exchange for group acceptance, because they have had no experiences that make delay or sacrifice worthwhile.

Anna Freud expresses a similar opinion for a different setting: "If infants are insecure and lacking in response owing to a basic weakness in their first attachment to mother, they will not gain confidence from being sent to a nursery group. Such deficiencies need attention from a single adult and are aggravated, not relieved, by the strain of group life" (28, p. 60).

Information concerning a child's social hunger must be available before a child is assigned to group therapy. This information cannot be obtained from psychological tests alone. The usual clinical categories, such as psychoneurosis, anxiety state, and personality disturbance, are of little use in determining suitable candidates for group play-therapy, since children seldom, if ever, present clear diagnostic pictures. Therefore, in the selection of clientele, behavior patterns and symptom pictures are of particular significance. Such information can be obtained best from complete case studies of the children. The case studies should contain detailed descriptions of the complaints and symptoms for which the child was referred, his physical size and appearance, his level of maturity or immaturity, his typical modes of reaction to frustration, his adjustment to school and peers, and his characteristic use of leisure time. The assumption is that the child will show toward the therapist and group members some of the same behavior which he shows toward his parents and siblings. The case data enables the therapist to anticipate each child's behavior in the group and to plan specific remedial situations and responses.

Indications for Group Therapy

What follows are condensed descriptions of children deemed suitable for treatment in play-therapy groups.

Withdrawn Children

Group therapy is the treatment of choice for withdrawn children with varied psychodynamic constellations and etiologies. Under this heading are included children who, according to their manifest behavior, can be described as over-inhibited, schizoid, submissive, fearful, shy, isolated, uncommunicative, inarticulate, constricted, and meek. Many of these children are unable to express ordinary feelings of affection and aggression, have no friends or playmates, and avoid social give and take. The greatest affliction of these children is social isolation, and their greatest need is for an opportunity for free and safe interpersonal communication.

Withdrawn children find it difficult to relate to a therapist in individual treatment. They continue their habitual withdrawal patterns in the therapy setting and may spend many hours sitting silently in the corner of the playroom staring into space. When they do play, they choose quiet and safe activities and avoid spontaneity and risk.

Withdrawn children are reached more readily in group therapy than in individual therapy. The friendly adult, the enchanting toys, and the playmates make it difficult for them to stay within their shells. These mild pressures of the therapeutic group diminish their "isolationism" and induce them to participate in peer activities. An optimal group for withdrawn children is one that is active but mild.

Immature Children

This term covers children who are apparently wanted and loved by their parents as babies but not as growing individuals with self-originating needs. Such children are over-sheltered and unprepared for the realities of life outside their family incubator. These children crave social experience with contemporaries but do not develop adequate appreciation for the needs and feelings of others. They find it difficult to share possessions or to delay gratifications. They are spoiled and want what they want when they want it. Infantilized children inevitably create turmoil at school and in the neighborhood, as they are constantly embroiled in conflicts with contemporaries.

Group psychotherapy is of particular value to immature children. The group offers motivation and support for growing up as well as a safe arena for testing out new patterns of behavior. In the group they learn which aspects of their behavior are socially unacceptable and which elicit peer approval. As a result, they make an effort to adjust to the values of their peers. In the group they acquire a variety of essential social techniques: they learn to share objects, activities, and the attention of a friendly adult; they learn to compete and to cooperate, to fight and to settle fights, to bargain and to compromise. These techniques prepare such children to face their peers on equal terms.

Children with Phobic Reactions

Children whose anxiety is expressed in specific displaced fears, such as fear of dirt, darkness, or loud noises, benefit greatly from group therapy. Phobic children handle their anxieties by withdrawing from activities that seem dangerous to them. In individual therapy a phobic child can continue to escape his anxiety by avoiding frightening situations and objects. He may restrict his motility and confine himself to playing with a few "safe" toys. However, in group therapy, other children are likely to engage in activities that will require the phobic child to do something about his neurotic fears. Other children may shoot loud cap guns, cover themselves with mud, or turn out the lights. The group makes it hard for the phobic child to escape facing his problems, thus giving the therapist opportunities to deal with the phobic reactions as they occur. In individual therapy it may take a long time for the child even to confront his problem.

Effeminate Boys

In guidance clinics one sometimes encounters boys who were brought up like little ladies. They usually come from matriarchal households, where father is either weak or absent or where they were the only boy in a family of many females. Since their primary identifications have been with non-masculine models, these boys cannot help but play a feminine role. They are meek and submissive and lack the characteristic aggressiveness expected of boys in our culture. They are usually unable to mingle freely with other boys or to participate in normal boyish games. Because they shy away from aggressive play and prefer the company of little girls, they are nicknamed "sissies" and are socially stigmatized and emotionally scarred. They often grow up to be inadequate adults.

Group therapy with a male therapist is the required treatment for such boys. Individual therapy is counter-indicated because a close relationship with a male therapist may activate latent homosexuality, while a female therapist cannot meet the boy's needs for masculine identification. A non-intense relationship with a male therapist, masculine toys and activities, and the company of boys provide the optimal curative elements for treatment of effeminate boys. The group therapist serves as an identification model without strong libidinal ties. The materials and group members call forth the masculine components of personality without arousing anxiety. The setting as a whole encourages assertiveness without fear of retaliation.

Children with Pseudo Assets

Some children are referred to guidance clinics because they are "too good." They are obedient and orderly and over-generous. They worry about mother's health, are concerned about father's finances, and are eager to take care of little brother. Their whole life seems to be oriented toward placating their parents, and they have little energy left for gratifying their own wishes or for building relationships with their peers.

Children who exhibit pseudo assets need group therapy, at least at the beginning of treatment. In individual therapy such children may continue their established patterns of "altruistic surrender,"* relying mainly upon reaction formation to convert aggressive impulses into kindly behavior. In the playroom they are meek and gentle and spend much of the time propitiating the therapist, whom they fear. They bring him gifts, sing him songs, draw pictures for him, and keep the playroom clean. From the first session on, they tell the therapist how nice a man he is and how much they love him. The compliments and declarations of love cannot be taken by the

---

* This term was coined by Edward Bibring and quoted by Anna Freud (27, p. 133).

therapist as a triumph of rapid rapport or real relationship. They may rather be the children's way of saying how afraid they are of their own aggressive feelings and of the therapist's consequent retaliation. The process of transforming hostile impulses into their opposites, and of keeping them in check, consumes the life energy of these children.

Group therapy provides an effective setting for eliminating pseudo-positive behavior. It encourages children to give up dutiful compliance toward adults and to assume normal assertiveness. By observing the aggressive play of other children and the consistently non-retaliatory reactions of the therapist, these children slowly begin to allow their own impulses to gain some expression. First through "spectator therapy" and then through actual experience, these children learn that there is no need to be ingratiating and self-effacing. This frees them to discover their own wants, express their own feelings, and establish their own identity.

Children with Habit Disorders

Frequently parents refer young children to child guidance clinics with such symptoms as thumb-sucking, nail-biting, eating problems, and temper tantrums. When these are the main difficulty, and there is no evidence of more serious pathology, these transient habit disorders are frequently expressions of thwarted strivings toward independence. In most cases, these difficulties did not begin in infancy but appeared at a later stage, as a result of parents' inability to cope with their children's emerging independence. As infants, these children experienced love and security and developed social responsiveness. Children with habit disorders readily benefit from group play-therapy. Their strivings for independence are encouraged by the consistently permissive adult and by identification with more autonomous group members.

Children with deeper pathology may also manifest habit disorders in addition to other symptoms. For such children, the treatment of choice will depend on the differential diagnosis.

Children with Conduct Disorders

Many children are referred to clinics because of "conduct disorders," such as fighting, cruelty, truancy, and general destructiveness. The aggressive behavior may occur at home, at school, in the neighborhood, or in all these places. When the child misbehaves only at home but not outside of it (or vice versa), it may indicate that the core problem is a reactive and unconsciously retaliatory way of life against real or fancied mistreatment by parents. In such a case, group therapy is the treatment of choice.

The most difficult task in treating these children is to establish a relationship of trust with them. Because their parents failed them, they are suspicious of all adults. They fear the therapist, distrust his kindliness, and cannot tolerate his permissiveness. They aggressively avoid close relationship with him by acting obnoxious and hostile. The directness of individual treatment is too intense for children with conduct disorders. Because of its diluted relationships, group therapy is the more appropriate treatment method. "The group acts as an insulator for them, diluting much of the tension that would otherwise exist if the children had no means of escape from closer contact with the worker" (68, p. 19). At the same time, mild pressures from group members and the therapist's timely interventions help such children to achieve self-control.

Again it must be emphasized that the meaning and source of the child's aggression should be established before he is assigned to a group. This is particularly important, since we occasionally meet children whose aggression does not diminish with expression and whose destructiveness is unaccompanied by visible guilt. When aggression stems from psychopathy or other characterological conditions, it cannot be worked through in group therapy exclusively.

Counter-Indications for Group Therapy

What follows are brief descriptions of children deemed unsuitable for treatment in play-therapy groups.

Intense Sibling Rivalries

Children with intense hatred toward brothers and sisters are excluded from group therapy. They see all group members as substitute siblings and treat them accordingly. The permissive atmosphere encourages them to act out their intense hostility openly. In a thousand and one ways they victimize their playmates; they grab their toys, interfere with their play, and even abuse them physically. Such relentless hostility cannot be worked through in group therapy. These children must first be seen in individual treatment before they can relate to children in groups. Less intense sibling rivalry, however, can be treated in group play-therapy.

Sociopathic Children

Despite the general reluctance to label children as sociopaths, nevertheless, in clinical practice one encounters children as young as seven or eight who act as though they had no conscience. These children are shallow, selfish, impulsive, and capable of committing extreme cruelties without apparent guilt or anxiety. They seem to lack the capacity for empathy and are strikingly unconcerned about the welfare of others. They may appear charming and solicitous, but they are cold and distant. They are, as one mother put it, "all take and no give."

Sociopathic children like to come to group therapy. They seldom miss a session. However, they make life miserable for the other children. They bully playmates, attempt to manipulate the therapist, monopolize materials, steal toys, and in general, create hate in group members and frustration in the therapist. They effectively block progress in therapy by preventing other children from autonomous play and activity. Therapeutic limits are ineffective with sociopathic children; they sneak past them and continue their corrosive acts. Neither reflection of feelings nor direct interpretations have beneficial effects on these children. They actively resist introspection and are quick to change the subject when the meaning of their behavior is discussed. They also interrupt discussions of other children's problems, as though they were afraid of any insight. Even direct censure and criticism have little effect on sociopathic children, because they are indifferent to what others think of them.

Ordinarily, sociopathic children must be excluded from permissive play-therapy groups in order to prevent group disruption. However, the young child under eight, whose personality seems to forebode sociopathic trends, is still a child whose character is not fully crystallized, and it is therefore feasible to place such a child in a group on an experimental basis. It is important that only one such child be in a group and that the rest of the group consist of children without deep pathology. Individual play-therapy that calls for close interpersonal relations is unsuitable for socio-pathic children. Because of their rejection of all authority, they cannot accept the therapist either. Slavson suggests that older sociopathic children should be seen not in clinical settings but in a group "of an authoritarian nature such as institutions provide." In such groups, "restraints, inhibitions and punishments are applied consistently. Instinctual fear is aroused and the authority symbols that should have been established earlier in life are now supplied by the institution and its staff. The total setting is of such nature that one has to find some way of adjusting to it in order to survive" (72, p. 106).

Children with Accelerated Sexual Drives

Some of the children seen in a guidance clinic evidence maladjustment that stems from impaired psychosexual development. These are children who have been exposed to sexual over-stimulation; they may have been fondled erotically by unconsciously seductive parents, or they may have slept in their parents' bedroom and witnessed intercourse. At any rate, they show premature sexual interests and activities. These children need treatment in depth and should be seen in individual therapy before assignment to a group. Children with such libidinal distortions need the strong transference relationships, the direct interpretations, and the insights that only individual therapy can provide.

Children Exposed to Perverse Sexual Experiences

Children who have actively engaged in homosexual relations are excluded from group therapy. They may activate latent homosexual tendencies in others or initiate children in undesirable practices.

Children Who Steal

Children with long histories of stealing are excluded from group play-therapy. Persistent stealing is a serious symptom, often representing intense hostility against society. Such ingrained hostility cannot be diluted or dissolved easily. These children carry over into the miniature society of the group their deep resentment against adult society. They may steal from group members, the therapist, and the playroom. They may also initiate other children into the art of thievery.

Slavson suggests that children who steal only at home may be placed in group therapy. Stealing at home may just be a bid for affection or an act of revenge for unkind treatment. "The accepting atmosphere of the group, the family substitute, meets in most cases the love needs of the child, and the stealing impulse subsides" (71, p. 115).

Extremely Aggressive Children

The meaning of a child's aggression must be thoroughly evaluated before psychotherapy can be initiated. If the aggression stems from deep-rooted hostility, homicidal tendencies, psychopathy, or a masochistic need to activate punishment, group therapy is counter-indicated. The permissive atmosphere of the group only encourages the destructive impulses of such children. These children cannot be allowed even the usual leeway for acting out, as free discharge of aggression brings them neither relief nor insight but leads to further disorganization of personality. Forceful restraints must be put on their acting out, to compel them to "look before they leap" and to think before they act. This policy cannot be carried out in a permissive group setting because of the detrimental effect that it may have on other children.

Gross Stress Reaction

Children exposed to severe trauma or sudden catastrophe may develop acute symptoms even in the absence of underlying personality disturbance. A child may react with overwhelming anxiety to a fire, an auto accident, or the death of a beloved person, and he may develop dramatic symptoms that differ only in etiology from the symptoms of neurosis or psychosis.

Prompt individual therapy is the preferred treatment method for these traumatized children. Anxiety generated by recent traumatic events can be dissipated by the child's repeated symbolic re-enactment of the events. Resolution of intense anxiety and recession of acute symptoms occur more readily when the child can focus his symbolic play on the content of his trauma. This can best be accomplished in a setting where there are no distractions from other children and where the therapist can give his undivided attention to the frightened child.

Summary

This chapter formulates criteria for the selection and rejection of children for group play-therapy. The main consideration for accepting children for group therapy is their capacity for social hunger. Children who in their babyhood missed close contact with a mother figure are excluded from group therapy. Unsuitable for group therapy are children with murderous attitudes toward siblings, sociopathic children, children with accelerated sexual drives, children exposed to perverse sexual experiences, children who habitually steal, extremely aggressive children, and children who exhibit gross stress reactions.

Children who have a potential need to gain acceptance by peers can benefit from group treatment. The following types of children are deemed suitable for treatment in group play-therapy: withdrawn children, immature children, children with phobic reactions, effeminate boys, children with pseudo assets, children with habit disorders, and children with conduct disorders.

Selected References

2. Axline, Virginia M. *Play therapy.* Boston: Houghton Mifflin, 1947.
21. Dorfman, Elaine, "Play therapy." In C. R. Rogers, *Client-Centered Therapy.* Boston: Houghton Mifflin, 1951, pp. 235–277.
27. Freud, Anna, *The Ego and the Mechanisms of Defense.* New York: International Universities Press, 1946.
28. Freud, Anna, "Nursery School Education: Its Use and Dangers." *Child Study,* Spring, 1949, pp. 35–36, 59–60.
49. Lippman, H. S., *Treatment of the child in emotional conflict.* New York: McGraw-Hill, 1956.
68. Schiffer, M., *Special Group Processes in Guidance.* Unpublished manuscript.
71. Slavson, S. R., *An Introduction to Group Therapy.* New York: The Commonwealth Fund and Harvard University Press, 1943.
72. Slavson, S. R. (Ed.), *The Practice of Group Therapy.* New York: International Universities Press, 1947.
73. Slavson, S. R., *Analytic Group Psychotherapy With Children, Adolescents, and Adults.* New York: Columbia University Press, 1950.
74. Slavson, S. R., *Child Psychotherapy,* New York: Columbia University Press, 1952.
77. Slavson, S. R., "Criteria for Selection and Rejection of Patients for Various Types of Group Psychotherapy." *Int. J. Group Psychother.,* 1955, 5:3–30.
78. Slavson, S. R., *Child-Centered Group Guidance of Parents.* International Universities Press, 1958.

Studying the Elementary Guidance Program

Harry Smallenburg

Many of the problems that concern teachers are related to guidance. If you were to ask the faculty of an elementary school to indicate some of the major areas with which they need help, you would receive a number of comments such as these:

"We should know more about the children we teach."

"I think we need to use our test results better."

"If someone would help me with just two or three of the youngsters in my class, I could do a better job of teaching the others."

"I need to know more about how to talk with Johnny's parents about his work in school."

"How can I obtain the findings of research studies in psychology, growth, and development?"

"We've been doing a better job of teaching the various subject areas. Now we need to do a better job of teaching our pupils."

Such comments as these add up to a need for a better school guidance program. They reflect a concern for understanding children better and for developing techniques of providing more effectively for their varying needs. A carefully developed and implemented guidance program can do much to help teachers work more successfully with children and to aid pupils in their emotional, physical, social, and intellectual development.

A faculty who want to strengthen the school guidance program should consider carefully the purposes, characteristics, and techniques of effective guidance services in the elementary school. They should ask: "Why is

"Studying the Elementary Guidance Program," *The National Elementary Principal,* 43, 5 (April 1964) 15–18, has been reprinted with the permission of the author and of the publisher. Copyright 1964, Department of Elementary School Principals, National Education Association. This article also appeared in *Selected Articles for Elementary School Principals,* published in December 1968 by the Department of Elementary School Principals, National Education Association. Harry Smallenburg is Director of Research and Guidance for the Los Angeles County Schools, Los Angeles, California.

guidance important in a modern educational program? What are some of the major characteristics of a good elementary school guidance program? What is the guidance role of the classroom teacher? What is the role of the elementary school counselor? Of the school psychologist? Of the school social worker? How can we develop a team approach to guidance?"

This article discusses each of these major questions in a modified outline form. The format may be particularly useful for principals and teachers who undertake a similar study.

Why Is Guidance Important?

The importance of guidance in a modern educational program is evident from the study of current literature.

(1) "No society can afford to ignore the fact that one out of every seven men was judged to be mentally and emotionally incapable of serving effectively in its armed forces in time of war," admonished the President's Commission on the Conservation of Human Resources. In its analysis and study of factors most predictive of ineffective performance, the Commission found positive correlation between armed service rejections and separations of men with moderate or acute emotional distress and their poor educational backgrounds.[1]

(2) In a report summarizing twenty-eight different studies of California school dropouts and graduates, a basic recommendation was that "identification of potential dropouts should begin in the elementary grades. Ways of doing this in time to apply procedures are needed."[2]

(3) Between 5 and 10 percent of the children enrolled in the public schools have emotional handicaps of sufficient severity that they are unable to learn in school in the way children not handicapped can and are unable to employ the type of behavior required in the classroom.[3]

(4) Emotionally handicapped pupils who are not identified early and given the help they need to eliminate their handicaps leave school just as soon as they find any opportunity to do so.[4]

(5) A team of social scientists who surveyed a section of midtown Manhattan, New York City, reported that 23.4 percent of 1,660 persons interviewed had "marked, severe, and incapacitating symptoms." Another 58.1 percent were found to have "mild to moderate symptoms." This second figure is not so alarming as it sounds. A survey of physical fitness would probably show few people without some physical ailment or impairment, such as rheumatism or defective vision.[5]

(6) The elementary school is in a favorable position to provide valuable guidance services to children. Parents can approach contacts with school personnel optimistically and constructively. Teachers who work with the children on a total-day basis can know their needs better and make adjustments to provide for optimum growth. The children themselves can change patterns

more easily because of their youth and the lessened effect of "typing by their peer group."[6]

What Are the Characteristics of a Good Guidance Program?

An effective guidance program in the modern elementary school should:

(1) Relate to and support the broad objectives of the total educational program.

(2) Focus upon the characteristics of pupils—their differences and similarities—physical, emotional, intellectual, and social.

(3) Provide systematic ways of gathering information about pupils: for example, cumulative records; standardized tests; interviews, case studies; observation and anecdotal records; conferences with parents; sociograms; and autobiographies.

(4) Provide systematic ways of using information with groups: grouping within the class; placement in grades and in classes; and group guidance.

(5) Provide systematic ways of using information with individuals through counseling—educational, vocational, social, and emotional.

(6) Provide for all pupils but make special provision for the exceptional child.

(7) Provide specialized assistance to classroom teachers, such as a counselor, a school psychologist, or a school social worker.

(8) Assist teachers and administrators in working with parents through: parent-teacher conferences; PTA meetings; and grade level meetings.

(9) Assist teachers and administrators in working with community agencies.

(10) Provide for on-the-job growth of the teaching staff in guidance skills.

(11) Provide opportunities for research to determine the effectiveness of the guidance program.

What Is the Teacher's Guidance Role?

The elementary classroom teacher is an extremely important guidance worker. This point is stressed in all of the literature on elementary school guidance. As a member of the school guidance team, the classroom teacher, according to *Guiding Today's Children:*[7]

(1) Observes children's behavior in daily situations.

(2) Uses a variety of methods to study children individually and in groups.

(3) Takes part in a systematic program of standardized testing.

(4) Contributes to and uses cumulative records for each child.

(5) Refers children for special study and guidance conference when help is needed.

(6) Recognizes children with exceptional needs and knows the special services provided for them.

(7) Meets with parents individually and in groups to understand children better and to involve parents in the education of their children.

(8) Evaluates the growth and learning of children and the effectiveness of the curriculum.

(9) Works with community personnel and agencies in providing for children's educational and social needs.

(10) Engages in professional growth activities to deepen his understanding of children.

What Is the Counselor's Role?

The responsibilities of the elementary school counselor are helpfully defined in an article by Robert N. Hart.[8] In his study, teachers ranked the importance of selected duties for the elementary counselor as follows:

(1) Counseling pupils with learning, physical, social, and emotional problems.

(2) Interpreting pupil data to parents.

(3) Holding conferences with parents regarding any pupil problems.

(4) Interpreting pupil data to faculty members.

(5) Assisting in placement of pupils in proper classes or in special classes when needed.

(6) Acting as a liaison person between school and community agencies on pupil problems.

(7) Coordinating the efforts of all specialists working on a case.

(8) Acting as a guidance consultant on pupil problems to all staff members.

(9) Interpreting pupil data to authorized community agencies.

(10) Reporting to the principal annually on what has been accomplished in guidance.

What Is the School Psychologist's Role?

The duties of a school psychologist vary in particular systems and will be influenced by the availability of other specialists, by his professional acceptance by teachers and community, and by the expectations of the administrator and school board. One list of duties representative of many systems states that the school psychologist:

Informs school personnel and parents regarding the special services he is prepared to render.

Accepts for study individuals referred to him by school personnel.

Studies the problems and potentialities of individuals referred to him, formulates procedures to be followed in the case of individual studies, and provides or helps to secure the treatment needed.

Confers with school personnel who are working with an individual studied regarding the results of the study, interprets his findings, recommends the treatment needed to correct the individual's difficulty, and suggests ways in which all can cooperate in giving the treatment.

Keeps informed regarding the various services available in the community that can be used in helping individuals to solve their problems and is prepared to secure the particular services for the individual who needs them.

Helps school personnel to understand the problems and needs that children commonly have at different age levels.

Helps school personnel to understand the causes underlying various kinds of behavior and methods of helping each child to develop desirable behavior patterns.

Helps members of the community to understand the causes underlying various kinds of behavior and to understand the intellectualness of children, youth, and adults.

Promotes and engages in the research that is needed to help each child and youth to work successfully at a rate and at a level commensurate with his potentialities.[9]

What Is the School Social Worker's Role?

Like the school counselor and the school psychologist, the school social worker is an important member of the guidance team. His work has been described as follows:[10]

. . . School social work functions as a profession within the profession of education. It attempts to use unique social work skills on certain problems of children in school. This contribution reflects current philosophy of the elementary school that includes not only the transmitting of knowledge and skills but social adjustment as well.

Such a goal is recognized when school personnel ask:

1. How can we understand and modify attitudes of children, parents, and teachers that hinder a child's progress in school?

2. How can we know more about the child when he comes to school?

3. How can we help children who are unable to learn because of some emotional disturbance?

4. How can we have a closer parent-school relationship?

5. How can we help teachers help individual children in their classrooms?

The school social worker can help in answering some of these questions because social case work functions as a helping process. Social case work promotes effective use of a meaningful relationship wherein mutual acceptance and growth take place. This process stimulates change toward a more satisfying level of experience.

How Can a Team Approach Be Developed?

The guidance committee approach to staff cooperation is worth considering.[11] Such a committee is an informal advisory group, interested in the study of problems, yet without administrative responsibility. As a "helping" group to teachers, it contributes to the study of children and encourages continuing professional growth. Guidance committees are most helpful if:

> The committee represents the varied competencies of the school staff. Staff members volunteer because of interest.
>
> Communication between the committee, the administration, and the entire staff is fostered.
>
> The committee's responsibilities and progress toward its goals are periodically evaluated.
>
> The committee is scheduled as an on-going professional activity within the school.

Through the guidance committee, teachers, psychologist, nurse, principal, and supervisor serve as a team to consider mutual problems. They enjoy working together and, of course, grow individually. The committee fosters a guidance point of view which recognizes the complexity of human behavior and avoids ready-made formulas. The interrelations of all members of staff come into sharper focus, and individualized help is extended to more boys and girls.

On the basis of an analysis such as this, a school faculty can plan specific steps to improve the guidance program. A guidance committee might be set up to survey the guidance services being provided in the school, using as criteria the characteristics outlined earlier in this article. The committee might then identify the two or three greatest needs and report the findings to the faculty. Once the total staff has agreed on priorities, consultant help can be sought.

If special guidance personnel are not available, the principal might discuss with the superintendent the possibility of obtaining such help. In doing so, he might submit data regarding the costs of such services and the values derived from it. If it should prove impossible for the district to employ the specialist help needed, it might be possible for someone already employed in the school district to be reassigned, provided he has the confidence of the teachers and the needed credentials.

Whether or not guidance specialists are available, the faculty who recognize the importance of guidance services in the modern educational program can accomplish a substantial amount if they will carefully study the elements of a good guidance program and plan specific, year-by-year steps for improvement.

Notes

1. Ginzberg, Eli, and others. *The Ineffective Soldier: Lessons for Management and the Nation.* New York: Columbia University Press, 1959. p. 314.
2. McCreary, W. H., and Kitch, Donald. *Now Hear Youth.* A Report on the California Cooperative Study of School Dropouts and Graduates. Sacramento: California State Department of Education, 1953.

3. *The Education of Emotionally Handicapped Children.* Sacramento: California State Department of Education, March 1961. p. 9.
4. *Ibid.,* p. 9.
5. *A New Report on Mental Health in the Metropolis: The Midtown Manhattan Study.* Leo Srole, et al. New York: McGraw-Hill, 1962. Reported in *New York Times,* March 30, 1962.
6. Martinson, Ruth, and Smallenburg, Harry. *Guidance in Elementary Schools.* Englewood Cliffs, New Jersey: Prentice-Hall, 1958. pp. 5–6.
7. *Guiding Today's Children.* California Test Bureau, Los Angeles County Superintendent of School's Office, 1959, p. 236.
8. Hart, Robert N. "Are Elementary Counselors Doing the Job?" *The School Counselor,* December 1961.
9. Bower, Eli M. "The School Psychologist." *Bulletin of the California State Department of Education* 24: 2–3; November 1955.
10. Spence, Louise Child. "Guidance Activities of the School Social Worker." *Guidance for Today's Children.* Thirty-Third Yearbook. Washington, D.C.: Department of Elementary School Principals, National Education Association, 1954. p. 111.
11. *Guiding Today's Children, op. cit.,* pp. 205–207.

Selected References

National Education Association, Association for Supervision and Curriculum Development. *Guidance in the Curriculum.* 1955 Yearbook. Washington, D.C.: the Association, 1954. 231 pp.

Barr, John A. *The Elementary Teacher and Guidance.* New York: Henry Holt & Co., 1958. 435 pp.

Cottingham, Harold F. *Guidance in Elementary Schools: Principles and Practices.* Bloomington, Illinois: McKnight & McKnight, 1956. 325 pp.

Detjen, Ervin W., and Detjen, Mary F. *Elementary School Guidance.* Second edition. New York: McGraw-Hill Book Co., 1963. 240 pp.

Froehlich, Clifford P. *Guidance Services in Schools.* Second edition. New York: McGraw-Hill Book Co., 1958. 383 pp.

Guiding Today's Children. California Test Bureau, Los Angeles County Superintendent of School's Office, 1959. 295 pp.

Knapp, Robert H. *Guidance in the Elementary School.* Boston: Allyn & Bacon, 1959. 394 pp.

Kowitz, Gerald T., and Kowitz, Norma G. *Guidance in the Elementary Classroom.* New York: McGraw-Hill Book Co., 1959. 314 pp.

Los Angeles City Schools. *Guidance in Elementary Schools.* Los Angeles: Board of Education, 1957.

Los Angeles County Schools. *Guidance Handbook for Elementary Children.* Los Angeles: Los Angeles County Board of Education, 1948. 158 pp.

Martinson, Ruth, and Smallenburg, Harry. *Guidance in Elementary Schools.* Englewood Cliffs, New Jersey: Prentice-Hall, 1958. 322 pp.

Ohlsen, Merle M. *Guidance: An Introduction.* New York: Harcourt, Brace & World, 1955. 436 pp.

Willey, Roy DeVerl. *Guidance in Elementary Education.* New York: Harper & Brothers, 1952. 322 pp.

Organizing for Guidance
in the Elementary School

Raymond Patouillet

The printed word possesses a subtle authority for no other reason than that it *is* printed. Also, it is quoted equally to support prejudice and bias and to uphold honest inquiry. And when this printed word is in the third person it takes on the added authority of impartiality. The end result is rather frightening, especially in the field of guidance, where "common sense" so easily leads us to accept uninvestigated hypotheses. So that what I have to say will be clearly understood to be personal, subjective reactions to the subject at hand, I shall use the first person through parts of my presentation.

The problem of defining guidance as this term is used in the school setting has plagued all of us in the field for a long time. Some like to think of guidance as a program of services which may be clearly "defined, recognized, administered and evaluated. It then is possible to define a guidance program as a program of services which is specifically implemented to improve the adjustment of the individuals for whom it was organized."[1] I must confess that this term "adjustment" concerns me a bit and leads me to ask rather bluntly, "Adjustment to what?" Other writers define guidance similarly, as "services to assist the teacher in knowing the pupil and to meet his needs better, as well as to aid the pupil in understanding himself. . . ."[2]

Others of us shudder at the word services and prefer to think of guidance as enlightened teaching.[3, 4] A recent book definies guidance as a viewpoint which brings about services which in turn result in an experimental process with pupils.[5] This statement, in a sense, is an attempt to bring together two schools of thought.

As the reader probably suspects, I neither agree nor disagree with everything that has been said above. In my opinion the proponents of

"Organizing for Guidance in the Elementary School," *Teachers College Record*, 58, 8, (May 1957) 431–438, has been reprinted with the permission of the author and of the publisher, the *Teachers College Record*. Raymond A. Patouillet is Professor of Education at the University of South Florida, Tampa.

services and the proponents of enlightened teaching are not really as far apart as they would like others to believe. They have simply chosen to stress different dimensions of the same thing. I do believe, however, that the point of stress may well determine the nature of the guidance program. Let's examine these emphases more closely. Both camps agree, for example, that a guidance program involves services. They agree also that the teacher plays a major role in the guidance program. The basic issue is one of relationships and organization. How do people and services in the school setting relate to each other for the good of children? I should like to present some of my thoughts on guidance and on people who are involved in this area, and to suggest a plan of organization as I discuss this question.

Guidance

Guidance is a term that is often coupled with another multi-meaning word, adjustment. This is a potentially dangerous association. We must first define what we mean by adjustment. Adjustment to the status quo, for example, is not necessarily desirable. In a rapidly changing society like ours, marked by high mobility of the population, it is inadequate preparation for the future. In a democracy it can be fatal, for a democracy is strong to the extent that each individual contributes his greatest potential, his uniqueness developed to the fullest. The democratic answer to manpower shortages is human development rather than identification of talents for assignment to currently critical areas. Guidance can therefore be defined as the maximum development of an individual's potential for his own personal happiness and the welfare of society.

Old and New Guidance

The idea of guidance is as old as the first teacher. A sound curriculum, adapted to the needs of youth, and appropriate to their level of maturity, is sound guidance. A program of activities aimed at the development of social competence is likewise sound guidance. In these phases of the school program teachers have always played, and will continue to play, major roles.

More recently, guidance has developed specific techniques which are used by administrators and teachers as well as by school personnel specifically designated as guidance workers. Some of the better known instruments are cumulative records, psychological tests, counseling and group work techniques, and skills in human relations.

Originally, guidance was largely a remedial function, concerned with those in difficulty. The subtle assumption then was that pupils not measuring up to externally imposed standards (of achievement, behavior, and so forth) needed extra help or guidance. Schools soon realized the futility and waste involved in waiting for the casualties, and guidance began to assume a preventive function. The task then shifted to one of identifying potential casualties before they actually got to the disability lists. But even this has proved inadequate. In the face of the titanic struggle between communism and democracy, the optimum development of the individual has become more than the goal of a minority of progressive educators; it has become a necessity for national survival. Guidance is now being forced to assume a developmental approach. This means that it can no longer be solely or primarily concerned with the relatively few severely retarded or disturbed; guidance must be concerned with all pupils and must contribute to the maximum development of each.

Thus, while guidance will continue to serve remedial and preventive functions, its primary focus will be increasingly developmental. For example, rather than emphasizing testing to identify or predict strengths and weaknesses, it will emphasize enriching experiences to stimulate development so that tests will have more to measure. And there's something else here which I should like to make clear. The teacher's role is very definitely not that of junior psychologist, but of one who can translate subject matter into exciting experiences for children. That is the teacher's greatest contribution to education and to guidance.

. . . Everybody's Business

When guidance assumes a developmental approach, it inevitably involves all individuals and agencies which contribute to an individual's development. It is likewise concerned with the many facets of development —emotional, social, and intellectual, for example. The school can no longer arrogate the right to be *the* guidance institution of society. Often, it unknowingly assumes this responsibility, but wise parents have never permitted this. The school does, however, play a critical role. Because it deals with all the children of all the people, it is ideally suited to play the role of coordinator of guidance efforts.

Specifically, the school does not provide therapy, but it does provide a therapeutic climate. It also refers parents and children who need therapy to community agencies organized to offer such aid. Where no appropriate agencies exist, the school assumes a leadership role in establishing them. Similarly, the school does not assume the role of clergyman, den mother, or parent, but it does coordinate their efforts for the good of the child in the school setting.

The Core of Guidance

If guidance is everybody's business, then someone is needed to coordinate and integrate this emphasis in the educational program. The logical person is the guidance worker, and his task involves primarily skill in human relations. This is not to say, of course, that the guidance person need not have unique knowledges and skills in such areas as child development and diagnostic techniques, but rather, that these unique contributions may never be utilized if the guidance person is unable to relate positively to teachers, parents, administrators, community agencies, and groups of children as well as to the individual child within the counseling cubicle.

The guidance worker, therefore, is essentially a consultant in human relations who involves in a cooperative enterprise all those who affect the development of the child.

Mental Hygiene and Human Relations

Good human relations within a school contribute to a mentally hygienic atmosphere, and a mentally hygienic atmosphere allows people to be their own best selves, thereby encouraging sound human relations. The two are inseparable, and guidance cannot survive where they are not present. In order to insert a wedge into this circular relationship for purposes of study, I shall attempt to define a mentally hygienic atmosphere. I think it might be defined as an atmosphere which promotes physical health, a feeling of personal worth, and communication among members of the school community.

If pupils and teachers are enjoying good physical health, they are released from an area of worry that can in and of itself be disabling and inhibiting to good teaching and learning. Healthy pupils enjoy physical activity and seek to develop physical skills. Children in poor health are apt to look upon physical activity as a threat to their very being and to avoid it. They may react, as all human beings do to frustrating situations, by aggression or by withdrawal, both of which are roads to emotional disturbances.

A feeling of personal worth is a second factor in a mentally hygienic atmosphere. This factor is enhanced when one feels accepted as a person— not despite his differences or even because of them, but, more basically, because he is a human being and by that fact alone clothed in dignity. I do not believe that man gives dignity to man. If that were true, then man could take away dignity from man, a morally untenable position. For example, to fail a child because he is unable by nature to learn a certain task is just as immoral as ruling that no child shorter than four feet six inches shall be promoted to the fifth grade. It should be added that not all experience with failure is of a negative nature. A school program in which one experienced only success would be poor preparation for life. But failure that leads to a feeling of hopelessness, in turn leads to the possibility of serious emotional upset.

A third characteristic of a mentally hygienic situation is communication. This means multi-directional communication, rather than one-way-to-one-person communication. Figures 1 and 2 may prove helpful at this point.

Represented in Figure 1 is an open society in which lines of communication are open. The lines in this figure should not be interpreted to be lines of responsibility or of authority, however, and the distinction should be kept clearly in mind. Unfortunately, most organizational charts usually clearly indicate lines of authority and little else. These tend to become

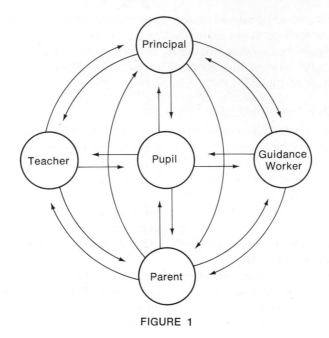

FIGURE 1

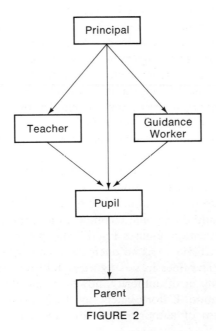

FIGURE 2

lines of communication as well (as shown in Figure 2) and suggest a one-way communication process from "top" to "bottom," even though this may not be the intention.

In a situation where there is limited intercommunication, there is obviously limited opportunity to develop interpersonal relations, and potential resources for child development are isolated. Also, where there is a hierarchy of communication, creative energies of those beneath the top tend to be submerged in a feeling of hopelessness.

Thus, physical health, a feeling of personal worth, and multi-directional lines of communication are basic to sound mental hygiene. In turn, a mentally hygienic atmosphere is basic to human relations and to the guidance program of the school.

Guidance Personnel

In this discussion I shall direct my comments to those people in the school setting who have major guidance responsibilities. If I don't discuss the custodian, it isn't because I think he is not important in the guidance program of the school. If I don't mention the children, it is not because I am unaware of the guidance implications of a first grader's cruel comment to a classmate, "You're not pretty. You can't play with us." I have to establish limits and I am concerned with organizational problems.

The Teacher

In the school setting, the teacher continues to be the key guidance person. Two procedures are especially rich in guidance possibilities: pupil–teacher planning and parent–teacher conferences.

Through pupil–teacher planning, which involves beginning where children are (taking into account their level of maturity, their varying abilities, interests, and other personal characteristics), pupils develop a sense of personal worth and learn the necessity of multi-directional communication. Children learn better when they are dealing with meaningful material and are actively involved in the setting up of course goals, procedures, and evaluation, with the teacher serving as guide and resource person.

Through parent–teacher conferences the guidance responsibility of home and school is clarified and a cooperative, consistent approach is maintained.

The Principal

It is the principal who takes the lead in setting the guidance tone of the school. He involves his staff in policy making, thereby letting them know that they count as individuals. His position as democratic leader demands that he release the creative energies of his staff, rather than project his own needs upon them. He is skilled in human relations, in guiding his professional team through activities aimed at professional development. It has been said that "we do unto others as we have been done unto." This is especially appropriate in the field of teacher–administrator relationships. Teachers find it difficult to accept children as individuals if they themselves are not so accepted.

The Guidance Worker

The school guidance worker (counselor, psychologist, visiting teacher) works primarily with and through teachers as well as with parents and the principal, serving as consultant and resource person to them. The guidance person works with children through the class setting, although individual conferences with parents and children are held if referral to an outside agency is indicated or if individual testing or interviewing is agreed upon by the teacher and guidance person.

I have grouped counselors, psychologists, and visiting teachers together under the general heading of guidance worker because I see an increasing number of similarities and a decreasing number of differences among their respective roles.

The term guidance counselor was probably first used in secondary schools with strong vocational emphases. The guidance counselor now finds himself involved in matters pertaining to educational planning and to personal and social development. He also finds that he is working with teachers, parents, community agencies, and groups of children, as well as with individual children. The term counselor therefore no longer adequately describes his function if we think of counseling as a one-to-one relationship. Thus, the guidance counselor has broadened his area of concern and is beginning to move into the elementary schools.

The role of the school psychologist too is assuming broader proportions. Initially, the psychologist was concerned primarily with the individual exceptional child.[6] He continues to be concerned with testing but has extended his concern to include the mental hygiene of the school. He works with teachers, parents, community agencies, and groups of children as well as with individual children. His area of operations is no longer restricted to the elementary school.

The school social worker or visiting teacher is moving in new directions too. Interest in prevention rather than remediation, wider use of referral rather than direct handling of cases, a realization of the need for visiting teachers in other than low-income areas, the growing use of visiting teachers in a consultative capacity, broadening the scope from trying to prevent truancy and delinquency to "helping all children with personal and adjustment problems,"[7] the extension of social work upward through high school—all of these trends seem to be drawing the visiting teacher closer to the guidance counselor and school psychologist.

It is clear that the teacher is the one who works with the guidance personnel and if she is to be helpful, guidance workers must understand her needs. The following list of functions prepared by a teacher attending the Thayer Conference of school psychologists is pertinent for all guidance workers.

> What do I want of a school psychologist?
> I want a person to help me with classroom problems on which I need help.
> I want one to help me with a solution to my problem rather than give me a *diagnosis* of my problem.
> I want one to *help me* solve my problems *within* my classroom setting (as much as possible) rather than to take my problem *from* my classroom.
> I want one who may give me ideas on new techniques of teaching but not one who would do them for me.
> I want one to give me advice on my relations with my fellow staff members if I need it.
> I want one who would be a member of my staff, rather than an *assistant* in the administrative office.
> I want one who would be a member of the *team.*
> I want one whose personality traits are outstanding.
> In teaching, we start with the child and get back to the child. *We are all in this together.*[8]

From a study conducted by the National Association of Guidance Supervisors and Counselor Trainers[9] I was interested to learn that school systems were recommending the hiring of more guidance counselors, more psychologists, and more visiting teachers for our elementary schools. Frankly, I asked myself whether the schools responding to the questionnaire had comparable perceptions of these different guidance workers. In view of the discussion above, I think we can conclude that the teachers who responded were clearly indicating a need for assistance.

Guidance Organization

Let us assume for a moment that we are in an elementary school of 900 pupils; that we have a guidance counselor, a school psychologist, and a school social worker. Figure 3 represents these people. Theoretically, the triangle is taking care of the guidance counseling needs of 900 pupils, the square is responsible for the school psychology needs of 900, and the diamond is prepared to meet the visiting teaching needs of 900. In view of the preceding discussion we know that much overlapping of work will prevail and the teacher will not feel that she is getting any concerted assistance.

An alternative plan of organization would be to have three "helping teachers" or "child development consultants," each responsible for the developmental needs of 300 children. Both children and teachers would then stand a better chance of being served.

Of course the question that immediately arises is, What sort of training will these child development consultants need? My answer at this

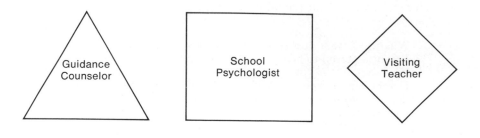

FIGURE 3

point would be a two-year program of graduate study including courses in guidance, developmental psychology, school psychology, social work, administration, and curriculum (including reading, an area in which teachers say they need help). Such a program is currently offered on an experimental basis at Teachers College, Columbia. The fully qualified school psychologist (a graduate of a four-year program) would still be needed of course, and would serve as consultant in our imaginary school to our three child development consultants. The proposed plan perhaps fills the need for more immediate assistance to teachers within reasonable financial limits.

An intermediate step which is probably necessary for the present is charted in Figure 4. While called child development consultants and per-

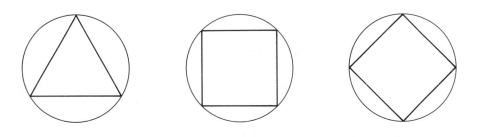

FIGURE 4

forming similar tasks, each individual represented might have a different background and contribute unique strengths. The circle surrounding the triangle is the person who has had two years of graduate work in guidance; the one around the square is the two-year psychologist; and the one with the diamond in the center is the graduate of a two-year master's program from a school of social work. These three would work as a team, each serving as consultant to the other two.

Summary

The great need in the elementary school guidance field is to ask ourselves some critical questions. How can we organize more effectively to meet the challenges of our dynamic society? Perhaps an analogy would be helpful. If we use a rowboat to transport four men across a pond, do we use twenty-five rowboats to transport 100 men across an ocean or do we even build one huge rowboat? Perhaps we need to develop new means of transportation.

Whatever is done will have to be done with a thorough understanding of our children and our available resources. And it will challenge the efforts of *all* of us, working cooperatively, to establish the optimal relationship between the two.

Notes

1. Raymond N. Hatch, *Guidance Services in the Elementary School* (Dubuque, Iowa, William C. Brown Co., 1951), p. 14.
2. Harold Wright Bernard, C. Evan James, and Franklin R. Zeran, *Guidance Services in Elementary Schools* (New York, Chartwell House, 1954), p. 5.
3. Janet A. Kelley, *Guidance and Curriculum* (New York, Prentice-Hall, Inc., 1955).
4. Esther Lloyd-Jones and Margaret Ruth Smith (editors), *Student Personnel Work as Deeper Teaching* (New York, Harper and Brothers, 1954).
5. Harold F. Cottingham, *Guidance in Elementary Schools* (Bloomington, Ill., McKnight and McKnight Publishing Co., 1956), p. 3.
6. Norma E. Cutts, ed., *School Psychologists at Mid-Century* (Washington, D.C., American Psychological Association, 1955), pp. 16–25.
7. Jean Pearman and Albert H. Burrows, *Social Services in the School* (Washington, D.C., Public Affairs Press, 1955), p. 9.
8. Cutts, *op. cit.*, p. 71.
9. National Association of Guidance Supervisors and Counselor Trainers, *A National Study of Existing and Recommended Practices for Assisting Youth Adjustment in Selected Elementary Schools in the United States* (Ann Arbor, Michigan, Ann Arbor Publishers, 1953).

A Psychologist Views the Preparation and Potential of an Elementary School Counselor

Eli M. Bower

Somewhere in one of Freud's early lectures on psychoanalysis to medical students he presents the onslaught of new concepts on man's ego. According to him, persons who changed our picture of the nature of the world such as Copernicus, Galileo and others, and persons who changed our picture of the nature of man such as Darwin, Wallace, and others met with great resistance and hostility. And Freud himself who suggested man look at his own self did not win any popularity prizes in his day.

I think our present problem is best conceptualized as: how do we make more human beings out of potential human beings? How do we do this in such a way that the human being is not only effective but creative and utilizes whatever biological potential he has? In this humanizing process we are aware that we have failed in many ways, that we have large numbers of people who just don't make it.

We have attacked the problem very much like the engineer who investigated recurring floods produced by a river and decided that the best way to deal with this problem was to build a dam at the mouth of the river. We have a tremendous number of investigations of crime, delinquency, and mental illnesses. Many who are reminded of delinquency think about "streets full of gangs," and what to do about them, and many who think about dropouts ask, "What do you do about the child who is one hour away from leaving school?" Those who consider mental illness concern themselves with what to do about a person who needs immediate hospitali-

"A Psychologist Views the Preparation and Potential of an Elementary School Counselor" was presented at the Invitational Conference on Elementary School Guidance held in Washington, D.C., March 31–April 2, 1965, and is reprinted with the permission of the author. Eli M. Bower is Professor of Education at the University of California, Berkeley.

zation. It is remarkable to me that it has taken us so long even to consider the value of such a program as Operation Head Start which is a mild beginning but nevertheless a beginning, or even to conceptualize a notion of an elementary school counselor, or even to conceptionalize the elementary school as part of the whole system. Do we have a kind of culture blindness or is there something missing in our psyche or intellect? What I want to do is to give you some idea of some of the research that is pertinent to this problem, some of which we did in California, and some of which has been done elsewhere.

One of the reasons why I am here, by the way, is that I have a certain amount of anxiety about the elementary school counselor. My problem is that I tend to talk to myself about it.

I am reminded of a young father who was asked by his wife, as a sort of a punishment, to take his two-and-a-half year-old son to the market for shopping. Of course the youngster was grabbing and spilling and running and crying and yelling, and the poor distraught father who wasn't used to this kind of thing finally got his purchases collected and put the boy in that little seat of the shopping cart. He got in line and as he kept pushing the boy and the basket up toward the person who takes all your money, he kept saying, "O.K., Albert, relax. Just relax, calm down. We'll be out of here soon. Don't let this thing get you."

And lo and behold, pretty soon the little boy quieted down. The woman who was standing behind him was amazed at this unexpected turn of events and tapped the young father on the shoulder. "It is amazing," she said, "Albert has really calmed down." The young father turned around somewhat slowly. "Lady," he said, "I'm Albert." That's the kind of counseling I've been involved in.

In looking at the school and its relationship to the elementary school counselor, the thing that has been uppermost in my mind—the thing that I've been counseling myself on is this. Occasionally I talk with a group of principals and they say to me, "We need some help in the elementary schools; we need elementary school counselors." And I say, "O.K., what do you want them to do?" They want a group of people to man the ambulances so that the learning casualties can be carted out.

Then I talk to parents. And what do they want? Well, they want somebody who can enhance the intellectual development of their child, so that by the time he gets through the second grade he is well on his way to Princeton. Of course, the parent says, "I'm a parent, so I should know what a counselor ought to do."

Before deciding how to use a counselor, I think we have to conceptualize the school as a social system. Where does it have its flaws? Where are the chinks in its armor? Where does it need some reinforcement? Who are the children that are falling out, and why are they falling out?

I will review some pertinent research very quickly. We tried to discover the places in the school where children were being pushed out of the system. We made several assumptions. One was that this is a system that is mandated on all children, and that children have no choice in attendance or in learning how to learn. You have heard of court cases where children are asked with whom they wish to live and there is a variety of possibilities. But when they reach school age, it's mandatory that they go to school. And that's for every child in the United States with few exceptions. Even severely retarded children go to school. And cerebral palsy children with tremendous physical and mental complications go to school in most states.

If the child has no choice, then we have no choice. We have to find out where in the system children are not succeeding, and why. To do research on this, we assembled a group of directors of guidance in the state of California, all tried and true men and women, and we asked, "Can you identify for us a specific number of children who are having marked learning problems?" We asked the largest cities to identify the largest number of children and we gathered a pretty good sample. We said to the directors, "Identify those children who are being seen clinically and who are, in the judgment of clinicians (usually child guidance people), children who have moderate or severe problems." They all did this in the spring of the year. In the fall we identified all the classrooms in which these children were students and we asked the teachers to collect some information on every child in these classes. We wanted to find out what information the teacher had which was relevant to the identification of developing difficulties of children in a school system, information a teacher had that she could use, or the counselor could use in helping her make a reliable, valid judgment of the positive or negative growth of the child. These data were collected by the teacher without our giving her any specific information as to why we wanted this information about the children. It was done on forms and the information was recorded. It was the kind of procedure that would delight a fastidious research person!

We chose 10 pieces of data that we thought were relevant. First of all, we included the socio-economic status of the child which was recorded as the father's occupation. We spent a long time with the teachers to be sure that they understood that the father's occupation was something that he did, not an organization for which he worked. Very often, nevertheless, a space was filled with "Standard Oil." We didn't know whether the father was president or one of the oil field roughnecks.

We used the score on an IQ test that was usually the California Test of Mental Maturity. We used the chronological age divided by present grade, and the number of absences in the four-month period. We discussed whether we should differentiate between excused and unexcused absences. Because of the variety of ways in which this was interpreted we decided that it wasn't worth all the trouble, and we just used "total absences."

We had two ratings, two very quick ratings by the teacher. One was the behavioral status of the child with respect to others in his class. This was not a rating of the mental health of the child, but the behavior of the child in relation to other children. The other rating was the physical status of the child. Did the child have any visual difficulties, hearing difficulties, speech difficulties? And we asked for other information known to the teacher about the child's physical status.

Then we had a role rating which we developed—a little instrument called "The Class Play." We also had the score on a standard reading achievement test, and a score on an arithmetic test. These were the ten pieces of information we used.

Now, in every class there was one child whom we had identified previously as being a serious problem. We analyzed the data to find out which of these kinds of information was significant in separating this child from the others. We didn't assume that there were not others in the classroom that were having just as much difficulty as the child whom we had selected, but we needed a criterion group, and this was the way we did it.

The question we were trying to answer was, "Could we use this information to activate the teacher to use some behavioral scientist or school counselor to help her, so that the interaction between the teacher and the child would take place prior to the full development of the problem?" We wanted the teacher to become anxious in a positive sense before she was fully frustrated and reached the point of saying, "Take this child out of my class. I've had enough."

In other words, could we introduce a positive perception of intervention by making it a lot easier for the teacher to work with a child when the problem had not become overwhelming or when the ego development of the child had not become so pathological that the teacher's investment in helping was often wasted?

We found that a lot of the data were relevant. We used the IQ score —not the IQ—just the score that the child got. We also administered individual tests to the criterion group and, of course, we found that group tests were at least ten points below individual tests.

The reading test told a significant story. When you take the reading score for a particular grade and compare the group identified as problems, you find that the differences get larger as you go up in grades, which is an indication that the system tends to reinforce those who are succeding while at the same time it punishes those who are failing. The system itself is set up in such a way that those who fail get punished and those who succeed get rewarded. It's a good system if you can make it. And the ones who enter the school who are already inefficient in the system, of course, have no way of rectifying their deficiencies.

Of course, the school is an institution that doesn't have this as a goal. It has as its goal the success of everyone, but unfortunately it doesn't often operate this way. This is not to say that anybody is lax; if you study the school as a social system, this is the way it often turns out.

Perhaps the teacher can be activated to do something about children who are developing problems at a time when a change is possible. If so, what sort of person might be introduced to assist the teacher?

The payoff is going to be in the kinds of people that become elementary school counselors and the training programs that are set up. I think this is the greatest single program in the field of prevention that we can manage at the present time. And why we have been waiting for this, for these many years, is puzzling. Maybe it isn't puzzling, but certainly it is something that an anthropologist from outer space would have difficulty in understanding.

Now I want to discuss implications, and kinds of things we want the counselor to do. In the first place, I think that a counselor has to be thought of in relation to the school as a system, and not in terms of what a principal wants, or what a parent wants, or what a teacher wants. They all want different things, and they certainly should have them. When the principle says, "I need someone to take care of this schizophrenic child; I can't keep him in my school," he certainly is legitimate in asking for that help. On the other hand, to place a group of counselors in the school system in charge of problems which emerge is not going to be the best way of using such counselors.

It used to be thought that if there was a child guidance clinic right in the school, that was great because then one wouldn't have to send the kids far if they needed help; one could always send them to the child guidance clinic. And so the clinic got a large room for a waiting room, and many children were sent there.

It didn't change the system in any way. In fact, it made it easier to push out the children who were causing trouble or having difficulties because there was some place to send them. And anytime one provides services to a system by which the system can manage to get out of itself the things that are irritating it, it means that the system does not have to correct itself in any way; it can always push on to another system the things that are irritating and annoying. Nothing is going to be done if a program is instituted so that the system doesn't have to change.

What I am saying is that the elementary school counselor has to be looked upon as someone who is going to make an impact on what goes on in the school. To accomplish this will necessitate two things. One—focus on problems prior to the full development of them. Two—focus on the prime person in the system, the teacher. I think that the elementary school counselor has to be and do the following things: first of all, this person should be a behavioral science specialist, not a curriculum specialist—a person who knows a lot about human behavior and can assist the teacher in this relationship, can understand what goes on with certain children, the reason for lack of learning, and the difficulty in behaving. The counselor is not a supervisor, not an administrative assistant; he is a counselor in the real sense of the word, somebody one can talk to who has know-how and competence in this particular field. His main impact would be on reinforcing the teacher's competency in being more effective with all kinds of children, and as a result, in being more effective as a teacher.

If I were to institute a training program at this time, how would I build it? What sort of person do I see the counselor becoming? First of all, the elementary school is a different system from the high school. I see the counselor chiefly as a consultant to the teacher, not a person who takes on individual cases per se. Whatever he does in relation to children must be done to assist the teacher to be more effective in day-to-day operations.

I would accept into the training program anybody who has sensitivity, first of all (not necessarily training), and place him immediately in a variety of counseling situations for two or three hours in each morning, and then I'd arrange seminars in the afternoons with a group of behavioral scientists, mostly from the clinical field. I would include some anthropologists and I would try to relate the counselor's experiences to the content of behavioral sciences. I would also have a basic, didactic course in personality dynamics. I would spend the whole year on these aspects of training and I would alternate the experiencing and the conceptualization so that each would fit with the other.

I would make the afternoon sessions flexible enough so that if the group said, "Look, we have been having some concerns with reading. What is this business of reading all about? Could you get somebody here who knows something about the relationship between personality development and reading? This is something we ought to know about. Let's spend two or three weeks on this." This would be up to the group of trainees. They would also assume some responsibility for pinpointing the needs for the development of all counselors, for staffing the sessions, for determining the areas in which the counselors were effective and in which they were in need of assistance. That would occupy a whole year.

I believe that it would also be helpful to have a kind of National Training Laboratory experience. This is the only way I know of getting some understanding or think-back into one's self. Since one's self is going to be a critical instrument in working with teachers and others, anything that can be done to enhance this aspect of the personality would be helpful to the counselor. A National Training Laboratory experience for two weeks, then reinforced again a year later in another two weeks session, would be beneficial to any elementary school counselor. This role is going to be very exacting for the individual's professional competence and his understanding of himself and the way he uses himself in relation to teachers.

In addition, I think that a good counselor ought to have somewhere in his mind an array of alternatives which are related to possibilities in managing children in the system. Sometimes, alternatives are there but nobody seems to recognize them as alternatives. There are time, space and content alternatives; there are placement alternatives; there is a whole array of other alternatives, and if one doesn't possess them I think he must develop them. The flexibility of a program for inflexible children has to be increased. One can't do much in a system which is so tight that there is no possibility for arranging things in a different way. I think for young children there is need for environmental manipulation, of placing the child in situations from which the conflict-free parts of the ego can be developed, where children can get some zest in life, especially in the school system from which they can't withdraw. We've got to find places in the school system where some positive things can take place especially for those who have very few opportunities outside of school.

I also think that one of the strong competencies of the school counselor will have to be in the whole field of individual parent counseling and parent counseling in groups, and in the major area of inservice education of teachers. I don't think that the counselor necessarily has to counsel parents himself, although he may, but his main impact will be in working with a teacher who is seeing a parent so that, that teacher will be better able to work with other parents. However, there are potential preventative possibilities in bringing together a group of parents for two hours a week when children are just beginning to show some signs of difficulties.

We need help in conceptualizing for the future. We've reached the end of the rope with respect to diagnosis and studies of individual children based on irrelevant or out-dated conceptual schemes. In training counselors, the conceptual scheme by which individual studies are to be made must be oriented to some positive conception of development, and it must be related to program possibilities. One must tie individual studies to programs in order to get a feed-back. For example, in the UCLA Medical School program for severely disturbed children, there is a placement plan by which each child, when he enters, is placed in a specific program. There is, of course, some relationship between what is known about the child and where the placement is made. This may not work all the time but at least there is some way of organizing the data about children and trying it out in relation to success in the system.

Also I believe that the training of counselors should give an understanding of the ego development of children, the ego strength rather than the pathology. There are lots of children with problems in the school system. I think we need a concept that helps to answer the question, "how do you build ego development?" rather than, "how do you repair ego defeat?" When we think about the term "therapeutic" we have to consider that what is therapeutic will be learning experiences that increase the cognitive-affective development of the child—and I never separate those two words. Education *is* cognitive-affective development. What a school counselor does must contribute to this effort and goal.

Instruction needs to be based on educational needs. We talk about all kinds of pathology, about brain-injured children, about retarded children, emotionally disturbed children. This doesn't tell us anything. What we need is an assessment of the child in terms of his functioning in the social system. This has been done, by the way, in a classification by the American Heart Association relative to making decisions about heart patients. It includes along with the disease itself environmental factors, things that the person can do that can lead him on to more effective living. I think we are going that way in the behavioral sciences in looking, perhaps, not so much for the etiology but for information about people in order to make effective decisions regarding them in this social system.

I mentioned that the elementary school requires a tremendous variety of flexibility. We need to be able to make adjustments for children who are not going to make adjustments for themselves, and the impact of the counselor who makes the changes must come through the educational processes which the school tries to enhance for all children.

Some teachers believe that every time a behavioral specialist enters the school he eats away part of a teacher's competency. A good counslor must enhance the teacher, making the teacher feel more competent after the counselor leaves than he was before. It may seem sometimes that we are telling the teacher she does not know enough. Let's be aware of this pitfall.

Lastly, I think we need to learn how to be preventative in our approach in the school system, rather than always trying to dam up the Mississippi at New Orleans. I think we have to be a lot more imaginative. We have to get back to our basic goals. Development of the human being starts at the beginning. It has roots like a tree that are set by the time the child goes to school and certainly a lot more set by the time the child gets to high school. Let's put our money down where we are going to get the highest payoff. The elementary school counselor, I think, is going to be a highly significant professional person in our society.

PART IV

Educational Psychology—
A Related Area of Study

FOCUS ON THE CHILD

Educational psychology is a broad field—perhaps too broad. It draws knowledge from measurement, human growth and development, personality, learning, social psychology, and adjustment psychology. Such a broad approach to classroom psychology may confuse the beginning counselor, particularly since the discipline suffers from growing pains. Not too far in the past, personality, measurement, and learning were the cornerstones. This emphasis remains, but others such as the study of deviant children have been added. New ideas and theories are welcomed as they add to the psychology of the classroom making for more effective teaching. In the future, theories and empirical studies of instruction may be as commonplace as theories of learning are today. Perhaps that day is not so far away.

For the elementary school counselor human growth and development aligned with personality study resides at the apex of the counselor's priorities in educational psychology. Indeed, our focus is the growing, developing child. Through counseling our hope is to personalize the educational process. Extensive study of children aids the elementary counselor in understanding children's wants, needs, desires, and action tendencies. As a result of his understanding the counselor facilitates the growth of children. This being our basic aim in elementary counseling one can readily see its close alignment with human growth and personality development study. So, this is our beginning for counselor study and must be pursued in depth. Also, since educational psychology is a broad discipline, other aspects must not be omitted. Therefore, this section opens with the problem of identity in early life, moves on to articles on personality and school adjustment, and ends with suggestions for a mental health program in the elementary school. Again, let me emphasize that our focus on understanding the child can best be achieved through study of human growth and development.

His Struggle for Identity

Jerome Kagan

The newborn child is a remarkably capable organism from the moment he begins to breathe. He can see, hear, and smell, and is sensitive to pain, touch, and change in position. The only one of the five senses that may not be functioning immediately at birth is taste.

The newborn's behavioral equipment is also remarkably well developed. When only two hours old, he will follow a rapidly moving light with his eyes; his pupils will dilate in darkness and constrict in light; he will suck a finger or nipple inserted into his mouth; he will turn in the direction in which his cheek or the corner of his mouth is touched. He can cry, cough, turn away, vomit, lift his chin from a prone position, and grasp an object placed in his palm. His body will react to a loud sound. He can flex and extend his limbs, smack his lips, and chew his fingers.

It is fortunate that the infant is so competent at birth because his new environment outside his mother's body subjects him suddenly to such unfamiliar stresses as hunger, heat, cold, and pain. During the first weeks of life, most of his behavior is in direct response to the unexpected interferences with his equilibrium. If he is hungry, he cries. If he is excited, he babbles. If he is in pain, he cries to the accompaniment of thrashing arms and legs.

These innate reactions alter his environment significantly by bringing another person to tend him. When this happens, the child—who instructed his mother more than she instructed him during his period in the womb—enters the active influence of the society to which he belongs. Thenceforth, according to the talents of those who serve him, certain of the infant's behaviors will be selectively strengthened and certain others will be selectively weakened.

The relation between infant and mother is a ballet, in which each partner responds to the steps of the other. If, when the infant cries, the

"His Struggle for Identity," *Saturday Review* (December 7, 1968), 80–82, 87–88, has been published with the permission of the author and of the publisher. Copyright 1968 Saturday Review, Inc. Jerome Kagan is Professor of Psychology at Harvard University, Cambridge, Massachusetts.

mother bestows care and affection, the infant will be likely to cry on the next occasion when he is distressed. Thus the mother's actions are molding the infant's behavior. But the frequency and regularity with which the mother acts toward the child are also being affected by the infant. The mother is more likely to leave the living room and go to the infant's room if the infant cries than if the infant is quiet. As a result, irritable babies, who are more often boys than girls, typically share their mother's company more often than do placid, quiet babies. If a mother's attempts to soothe her infant are successful, she is more likely to come to the infant when he calls. The infant who smiles will elicit more smiling from the mother than a non-smiling baby. The infant girl who babbles provokes more imitative babbling from the mother than the infant who is quiet. In this sense, the infant is clearly shaping the mother's behavior as much as the mother influences the infant.

Another major determinant of the mother's actions, in addition to the child's moment-to-moment behavior, is her set of goals for the child. Most American middle-class mothers want their boys to be independent and self-reliant because contemporary American society rewards independence and competitiveness. Most Japanese middle-class mothers, by contrast, want their sons to be interdependent with the family and less self-reliant. The mothers' actions flow from these idealized models. Each mother loves her child equally and thinks she is doing the best for him.

Each set of parents has the difficult task of deciding what kind of child they wish to create. The decision can become excruciatingly difficult in times of great flux, like those through which we are now passing. The increasing population density in our cities, coupled with growing alienation of citizens from a sense of community, is causing many Americans to question whether individualism, carried to present-day extremes, is healthy. How does a particular set of parents react to this question? Depending on the strength of their commitment to traditions of competitive individualism versus their eagerness to participate in evolution of new cultural designs, their values may conflict with the values of their neighborhood. And if the characteristics of the child do not adapt him to whatever values are accepted by the parents, there is conflict within conflict.

The child whose personality traits do not match the values of his society is not likely to be well adjusted. Such a child might be much happier in a society governed by a quite different set of values. The parental decision regarding the child is an overwhelmingly moral one, not to be decided on scientific evidence alone. Parents should appreciate that there is no ideal set of personality characteristics for a child nor any ideal set of parental practices. Each is relative to its own time and cultural context.

The child's perception of whether he is loved or rejected is also relative. If the child knows that the parents are poor, and it is a sacrifice for them to buy him a toy worth $5 for Christmas, he will interpret receipt of that toy as an act of love and affection; for he recognizes that the parents have given him something that required a personal sacrifice. The child of an affluent family who receives the same toy is not likely to view it as reflecting any special affection. For this boy, perhaps, a long walk in the forest, which is a sacrifice for a busy executive father, is the gift that is symbolic of love. Love or rejection is not contained in any specific set of behaviors by a mother or a father. Love or rejection is relative to the child's perceptions; for love, like beauty, is in the mind of the beholder.

The same reasoning holds for punishments. There is no specific effect of a verbal chastisement, a spanking, or a banishment from the company of parents or siblings. The effect of each of these punishments on the child is always dependent on the child's interpretation of that punishment. Each parent will be better able to socialize his child if he has access to the "tote board" of values the child holds. It is not an easy accomplishment, but its attainment is worth great effort.

The first year of life is marked by rapid development of perceptual structures in the child. Although we now know that the newborn child is far from being an amorphous bundle of insensitive flesh and bone, our contemporary understanding of cognitive growth resembles the state of chemical theory in the seventeenth century, when a scientist could relate either natural or purposive causes to obvious changes in the color, weight, smell, or texture of substances but could not explain what happened to bring the changes about.

Long before anything at all was known about the human brain, pre-scientific philosophers taught that the heart was the seat of human personality. Therefore, it is interesting that modern scientific research with children should demonstrate—as it has—that the heartbeat is a dependable signal of the child's attention. Experiments in our own and other laboratories during the last decade have tracked the processes of the infant mind by noting the occasions when the child's heartbeat suddenly slows. The resting heart rate of infants ranges from 120 to 180 beats per minute, with an average of about 145 beats. Experience has confirmed that decelerations greater than six or seven beats are most often associated with an attentive posture, and facial or motor responses indicating surprise. By measuring the child's heart rate and the duration of his gaze at various events, one can easily see that the earliest determinant of the infant's attention is high rate of change in the physical parameters of a stimulus. Lights that blink on and off are more likely to capture his attention than is a steady light source. Intermittent tones of sound are more attention getting than continuous ones. Visual events with high black-white contour contrast possess more power to recruit sustained attention than stimuli with minimal contour contrast. These conditions produce distinctiveness naturally. They elicit attention without prior learning. These factors dominate the attention during the first twelve weeks.

After that time, the infant's reactions show increasing signs of being controlled by experience. In other words, the child is beginning to think about what he sees. Attention is focused more and more in relation to the degree to which the elements of an event are a distortion or discrepancy from an established schema.

A schema is a representation of an external event. Like a caricature, it is defined by a set of distinctive elements. If the distinctive elements change, the schema changes. The four-month-old child's schema of a human face probably consists of an oval outline and two symmetrically placed eyes. When an infant of that age is shown a sketch of a face with asymmetric eyes or a face with no eyes, the child smiles markedly less than he smiles at a face with symmetrically placed eyes, with or without the presence of nose and mouth. The smile seems to be his "Aha" reaction—his way of saying the stimulus is familiar to him.

A child pays maximal attention to an event that is a slight deviation from the distinctive elements of his schema. The four-month-old baby will look longer at a photograph of a face—regular or moderately disfigured—than he would at a randomly generated nonsense figure with a high degree of black-white contrast. Furthermore, his cardiac deceleration will be greater to it than to the black-white nonsense figures. Since each child develops his own schema at his own rate, it follows that information intended to command his attention must be tailored to fit his schema.

Let us consider some economic class differences in cognitive functioning in light of the above. Our Harvard laboratory has studied more than 160 first-born Caucasian infants from lower-middle-class, middle-class, and upper-middle-class families. Lower-class infants come from families where one or both parents did not complete high school and where the fathers were in unskilled occupations. Upper-middle-class infants came from families where both parents were college graduates.

Each infant was exposed to two visual episodes in the laboratory at four months of age. In the first episode, each child was shown each of four different achromatic depictions of human faces. The four stimuli were a photograph of a male face, a schematic outline of a regular male face, a collage of the photograph of the face, and a collage of the schematic regular face. After a short recess, each child was shown a series of three-dimensional sculptured faces painted flesh color, and four presentations each of four different faces: a regular male face; a collage of that face with eyes, nose, and mouth rearranged; a regular face with no eyes; and a completely blank face with neither eyes, nose, nor mouth.

The children from the lowest economic level displayed the smallest cardiac decelerations to all the stimuli. How are we to interpret this?

The lower-middle-class infants look as long at the faces as the upper-class babies do, but do not decelerate their heartbeats because the faces are not close enough to their schema for the faces of their parents. The favorite explanation for this difference in response is that the mother's face is a more distinctive stimulus for the upper-middle-class child than for the less privileged child. We believe that well educated mothers are more likely to engage in frequent, distinctive, face-to-face contact with their children, more likely to create conditions that will make the parent's countenance distinctive.

The most dramatic differences between lower- and middle-class children of pre-school or school age involve language skills. Documentation for this conclusion is everywhere. A fast and often glib interpretation of it rests on the belief that lower-class parents talk less often to their children. This may be too simple an interpretation. We certainly do not wish to reject the idea totally but we prefer to balance it with the possibility that lower-class children are not so much deprived of parental vocalization as they are deprived of distinctive vocalization. The lower-class child does not receive distinctive verbal stimulation from adults and, as a result, is less likely to attend to human speech.

Some of the lower and middle-class children mentioned above were observed with their mothers in their homes for a day when the infants were four months old. A selected set of mother and child variables was recorded every five seconds. The observer wore in her ear a small, inconspicuous battery-powered device which produced a brief auditory signal every five seconds, and the observer recorded, in five-second units, variables that belonged to a prearranged code. Some of the variables included: mother vocalize to infant, mother touch infant, mother vigorously manipulate infant, mother pick up infant, child vocalize, child extend limbs, and child thrash.

Computation of the percentage of time the mother vocalized to the infant, regardless of what else she was doing, or where she was in the home, disclosed only a slight and nonsignificant tendency for the upper-middle-class mothers to vocalize more often than lower- or middle-class mothers to their daughters. There were even less striking differences for sons. However, when we examined the distinctiveness of the mothers' vocalization—vocalization that occurred when mother was face-to-face with her infant and doing nothing else but talking to her—more dramatic differences appeared.

Let us describe a hypothetical experience of an upper-middle-class girl and a lower-class girl.

The middle-class child is lying in her crib in her bedroom on the second floor of a suburban home. She wakes, the room is quiet, her mother is downstairs baking. The infant studies the crib and her fingers. Suddenly the quiet is broken as the mother enters, looks down at her baby, and speaks. This auditory intrusion is maximally distinctive and likely to orient the infant to her mother and to the vocalization. If the child responds vocally, the mother is apt to continue the dialogue.

An infant girl in a ghetto is lying on a couch in a two-room apartment with the television going and siblings peering into her face. The child lies in a sea of sound; like the sea, the sound is homogeneous. The mother approaches the child and says something. This communication is minimally distinctive from background noise and, as such, is not likely to recruit the infant's attention. Many of the infant's vocalizations during the day are not likely to be responded to by anyone nor are they likely to elicit a special response.

This research generates implications for preschool enrichment programs for lower-class children. There is a zealous attempt to bombard the lower-class child with pictures, crayons, books, speech, and typewriters, as if an intellectual deficit was akin to hunger and the proper therapy required filling of his cerebral gulleys with stuff.

I would like to argue for a more paced strategy, a self-conscious attempt to intervene when the intrusion is likely to be maximally distinctive. For example, teaching reading or vocabulary should be individual or in very small groups, and background contexts should be simple so that the material to be learned has maximal distinctiveness. Instructional speech should be paced so that each communication holds the attentional stage solo and does not share the child's limited attentional capacities with other attractions. We must initiate explicit attempts to diagnose the content and articulateness of the child's existing schema and to plan interventions that are moderate discrepancies from his schema.

Distinctiveness of events recruits the child's attention and can maintain it for five, ten, or even twenty seconds. But sustained attention for minutes requires more than discrepancy; it requires the possession of structures or chains of cognitive units that are specifically activated by the event. When one sees a three-year-old devote a half hour to exploration of an old telephone, there is a temptation to smile and mumble something about the child's natural curiosity. However, long periods of sustained involvement are neither inherent in the event nor part of the child's natural equipment. It can be taken for granted that this particular child has either watched a telephone being used, or spoken into a telephone mouthpiece himself, or heard his parents explain what a telephone is for. Sustained involvement of any child is dependent on that child's previous acquisition of a set of hypotheses and reactions appropriate to the object. Without such prior learning, a potential thirty-minute exploration can be reduced to less than thirty seconds.

I recall a teacher who brought to class a dozen packs of Cape Cod seaweed stuffed with attractive samples of shells of diverse species. She gave each pair of six-year-old children one of these attractive toys and withdrew, expecting the pupils to display natural curiosity. Each child devoted less than ten seconds to the material before returning to his previous game. The teacher had failed to explain to the children that the shells were once inhabited by different kinds of animals, and that by looking carefully at a shell one could tell not only what kind of animal had lived there but how old the animal was when it left the shell.

A second anecdote is equally forceful. One of our graduate students raised an infant rhesus monkey from birth. The animal became in interesting sight around William James Hall on the Harvard campus. My daughter, twelve years old, begged to see the monkey. We arranged to have the student and monkey come to dinner. My daughter excitedly informed the neighborhood of the event. A few minutes after the student and monkey were seated in our living room, six children, from seven to eleven years of age, rang the doorbell. They ran to the monkey, looked and poked for about two minutes, and then casually walked off one by one to more interesting activities. We hadn't prepared the children to ask themselves logical questions about the monkey—what makes him afraid, what makes him run, what makes him smack his lips?

In short, curiosity may be only a romantic name for that phenomenon that occurs when a child tries out a set of acquired hypotheses on some new object that captures the child's attention.

In addition to the distinctive elements of new material, the child's motivation is another factor that controls the intensity of attention the child will devote to a task. The child's desire to be proud of his parents and similar to them in word and deed is one strong motivational force.

Lower-class parents may exhort their children to work hard for good grades in school, but the children do not perceive their parents as persons who publicly engage in or express a value in intellectual mastery themselves. As a result, the children cannot view mastery of intellectual skills as a way of being similar to their parents, or of gaining the adult resources of power and competence that the child perceives his parents to possess.

The peer group is not unimportant in the development of standards and motives surrounding intellectual mastery. The child selects models from among his classmates once he begins school. As with the lower-class family, the lower-class peer group is biased against school achievement in favor of those behaviors that the boys and girls themselves define as masculine or feminine. This situation has serious consequences for school performance. The child of six years wants to maximize his similarity to whatever standards his schoolmates set for his sex. The child has learned that he or she is called a boy or a girl and rushes to elaborate this operational definition.

How does the child decide what events, objects, or actions are masculine or feminine? He works by a reliable formula. He implicitly computes the ratio of males to females associated with an event or action. If the ratio is lopsided in one direction, that activity is assigned the sex role of the majority party. Fishing is masculine, sewing is feminine. Any five-year-old will tell you this. School is usually classified as feminine by six-year-olds because in over 90 per cent of the primary grades in this nation, the activity of the classroom is monitored by a woman.

One implication of these data argues for the wisdom of segregating the sexes, especially in the primary grades of school. In a sex-segregated class, each child might learn to maximize in the school experience the sex role appropriate to himself. The presence of a man in the classroom would obviously have the strongest impact on a boy. But even changing the content of the reading curriculum should have some benefit.

Aside from the importance of modeling, the peers mediate other mechanisms that engage the motive to master academic tasks. Most children, especially boys, have a strong motive for power, a desire to play the dominant role in an interpersonal dyad. The uncorrupted sign of power for all children is strength. Strength is the only legitimate currency of power which cannot be corrupted, and children recognize this principle. The culture, in its wisdom, preaches substitute signs for power. Prowess at athletics, skill at adult activities, signs of intelligence can function as badges of potency if the group accepts that currency. The middle-class child is likely to find himself in a peer group where the right to dominate is given to the child with good grades, to the child with a quick answer, to the child with a catalogue of facts. Lower-class peer cultures rarely adopt this translation of power. Thus the lower-class child, already unable to find models for intellectual striving in his parents, is further deprived of a primary motive to master intellectual skills.

The two themes in this brief essay stress the dramatic psychological growth that occurs in the opening years and the importance of the parent-child relationship for that growth. It is believed that a large share of the child's desire to adopt the values and skills of society, including the wish to master the tasks of the school, derive from a close parent-child relationship in the first few years of life. The child comes to value the parent and is, therefore, receptive to adopting the parent's motivations for him. There is growing interest in establishing day care centers for economically underprivileged mothers who wish to work and need a place where they can leave their infant for most of the day. We believe this plan has potential dangers for the child's growth, for it could produce a child who has a seriously diluted tie to his parents. It will also weaken the emotional involvement of the mother with her own child. It would perhaps be wise to consider paying the mothers to stay with the children and beginning strong educational programs for parents, to educate them into the nature of the child and the nature of his psychological growth.

However, implementation of this suggestion will not by itself ameliorate the awesome educational deficiencies of many economically deprived children. The poor progress of these children in school is probably the result of many factors, including low income, residence in a slum neighborhood, an unstable family organization, absence of a father, a peer group that does not value school success, and, in some cases, inadequate nutrition of the individual child. It is not possible to state with confidence which of these factors produces the child's problems in school. Cures are most effective when diagnoses are accurate. We must therefore be cautious about simple plans or devices that promise to solve "the problem" when we are still unclear about the fundamental nature of the problem.

The Lonely School Child

Dora Wayne

Elementary school teachers tend to underestimate their direct role in the formation of personality. Many view the childhood personality as an exclusive product of the home. Yet, school personnel can be initiators of purposeful action in counteracting negative patterns that originate outside the school's bounds. Sullivan defines personality as "the relatively enduring pattern of recurring interpersonal situations which characterize a human life."[1] He recognizes a hierarchy of biologic accomplishments, but stresses that man evolves a personality only through interpersonal situations in a social culture. Erikson also views the personality as developing . . . *according to steps predetermined in the human organism's readiness to be driven toward, to be aware of, and to interact with, a widening, social radius, beginning with the dim image of a mother and ending with mankind, or at any rate that segment of mankind, which "counts" in the particular individual's life.*[2]

Thus, the child's personality is the summation of all his experiences, both in and out of the home, and school personnel who are understanding can influence his psycho-social growth positively.

The developing character, according to some psychoanalytic thought, strives for the fulfillment of certain basic needs; among these are satisfaction and personal security. Satisfaction is primarily the appeasement of bodily wants. Personal security is dependent on the maintenance of self-esteem. Anxiety results if either goal is not achieved.

The infant first experiences anxiety through his emphatic relationship with his mother. He feels uncomfortable when she is anxious. Later he learns that certain of his behavior patterns gain him approval and others will result in disapproval. This disapproval causes him anxiety. The experiences which the child undergoes in this learning are all preparing him for his "orientation in living."[3] If the child lacks opportunities to

"The Lonely School Child," *American Journal of Nursing,* 68, 4 (April 1968), 774–777, has been reprinted with the permission of the author and of the publisher, the *American Journal of Nursing.* Dora Wayne is a school nurse-teacher at Pasadena School, Plainview, New York.

learn appropriate responses or if his parents approve inappropriate responses, he will have difficulties in relating with others. This can lower his self-esteem.

The school setting is similar to any other social community. It has its ingroups and its outgroups. Those children who are in the ingroup or on its fringes are fortunate. They are usually children of similar ethnic and economic backgrounds. Other children are popular because they are known to be good sports, good athletes, or of average or better intelligence, know the jargon of the day, and are able and willing to compete, cooperate, and compromise with their classmates.

The outgroup is composed of the lonely isolates. Loneliness first appears in the very young child. The infant needs human contact and tenderness. These needs are met by the mother as she gives protective care, sustaining her infant in his helpless state. As the child grows and becomes less totally dependent, the mother no longer responds in the same way. Some parents now tend to show disapproval when the child expresses his need for tender, loving care, often because they themselves are unable to feel and give affection.

The young child now turns to companions. From them, he demands approval, acceptance, models for learning, and most of all, a chum of the same age and sex. With this chum, he learns to exchange intimacies. Through this exchange, the child learns to validate his personal worth, to become sensitive to other people's needs, to form value judgments, to compete, to collaborate, and to love and care for another human being outside his family group. If the child is deprived of both his companions and family tenderness, he will suffer serious personality defects.

Some children have malevolent parents and have great difficulty trusting anyone. Others have parents who disparage everyone their children show interest in (it may be a teacher or another child), and thus they sow seeds of distrust, preventing their children from acquiring adequate standards by which to judge their own worth.

Lonely children are those who have had unsatisfactory interpersonal relationships. They have not learned appropriate behavior and are rejected time and again by their peers. This causes them anxiety. Yet they continue to attempt to seek companionship with others because, as Sullivan points out, "loneliness in itself is more terrible than anxiety."[4] Fruitless seeking, however, results in increased anxiety. Eventually, some of this anxiety may be expressed as somatic complaints. Every school nurse-teacher becomes familiar with this situation.

Anne

Anne was a lonely nine-year-old of medium height with a well-developed, stocky body. She was always well-dressed and neat. Her tortoise-shell glasses gave her a studious mien. Her adult vocabulary was astounding; one immediately assumed that she was of superior intelligence, yet she never achieved beyond an average scholastic level. She rarely smiled, and her voice always had a whining quality. Her parents were evidently quite mobile, for Anne had already been in several schools. She had been transferred to our school in the beginning of her fourth grade. This, too, served to handicap her socially.

It did not take Anne long to find me in the health office (about a week after the term had begun). She had various somatic complaints—backache, headache, stomachache—but no overt symptoms. Highly dramatic, she loved to give me a detailed description of each ailment. Anne seemed to enjoy her tête-à-têtes with me, but if another child approached me or if the telephone rang and I had to divert my attention from her, she would become angry and rudely interrupt. As her visits became more frequent (to the point of two a day), I noted a developing pattern. She came always during recess or gym, and she always was willing to return to her class when these particular periods had ended. Also, most hurt or ill children, in my experience, come with a companion. Yet, Anne always came alone.

As soon as this became apparent to me, I called Anne's mother. I requested that she come in for a conference, but she said no, she could not because of illness. Oh yes, she knew all about Anne's "illnesses" and bluntly told me to disregard her.

After that, when Anne came in, I tried to spend more time alone with her so that I could understand her problem and help her. She gradually told me about her mother, a semi-invalid as a result of a car accident several years previously in which she had sustained a back injury. She had had several operations and was now confined to bed most of the time. I believed that Anne was adopting her mother's physical symptoms in a bid for contact and tenderness, which were denied her at home. Her somatic complaints had become a pattern of behavior; she would learn to use them for every stress situation.

Concerned about Anne, I conferred with our school psychologist. She has two schools to service and is very busy with children who present either learning or behavior problems, neither of which category fit Anne. She suggested that I urge the parents to take Anne for private guidance. When Anne's father came to school for the next routine teacher-parent conference, I literally ushered him from the classroom to the health office, where he listened quietly while I told him that his child was becoming neurotic, showed hypochondriac tendencies, was extremely unhappy, and needed psychologic help. Then he talked. He told me about his wife's illness and how he had only part-time help and had to do the shopping and cooking for the family when he came home from work each evening. He said he realized that he and his wife were unable to give Anne the attention she needed. He said that he would think about getting help for her. Thanking me, he left.

The next day Anne told me that her father said he would get her a certain doll she desired, if only she would not come to see me for a whole month. Off she flounced. Needless to say, two days later she was back, doll forgotten.

I realized then that there was little help for Anne at home. Could we help her? I again spoke to the school psychologist. No, the teacher had not referred her. I then talked with her teacher, who was unaware that Anne had a problem. Yes, she whined. And the other children seemed not to like her. But she was not aggressive nor really withdrawn, and she was making "normal" progress scholastically.

We discussed Anne at length and decided to give the class a sociogram. Through this means we were able to discover another companionless child. The teacher arranged for them to sit next to each other and gave them joint chores and assignments. The gym teacher, agreeing to cooperate, paired them together for games and gave them a ball to share at recess. I also encouraged the friendship and suggested to Anne's mother (via the telephone) that she invite the other child to her home. She was happy to do so. Often, two lonely children can help each other.

As she was still able to be favorably influenced by outside forces, this friendship helped Anne tremendously. Her visits to me decreased markedly, although we remained friends.

Richard

Another lonely child, Richard, was unable to compete with the other boys. The importance of the development of the competitive spirit has been cited by Sullivan:

> There are two genera of learning which are practically the special province of the early school situation—competition and compromise. They are sufficiently important that certain provisions for them are made in the primary education of all cultures that value these things at all. . . . The juvenile society itself encourages competitive efforts of all kinds, and . . . such competition is natural. In addition, the authority figures encourage competition.[5]

Richard, a blond nine-year-old, was slight in build and manifested definite effeminate characteristics. He had a "pretty" face, gestured gracefully when he talked, and minced when he walked. He was very pleasant, spoke in a high-pitched voice, and preferred to play with the girls. The boys avoided him. Richard was unable to master simple gymnastic skills. When gym or recess became too anxiety provoking, he would seek me out.

He never failed to ply me with compliments. Very observant of clothes and hairdos, he would stand in front of my full-length mirror, comb his hair, and scrutinize himself carefully. He had dramatic swings in moods and complaints which took various forms. He would grimace as though in horrible pain and then smile cheerfully and relate some incident to me.

Richard had learned to utilize illness to gain attention and affection and as a way to avoid contact with other boys. In illness, he was able to elicit sympathy from the teacher (who then also made fewer demands on him), from the other students, from me, and from his working mother. Repeatedly asking me to call his mother, he would use the public hall telephone and call her himself whenever I refused.

I minimized his symptoms, but never ignored them. He began to confide in me. He "adored" his mother, he said. She was "beautiful" and "wonderful." He mentioned his older brother, a high-school athlete, very briefly and never spoke of his father.

Again I consulted our school psychologist and then asked Richard's mother to come in for a conference. She came willingly, seeking counseling. Indeed a beautiful woman, she seemed concerned about Richard's constant bids for her affection which she could not "understand." She told me that she spent a great deal of time with him, that they did everything together, that he had no friends, and that he "clung" to her possessively. Apparently overloaded with guilt, she was sure that she had committed some wrong in raising this child, but did not know what it was nor how to correct it. She told me that the father favored the older boy and would engage in sports with him. Richard refused to participate. She said they did not "get along."

The evident signs pointed to an unresolved Oedipus complex with a resulting inability to identify with the male parent. Erikson says:

> His danger, at this time, lies in a sense of inadequacy and inferiority. If he despairs of his tools and skills or of his status among his tool partners, his ego boundaries suffer, and he abandons hope for the ability to identify early with others who apply themselves to the same general section of the tool world. To lose the hope of such "industrial" association leads back to the more isolated, less tool-conscious "anatomical" rivalry of the oedipal time. The child despairs of his equipment in the tool world and in anatomy, and considers himself doomed to mediocrity or mutilation.[6]

I urged that she take Richard to a child guidance clinic or a private psychologist, because he needed help which we were unable to provide. She said she was willing but she could not make a decision without consulting her husband. Richard's pattern continued, and I called her again and again. She told me that the father was very resistant.

During the week of parent-teacher conferences, she brought her husband to see me. He was a tall, well-built man and good looking. He said he understood Richard's problem: his wife was overly solicitous of Richard, she "babied" him, she "spoiled" him, and psychologic help was not necessary. I reiterated that a child guidance clinic would help both of them to better understand Richard and would guide them to assist the child in changing his behavior. They thanked me and left.

I discussed Richard with his teacher, who considered him a "sweet, affectionate" child who presented no problems to her. Yes, he was alone most of the time. I consulted the gym teacher, who arranged to give Richard some individual time to help him develop such simple skills as running, catching, and throwing.

It took Richard's parents months before they made an initial move. This is not unusual. Most parents do not immediately accept the fact that their child needs psychologic help, even though they would call a pediatrician immediately if he were physically ill. I realized that we in school could not solve Richard's problem, which stemmed from his parents' difficulties. Several months later Richard's mother came in to see me and reported that they had arranged an appointment with a private psychologist. She thanked me again and apologized for her husband's resistance.

School Responsibility

When school personnel cannot directly help a child, it is their responsibility to counsel the parents to seek other assistance. The loneliness of both Anne and Richard originated outside the school, but this was not a valid reason for the school to be passive. When the school personnel are willing to spend more time with an individual child, to listen to him, and give him an opportunity to confide in them, he will often begin to discuss his problems. A teacher who notes both verbal and nonverbal signs, gestures, overt and covert behavior, and how the child interacts with his peers can help discover and aid the lonely child.

References

1. Sullivan, H. S. *The Fusion of Psychiatry and Social Science.* Introduction and commentaries by Helen Swick Perry. New York, W. W. Norton and Co., 1964, p. 237.
2. Erikson, E. H. *Identity and the Life Cycle.* New York, International Universities Press, 1959, p. 52.
3. Sullivan, H. S. *Interpersonal Theory of Psychiatry.* New York, W. W. Norton and Co., 1953, p. 243.
4. *Ibid.,* p. 262.
5. *Ibid.,* pp. 231–232.
6. Erikson, E. H. *Childhood and Society.* New York, W. W. Norton and Co., 1950, p. 227.

Starting Sex Instruction
for Sixth-Grade Boys

Marilyn E. Schima

"Dear father," the invitation began, "You and your son are invited to a father and son program at Kensington School." The invitation continued, "The topic of the program is an ever-timely subject called, 'For Growing Boys,' having to do with the growth and development of the young boy into manhood."

This was to be the first presentation sponsored by our parent-teacher association of a sex education program for sixth-grade boys.

The idea for a regular elementary school sex education program began several years ago when the PTA planning committee decided to sponsor a mother-daughter afternoon once a year. At many meetings, the original planners reviewed and discussed articles, pamphlets, films, and books. They decided the film, *The Story of Menstruation,* was the most suitable for the girls in our school. An introduction and a general period of questions and answers were part of the program.

This same format and content have been continued each year, and the mother-daughter afternoon is now a popular and permanent part of the PTA program in our community. This program was reported in a *journal* article, "Sex Education in Elementary School," in November 1960.

As the school nurse-teacher, I was aware of the need for a comparable program for boys. Many of the parents who were familiar with the success of our program for girls had commented to me on this need. These parents wanted guidance in teaching their sons about sex.

Many sixth-grade teachers reported seeing evidence of vulgarity, curiosity, titillations, all of which pointed to intense curiosity about sex, Because of the onset of menstruation, the girls' need for sex education is

"Starting Sex Instruction for Sixth Grade Boys," *American Journal of Nursing,* 62, 9 (September 1962) 75–77, has been reprinted with the permission of the author and of the publisher, the *American Journal of Nursing.*

commonly recognized by most parents, but boys are frequently neglected. Yet, by the time boys reach the same age, they are experiencing growth spurts themselves. By the time they reach the sixth grade, they are generally ready for introductory sex education.[1] They see the physical changes taking place in the girls, and they become aware of the current trend of dating and parties at the elementary level.

Parents Approval

When the idea for the father-son program was brought to the PTA planning committee, it was immediately adopted. After we obtained approval from the school principal and from the PTA executive committee, we set about to gather and review various films, filmstrips, and other materials. The list of books and pamphlets we reviewed and accepted is included at the end of this article.

While this preliminary work was being done, I thought that it might be a good idea to get a sampling of opinion in the school community regarding our proposed program. I drew up a questionnaire for the committee to distribute to the parents. It was, of course, a limited survey intended primarily to help us evaluate attitudes and reactions of parents whose sons attended Kensington School.

We did not request that anyone sign the questionnaire, except voluntarily. We requested such information as religious preference, age, number of children, and education. This was done to detect any significant pattern in any particular group. We thought that such patterns might influence the content we should include in the program. Both the questionnaire and the response to verbal inquiries produced an emphatically favorable response for the program.

In reviewing our films, we concluded that none of them quite covered the information we wanted to present in the way we wanted. We had agreed about two basic aims in the program. First, we wanted to establish an intellectually permissive atmosphere in which to discuss relatively simple information about sexual development. Second, we wanted to encourage closer father-son relationships and provide fathers with a starting point for offering further guidance and counsel.

Since our presentation was to be at a single extracurricular meeting with a large audience rather than a small group and did not allow for a subsequent meeting, we decided to use a speaker instead of a film.

We decided against asking a physician to talk. We did not want the boys to get the impression that a speaker on this topic needed to be medically trained, but rather that any well-prepared person could discuss the subject. We believed it more important that the person be an educator. Consequently, we chose a capable and interesting speaker, who was the head of the health education department of one of the senior high schools.

A PTA mother, who was an artist, made drawings for projection on a screen to help our speaker illustrate specific points during his talk. In the meantime, mimeographed invitations were sent to all fathers. I prepared a bibliography on sex education to distribute to fathers after the program.

At our first presentation, we had 50 fathers, 52 boys, and 17 guests. The guests were parents from other schools in the community, health educators from the secondary schools, and representatives from interested groups such as the tuberculosis association.

Our speaker gave a 40-minute talk in which, with the use of slides, he explained the various types of growth—intellectual, social, emotional, and physical. He explained the functions of the glands and reproductive organs and the transition from boy to man. Seminal emissions and masturbation were discussed. Also, he described the changing interests, relationships, and needs of a growing boy, and how such factors as external environment, heredity, and health habits influence all these things.

After the talk, our speaker conducted a lively question and answer period in which both fathers and boys participated. Following are some of the questions which were asked and discussed: Can you have a seminal emission during the day? Could you have a seminal emission and not know about it? Is it bad to masturbate? Isn't it normal for all boys to masturbate at some time? (One father expressed the opinion that the boy who did not masturbate at some time was abnormal.) When should boys start to date girls? Why is it important for boys at this age to get enough sleep, and how many hours do they need? What are some health practices that are important for boys of this age to adhere to and why? Perhaps one of the most significant questions, culturally, was this: Should sixth graders "go steady"?

Because this was our first program, we circulated another questionnaire at the meeting to secure fathers' reactions and suggestions for improvement. Later, we were sorry that we had not made one for the boys, because they were so eager to express their opinions. Many of them filled in the questionnaires and wrote, "Boy," across the top.

Responses to the questionnaires showed unanimous agreement that the program should be continued in the future. Ninety-seven percent said that the program met their specific needs for this kind of information. Ninety percent of the fathers said that the program would make it easier for them to discuss sex with their sons. A majority said that the program should be continued as presented rather than broken into two or more separate meetings—that is, fathers, then sons, and then sons and fathers together.

Tangible Results

We were all very elated over the response to our program. The following day, I began to observe its tangible results. Three sixth graders came into the health office for first aid and, almost immediately, they began to tell me about the meeting and how much they had learned.

Freely and without embarrassment, they discussed points about which they were confused or didn't quite understand, and all three were eager to "meet with that guy again." Gone were the giggling innuendos and the street-corner terms. Instead, there was a new respectfulness and frankness which was gratifying to note. In the following days and weeks, I found the same thing to be true with other sixth graders who discussed the program with me.

Much work remains to be done, testing new approaches and improving the presentation. But I believe that we have successfully added another part to our expanding sex education program.

Note

1. Gesell, Arnold and others. *Youth, The Years from Ten to Sixteen.* New York, Harper and Brothers, 1956, p. 78.

Suggested Reading for Parents and Sons

For Parents

Baruch, Dorothy. *New Ways in Sex Education.* New York, McGraw-Hill Book Co., 1959.
Bibby, Cyril. *Sex Education.* New York, Emerson Book, 1946.
Child Study Association. *Facts of Life for Children.* Indianapolis, Bobbs-Merrill Co., 1954.
Kirkendall, Lester. *Sex Education As Human Relations.* New York, Inor Publishing Co., 1950.
O'Brien, J. A. *Sex Character Education.* New York, Macmillan Co., 1952.

For Junior High School Boys

Armstrong, D. W. *Questions Boys Ask.* New York, E. P. Dutton and Co., 1955.
Bundesen, H. N. *Toward Manhood.* Philadelphia, J. B. Lippincott Co., 1952.
Dickerson, R. E. *Into Manhood.* New York, Association Press, 1954.
Rice, T. B. *Story of Life.* Chicago, American Medical Association, Bureau of Health Education, 1948.
Richardson, F. H. *For Boys Only.* Atlanta, Ga., Tupper and Love, 1952.

For Preschool and Elementary Boys

DeSchweinitz, Karl. *Growing Up.* New York, Macmillan Co., 1953.
Gruenberg, Sidonie M. *The Wonderful Story of How You Were Born.* Garden City, N.Y., Doubleday and Co., 1952.
Redmond, Louis. *What I Know About Boys.* Garden City, N.Y. Doubleday and Co., 1952.
Selsam, Millicent. *All About Eggs.* New York, William R. Scott, 1952.
Strain, Frances B. *Being Born.* New York, Appleton-Century-Crofts, 1944.

The Relationship Between "Causal" Orientation, Anxiety, and Insecurity in Elementary School Children

*Rolf E. Muuss**

This paper presents the findings of a study designed to investigate the relationship between "causality" and such indices of mental health as anxiety and insecurity in fifth- and sixth-grade children. The concept, causality, constitutes the theoretical framework of the Preventive Psychiatry Program at the State University of Iowa. The Preventive Psychiatry Program is designed to investigate the extent to which causal orientation contributes to mental health, and whether and to what extent an experimental learning program emphasizing the causal nature of human behavior produces causally oriented subjects.

Causality is defined as an understanding and appreciation of the dynamic, complex, and interacting nature of the forces that operate in human behavior. It involves an attitude of flexibility, of seeing things from the view point of others as well as an awareness of the probabilistic nature of knowledge. A causally oriented person is capable of suspending judgment until sufficient factual information is available; furthermore, he realizes that his behavior has consequences and that there are alternative ways of solving social problems (Muuss, 1960). It is assumed that a person who is aware of the dynamic and causal nature of human behavior is better able to solve his own problems and to meet social

* This study was completed while the author was with the Iowa Child Welfare Research Station, State University of Iowa. Appreciation is expressed to the Grant Foundation for their support of this research project.

From: Rolf E. Muuss, "The Relationship Between 'Causal' Orientation, Anxiety, and Insecurity in Elementary School Children," *Journal of Educational Psychology*, 51, 3 (June 1960), 122-129. Copyright 1960 by the American Psychological Association, and reproduced by permission. Rolf E. Muuss is Professor of Education at Goucher College, Baltimore, Maryland.

situations. This study purports to investigate a limited aspect of this assumption.

Explicitly stated, our hypotheses are that Ss who are highly causally oriented (as measured by paper-and-pencil tests) will differ from Ss who show a low degree of causal orientation on the following criterion variables:

> Hypothesis 1. They will demonstrate less insecurity as measured by the Kooker Security-Insecurity Scale (Kooker, 1954).

> Hypothesis 2. They will show less anxiety as measured by the Children's Manifest Anxiety Scale (CMAS) (Castaneda, McCandless, & Palermo, 1956).

> Hypothesis 3. They will make fewer L responses as measured by the L scale which is part of the CMAS.

The rationale for these hypotheses is based on the assumption that a lack of insight into the dynamics of one's own behavior and an unwillingness and/or inability to understand the problems and the behavior of others tends to increase the level of anxiety and the degree of insecurity. If other people's behavior is not understood it will tend to be threatening, as are physical events which an individual experiences and does not understand. A lack of insight into the dynamics of behavior will tend to make it difficult to react logically to the behavior of others. Furthermore, if behavior is not understood, it may be misinterpreted and the individual may react in such a way as to produce a threat to the other person's security and self-respect. This then might tend to generate conflict which would add further to the difficulty of the situation. If at times a person does not understand his own behavior and the factors that influence him he naturally feels threatened, insecure, and anxious. Once a person does understand himself and others he is more willing to agree with such statements as: he sometimes gets angry, he does not always tell the truth, he does not like everyone, and similar items that make up the L scale.

> Hypothesis 4. Furthermore, it is hypothesized that these differences—if they have any generality at all—will be equally obvious for fifth- and sixth-grade Ss.

> Hypothesis 5. The two measures used, insecurity scores and anxiety scores, will show a positive relationship to one another.

> Hypothesis 6. Since about half of the Ss have been exposed to an experimental learning program and half have served as controls in another research study, it is hypothesized that a significantly larger portion of the high causally oriented Ss came from the experimental classes and that a larger portion of the low causally oriented Ss came from control classes.

Procedure

In order to investigate the above stated hypotheses, two sets of tests were administered to 280 sixth- and 179 fifth-grade Ss in the schools of a midwestern community of 80,000. 224 of these Ss had been exposed to an experimental learning program designed to develop a causal orientation, while 235 Ss came from regular classrooms and served as controls in another research study. The fact that the Ss came from both experimental and control classes was only utilized in testing the sixth of the previously stated hypotheses. However, there is some justification in utilizing Ss from two different groups since there is evidence (Stiles, 1950) that children from regular classrooms do not have much of an understanding and appreciation of the causal nature of human behavior. Therefore, in order to obtain a wide range of causal orientation, the experimental and the control Ss were combined so that differences between high and low causally oriented Ss could be studied more effectively.

The following two tests served as selection criteria to determine high causally oriented and low causally oriented Ss:

(1) The Social Causal Test*
(2) The Physical Causal Test†

Of these two tests only the Physical Causal Test had a significant correlation ($r = .58$, N 251) with IQ. This might explain that the high causal group differed significantly from the low causal group in terms of IQ scores. However, this is not a serious shortcoming since it will be shown that the criterion variables, insecurity, anxiety, and L scores, have a relatively low relationship to IQ. The high causally oriented Ss, for the purpose of this study, are defined as all those Ss who fell above the corresponding grade mean on *both* the above described selection criteria, low causally oriented Ss as those Ss who fell below the corresponding group mean on *both* selection criteria.

The second set of tests, constituting the criterion variables, consisted of:

(1) The Kooker Security-Insecurity Scale. Kooker ratings are obtained by a trained observer who follows the Ss during the whole school day for a period of five days, and who rates the child on a series of 19 behavior items indicative of security or insecurity as to frequency of occurrence. When several observers independently rated the same Ss, between rater correlations ranged from .63 to .86 (Kooker, 1954).

(2) The Children's Manifest Anxiety Scale (CMAS) (Castaneda, McCandless, & Palermo, 1956).

(3) The 11 item L scale which is administered interspersed with the CMAS.

The Design of the Study

From the 280 sixth-grade Ss 90 met the selection criteria and were classified in the high causal group; 72 fell below both group means on the selection criteria and were classified as the low causal group. Similarly,

*The Social Causal Test is described elsewhere in the literature (Lyle & Levitt, 1955) (Ojemann, Levitt, & Whiteside, 1955).
†The Physical Causal Test was developed in part by the author. Part of the test was modified by the author for use with fifth- and sixth-grade Ss from Clark (1953).

TABLE 1
Distribution of Original and Corrected Number of Cases in the Factorial Analysis of Variance

Grade Level	Original N for the Security Scores		Original N for the Anxiety and L Scores		Corrected[a] N in Order to Obtain Proportionality	
	Degree of Causality		Degree of Causality		Degree of Causality	
	High	Low	High	Low	High	Low
5th grade	59	41	58	45	60	45
6th grade	89	72	89	71	88	66

[a] This corrected distribution was used for all three sets of scores: anxiety, security, and L scores (see text).

from the 179 fifth-grade Ss, 59 met the criteria for the high causal group, and 45 fell in the category low causal group. In order to test for the effect of grade level (G) (fifth or sixth grades) and the degree of causality (C) (High and Low as defined above) an analysis of variance was computed for each of the three criterion variables, insecurity, anxiety, and L scores. A factorial analysis of variance design was utilized for all three sets of scores. Since this design requires either an equal number of cases in each cell or proportionality of cases from column to column or from row to row (Lindquist, 1953), the data had to be adjusted. Proportionality could be obtained with the least loss of cases by utilizing the corrected distribution shown in Table 1. Proportionality of cases—as illustrated in Table 1 under Corrected N—was obtained by either randomly omitting cases from the original N, or by adding cases made up of the corresponding cell group mean of the original N. The original N's for the security and the anxiety scores are also presented in Table 1.

Results

The analysis of variance data are reported in Table 2. Inspection of Table 2 reveals that there is a highly significant ($p < .001$) difference in the predicted direction between the high causally oriented and the low causally oriented Ss on the security variable. Table 3 contains the means and standard deviations. The summary table (Table 2) also shows a significant difference ($p < .025$) between fifth- and sixth-grade Ss. It is interesting to observe, however, that the fifth-grade Ss appear to be more secure ($M = 9.16$) than the sixth-grade Ss ($M = 10.90$). One might speculate as to whether or not the onset of pubescence in sixth-grade Ss contributes to this unexpected finding or whether the anticipated change to Junior High School is a factor contributing to insecurity. The grade by causality interaction effect is nonsignificant. Independent t tests for fifth-

TABLE 2
Summary of Analysis of Variance of Insecurity, Anxiety and L Scores
(N 259)

Types of Scores and Source of Variance	df	Mean Squares	F	p
Insecurity Scores				
Grades (G)	1	187.76	5.25	<.025
Causality (C)	1	753.19	21.04	<.001
G×C Interaction	1	50.89	1.42	NS
Within cells (w)	250*	35.79		
Anxiety Scores				
Grades (G)	1	233.05	5.62	<.025
Causality (C)	1	862.22	20.80	<.001
G×C Interaction	1	.93	.02	NS
Within cells (w)	253**	41.45		
L Scores				
Grades (G)	1	.02	.004	NS
Causality (C)	1	132.20	26.73	<.001
G×C Interaction	1	6.57	1.33	NS
Within cells (w)	253**	4.95		

* Five degrees of freedom deducted from df for error since five mean values were added in order to obtain proportionality.
** Two degrees of freedom deducted from df for error since two mean values were added in order to obtain proportionality.

and sixth-grade Ss (Table 3) result in significant differences for both groups. The data in Table 3 further show that homogeneity of variance may be assumed. Thus, we feel justified in concluding that high causally oriented Ss are more secure than low causally oriented Ss as measured by the Kooker Security-Insecurity Scale.

The analysis of variance summary relating to the second hypothesis —that high causally oriented Ss have less anxiety than low causally oriented Ss—is also reported in Table 2. There is a significant ($p < .001$) difference between the high causally and the low causally oriented groups on the anxiety variable. As Table 3 indicates the difference is in the predicted direction, high causally oriented Ss manifest less anxiety as measured by the CMAS than low causally oriented Ss. Again there is a significant difference ($p < .025$) between fifth- and sixth-grade Ss. However, the trend on the anxiety scale is in the opposite direction from that on the insecurity measure. Sixth graders are more insecure than fifth graders, while sixth graders are less anxious than fifth graders. This finding throws some doubt on the fifth hypothesis which stated that anxiety and insecurity are positively related variables. The grade by causality interaction effect of CMAS scores is nonsignificant. Independent t tests for fifth- and sixth-grade Ss demonstrate significant differences ($p < .005$) for both classes. Tests for homogeneity of variance show that the assumption of homogeneity of variance is justified. In conclusion, the evidence supports the hypothesis that high causally oriented Ss are less anxious as measured by the CMAS than low causally oriented Ss.

The third hypothesis predicted that there would be a relationship between causality and L responses on the L scale. The summary Table 2 demonstrates that there is a significant difference ($p < .001$) between the high causal and the low causal groups on the L variable. The score on the L scale is obtained by counting the L responses. Thus, a low L score might be interpreted as honesty, a high L score as faking, dishonesty, or as lacking self-insight. Inspection of the mean (Table 3) demon-

TABLE 3
Comparison of the Mean Scores of the High and Low Causally Oriented Groups on the Kooker Security-Insecurity Rating Scale, the Manifest Anxiety Scale and the L Scale

	High Causal Group			Low Causal Group			
	N	M	SD	N	M	SD	t
Security Scores[a]							
5th-grade Ss	60	8.15	5.26	45	10.51	5.86	2.11*
6th-grade Ss	88	9.10	5.22	66	13.29	7.27	3.94**
Total	148	8.72	5.22	111	12.16	6.81	4.42**
Anxiety Scores[b]							
5th-grade Ss	60	11.63	5.65	45	15.47	6.23	3.21**
6th-grade Ss	88	9.81	5.94	66	13.39	7.67	3.13**
Total	148	10.55	5.86	111	14.23	7.13	4.42**
L Scores[c]							
5th-grade Ss	60	2.10	1.96	45	3.93	2.44	4.09**
6th-grade Ss	88	2.40	2.25	66	3.58	2.22	3.22**
Total	148	2.28	2.13	111	3.72	2.30	5.14**

[a] Low Kooker scores imply greater security.
[b] High scores reflect high anxiety.
[c] High scores indicate many L responses.
* Significant at the .05 level.
** Significant at the .005 level.

strates that the differences are in the predicted direction. The mean L score for the high causal group is 2.28, for the low causal group it is 3.72. There is no significant difference between fifth and sixth grades and there is no significant interaction effect between grade level and causality. Independent t tests for fifth and sixth grades demonstrate significant differences between the high and low causal group. Homogeneity of variance may be assumed since the variance ratio is nonsignificant. Thus, there is support for the hypothesis that high causally oriented Ss give fewer L responses, as measured by the 11 item L scale, than low causally oriented Ss.

TABLE 4
Intercorrelations of the Criterion Variables and IQ for Fifth-Grade (N 137) and Sixth-Grade Subjects (N 232)

	Security	Anxiety	L Scores
IQ			
5th grade	−.30**	.09	−.40**
6th grade	−.28**	−.20**	−.13*
Security			
5th grade	−	.002	.10
6th grade	−	.13*	.07
Anxiety			
5th grade	−	−	.11
6th grade	−	−	.13*

* Significant at the .05 level.
** Significant at the .01 level.

The *F* ratios which show the interaction effect of grades by causality in Table 2 are nonsignificant and thus support the fourth hypothesis. This is equally true for all three variables: security, anxiety, and L score. This finding and the *t* values reported in Table 3 provide justification for accepting the hypothesis that in this study high causally and low causally oriented Ss respond differently to such indices of mental health as insecurity, anxiety, and L responses, irrespective of whether the Ss come from the fifth or the sixth grade.

Table 4 reports the intercorrelations of the three criterion variables, as well as the correlation between IQ and each of the variables separately for fifth- and sixth-grade Ss.

There is only a small positive correlation of .13 between anxiety scores and insecurity scores for sixth-grade Ss, which barely reaches the .05 level of significance. The magnitude of the correlation does not change when analyzed separately for boys (*r* = .13, *N* 120) and girls (*r* = .16, *N* 112), but with smaller *N*'s the correlations are no longer significant. The correlation between anxiety scores and security scores for fifth-grade Ss is, for all intent and purpose, zero. Thus, we do not have conclusive evidence that our measures of anxiety and security are positively related. The data might indicate that both tests measure different and unrelated aspects or traits. However, we might also consider an alternative explanation arising from the different nature of the two test instruments, namely, that the anxiety scale is a paper-and-pencil test, consequently acquiescence, faking, rationalizing, and a deliberate attempt to give the socially desirable response might operate in a systematic fashion, while the Kooker scale uses the rating of behavior by trained observers. Possible shortcomings of this scale such as rater bias and halo effect would be operative in a different fashion. Bruce (1958) using the same tests with sixth-grade Ss obtained a correlation of .26 (*N* 184) significant at the .01 level, thus giving some indirect support for our hypothesis.

Furthermore, his finding is basically in agreement with our data obtained for sixth-grade Ss. All that can be said at this point is that there are sufficient indications to warrant further investigation of the relationship between anxiety and insecurity as stated in our fifth hypothesis.

The correlation between insecurity scores and L scores is nonsignificant for both grade levels. The correlation between anxiety scores and L scores is nonsignificant for fifth graders and barely reaches the .05 level of significance for sixth graders. If the sixth-grade data are broken down into sexes the correlations are for boys $-.11$ (N 120) and for girls $-.21$ (N 112), both nonsignificant. Thus, the correlations of the anxiety scores with the L scores are not in disagreement with those reported by Castaneda et al. (1956) who found for sixth-grade boys $r = -.10$ (N 65) and for girls $r = .22$ (N 49), both nonsignificant, even though he reports a positive correlation for girls, while ours is negative.

As was indicated previously, the relationship between IQ and the criterion variables is relatively low and not always consistent for fifth- and sixth-grade Ss. The correlation of the Kooker Security-Insecurity Rating Scale and IQ is $-.28$ for sixth- and $-.30$ for fifth-grade Ss, both significant at the .01 level. Thus, there is a tendency for the more intelligent child to be rated as more secure. However, a correlation of .30 accounts for only 9% of the variance.

The correlation between anxiety scores and IQ is $-.20$ (significant) for sixth graders and $+.09$ (nonsignificant) for fifth graders, thus not only small in actual size but operating in different directions for the different grade levels. McCandless and Castaneda (1956) report correlations between IQ and anxiety scores for sixth-grade boys $-.16$ (N 55), nonsignificant, and for sixth-grade girls $-.43$ (N 45), significant.

The L scores show a moderately high significant correlation ($r = -.40$, N 137) with IQ for fifth-grade Ss, but only a barely significant correlation ($r = -.13$, N 232) for sixth-grade Ss. Again we feel justified in concluding that only a small amount of the variance is attributable to differences in IQ's. For a correlation of .40 only 16% of the variance can be accounted for in terms of IQ. However, there is a small tendency for the less intelligent children to give more L responses than the more intelligent Ss.

In order to further eliminate the influence of IQ on the data, Ss from the high causal group were matched with Ss from the low causal group on the IQ variable. Sixth-grade Ss were paired with sixth graders and fifth graders with fifth-grade Ss. The IQ score difference between each pair was never greater than plus minus one IQ point. The data in Table 5 are based on 31 matched pairs of sixth graders and 19 matched pairs of fifth graders. The t test between the high causal and low causal Ss matched on IQ is computed by way of the standard error of a difference between correlated means. The data indicate that IQ has no effect on the security data. The difference between the means is significant at the .005 level. The group means for the high and low causal Ss are almost identical for the total 259 Ss (Table 3) with the group means for the 100 Ss who are used in the pairing (Table 5). Intelligence scores do not influence the results obtained in this study with the Kooker Security-Insecurity Scale.

For the anxiety data—even though the correlations between IQ and anxiety scores are lower and less consistent in magnitude and in direction for fifth- and sixth-grade Ss than for the security scores (Table 4)— the t ratio between matched groups is not significant, but approaches the .05 level of significance. However, the correlation between IQ and anxiety scores for thc 99 paircd Ss only is −.13, not significant. Thus, even though IQ scores appear to have some influence on the obtained differences on the anxiety data, this influence appears to be negligible.

The difference between the high causal and low causal Ss matched on IQ for the L scores is significant at the .02 level. The L score means for the matched groups (Table 5) are about the same as the means for the total groups (Table 3).

TABLE 5
Comparison of the Mean Scores on the Kooker Security-Insecurity Scale, the Manifest Anxiety Scale and the L Scale for Causally and Low Causally Oriented Subjects with Matched IQ's (N 100)

	High Causal Subjects			Low Causal Subjects			
	N	M	SD	Na	M	SD	tb
Security Scores	50	8.60	5.51	49	12.35	7.85	3.05***
Anxiety Scores	50	11.62	6.19	49	14.06	8.04	1.79*
L Scores	50	2.48	2.17	49	3.59	2.38	2.55**

a The security score for one child, the anxiety and L scores for another child were not available.
b Since individuals are matched on the basis of IQ the standard error of a difference was computed for correlated means.
* Significant at the .10 level.
** Significant at the .02 level.
*** Significant at the .005 level.

We thus can conclude that the results obtained in this study cannot be explained on the basis of differences in intelligence which existed between the original high causal and low causal groups.

So far the discussion has dealt only with the relationship between the degree of causality and indices of mental health, such as insecurity, anxiety, and L responses. No attention has been directed to the effects of a causal learning program in producing causally oriented Ss. In line with the sixth hypothesis one might ask: To what extent did the experimental classes contribute subjects to the high and the low causally oriented groups? As noted in Table 6 chi square analysis indicates for both fifth and sixth grades a preponderance of cases from the experimental

TABLE 6
A Comparison of Fifth- and Sixth-Grade Subjects from Causal and Regular Class-rooms with Respect to the Selection Variable

	Causal	Regular	Total	Chi Square	P
Fifth Grade					
High Group	44 (29.2)[a]	15 (29.8)	59		
Low Group	8 (22.8)	38 (23.2)	46		
Total	52	53	105	31.65[c]	<.001
Sixth Grade[b]					
High Group	61 (46.5)[a]	32 (46.5)	93		
Low Group	23 (37.5)	52 (37.5)	75		
Total	84	84	168	18.88[c]	<.001

[a] Figures in parentheses are expected frequencies.
[b] Reproduced with permission from Child Development Publications from a previous publication of the author (Muuss, in press).
[c] Chi Square with Yates correction for continuity.

(causal) classes in the High Causal Cell and a preponderance of cases from the control (regular) classes in the Low Regular Cell, far beyond the number of expected frequencies.

Bruce (1958) demonstrated that sixth-grade children who had participated for two consecutive years in an experimental learning program designed to develop a causal understanding were more secure and less anxious than control Ss who had not participated in such a program. He used the same tests which were used in this study but did not report the L scores. It is interesting to observe that he obtained significant differences only between the two-year group and the control group, but not between the one-year group and the control group. In this study a comparison was made between high causally and low causally oriented Ss— a method more sensitive to differences than the comparison of experimental and control groups, but yielding basically the same results.

Summary

Two tests, the Social Causal Test and the Physical Causal Test, served as selection criteria for high causally (N = 148) and low causally (N = 111) oriented Ss. A comparison was made between the high causal and the low causal fifth- and sixth-grade groups in respect to measures of security, anxiety, and L responses. Data were analyzed by a factorial analysis of variance design followed by t tests. The findings of the study may be summarized as follows:

(1) Fifth- and sixth-grade Ss who are high causally oriented respond to measures of security, anxiety, and L responses in the direction that might be considered as indicative of mental health. The high causally oriented subjects show more security, less anxiety, and give fewer L responses than low causally oriented Ss.

(2) The obtained differences are equally obvious for the fifth- ($N=105$) as well as for the sixth-grade Ss ($N=154$).

(3) The differences between grade levels are inconsistent: fifth graders are more secure, sixth graders are less anxious. There is no between grade level difference on the L scale.

(4) For sixth-grade Ss there is no correlation, for fifth-grade Ss there is a very low but significant correlation between insecurity and anxiety.

(5) Even though there are small but significant relationships between intelligence and the criterion variables, the obtained difference between the high causal and low causal groups on the criterion variables cannot be explained on the basis of differences in intelligence.

(6) The experimental classes designed to develop a causal understanding of the dynamics of human behavior contribute significantly more high causally oriented Ss, while the regular control classes contribute more low causally oriented Ss to this study.

References

Bruce, P. Relationship of self-acceptance to other variables with sixth-grade children oriented in self-understanding. *J. educ. Psychol.,* 1958, **49,** 229–238.

Castaneda, A., McCandless, B. R., & Palermo, D. S. The children's form of the Manifest Anxiety Scale. *Child Develpm.,* 1956, **27,** 317–326.

Clark, C. A. A study of the adolescent's conception of the nature of scientific knowledge. Unpublished doctoral dissertation, State Univer. Iowa, 1953.

Kooker, E. An investigation of security, insecurity, achievement, and boredom in elementary school children. Unpublished doctoral dissertation, State Univer. Iowa, 1951.

Lyle, W. H., Jr., & Levitt, E. E. Punitiveness, authoritarianism, and parental discipline of grade school children. *J. abnorm. soc. Psychol.,* 1955, **51,** 42–46.

Lindquist, E. F. *Design and analysis of experiments in psychology and education.* Boston: Houghton Mifflin Co., 1953.

McCandless, B. R., & Castaneda, A. Anxiety in children, school achievement, and intelligence. *Child Develpm.,* 1956, **27,** 379–382.

Muuss, R. E. Mental health implications of a preventive psychiatry program in the light of research findings. *Marriage and fam. Living,* 1960, **22,** 150–156.

Muuss, R. E. A comparison of "high causally" and "low causally" oriented sixth-grade children in respect to a perceptual intolerance of ambiguity test. *Child Develpm.,* in press.

Ojemann, R. H., Levitt, E. E., Lyle, W. H., & Whiteside, Maxine F. The effects of a "causal" teacher training program and certain curricular changes on grade school children. *J. exp. Educ.,* 1955, **24,** 95–114.

Stiles, Frances S. Developing an understanding of human behavior at the elementary level. *J. educ. Res.,* 1950, **43,** 516–524.

Research from Educational Psychology that Has Implications for Elementary School Guidance

Walter B. Waetjen

It is my purpose to present some research and ideas about learning and to show the possible relationship of these to the function of an elementary school counselor.

In doing this, I intend to look at some of the problems that occur in schools, and assumptions about causes of the problems with particular reference to: assumptions that teachers make about individual differences and assumptions that educators make about the nature of the classroom environment.

Prior to becoming involved in research on pupil personnel services, I conducted research on one aspect of individual differences, namely, the way in which the sexes approach the learning task. These sex differences in learning will become one part of my presentation. A second part of the presentation will be a discussion of motivation, with special reference to the way in which the classroom environment either promotes or prevents the development of motivation. Finally, there will be a discussion of the role of the elementary school counselor as suggested by the research findings on learning the motivation.

It is entirely too easy to believe that counseling is a natural social phenomenon that anyone can carry out. If this were true there would be no point in this conference. Counseling is somewhat akin to kissing in the respect that it occurs at all levels of experience and it's a pleasant thing

"Research from Educational Psychology that Has Implications for Elementary School Guidance" was presented at the Invitational Conference on Elementary School Guidance held in Washington, D.C., March 31–April 2, 1965, and is reprinted with the permission of the author. Walter B. Waetjen is Vice-President for Administrative Affairs at the University of Maryland.

to do. Counseling has further similarities to kissing in that almost everybody feels qualified to practice kissing and they do so at some time or another; and the objectives of kissing while not clearly stated are not entirely intangible. Another trap inherent in both counseling and kissing is that both are apt to be so satisfying that there is little tendency to evaluate them otherwise.

I have found myself through the years particularly interested in individual differences, which I viewed rather globally. It then became of interest to me to single out one of these differences because it is overlooked in our schools. We know full well that no matter how one defines an underachiever (and there are many different definitions of underachieving youngsters), there are far more underachieving males than underachieving females. Those who have been in elementary education are also sensitive to the fact that we have considerably more nonreading or poor reading boys than we have girls. Those who are involved in pupil personnel services can report on the youngsters who are in speech clinics for functional disorders such as stuttering and articulation problems. Ninety-eight percent of those cases are boys. The youngsters referred to counselors by teachers—not on a self-referral basis and not on a parental referral basis—are, in the majority, boys. Also, boys drop out before high school graduation more frequently than girls.

The point I am trying to make is this: There is an assumption in education that it really makes little difference whether the student we teach is a boy or a girl. The point is that it really *does* make a difference whether it is a boy student or a girl student. For example, it becomes quickly apparent that there is a marked superiority of females over males in the language area. This is of concern because, by-and-large, the school experience is verbal, symbolic, or linguistic in nature. Since girls have better language skills, then we have to say that girls have a running start on the school experience. That statement would be supported by the fact that almost any school statistic on the general academic progress of girls —whether in the elementary school, junior high, senior high, or in college —the females have a better grade point average than do the boys.

One study in particular demonstrated that girls have better language abilities than boys. Clark (5) sampled 150 youngsters in grades three, five, and eight out of 69,000 pupils from 48 states and gave them the California Test of Mental Maturity and the California Achievement Test. He found that the results obtained from the California Test of Mental Maturity manifested no sex bias. On the other hand, when he used the Achievement tests, the girls were consistently better in mechanics of English and spelling. He concluded the following: that in basic skill areas, of language, mechanics of English and spelling, girls do consistently better.

On the other hand, males are found to be somewhat better than females in the two curriculum areas of mathematics and science. The reason for this is that the cognitive skill that undergirds these two curriculum areas is analytical thinking. Here the research findings make clear the fact that boys are only somewhat better than females in mathematics and science, whereas in the language area, the girls are markedly superior to boys.

Males are somewhat superior to females in transfer of learning. Transfer of learning refers to the application of skill or knowledge to some new situation, that is, an adjustment to a new situation. I have reference particularly to the study done by Kostick (7) in which he found that there was a significant difference in favor of boys in terms of their ability to transfer learning. His conclusion was that this superior ability to transfer was not due to I.Q., previous knowledge, reading comprehension, reading preference, personal traits or practice effects.

All of this sounds very convincing, but one might properly raise the question as to whether in any way teachers are implicated in girls' superior performance in school. The answer to the question appears to be affirmative if teachers' grades are any indication.

When a standardized achievement test is given to a large group of youngsters, and a boy and girl having identical scores on the test are established as a matched pair, one might predict that teachers would give each member of the pair the same grade. However, it was determined that invariably, the girls receive higher grades, even though their level of achievement was either identical or highly comparable. The same study ascertained that it didn't make any difference whether it was a male teacher or a female teacher who assigned the grades. Apparently, the sex of the student is more important in the determination of grade than the sex of the teacher, which really means that both men and women teachers are equally biased in giving girls higher grades (4).

A perusal of honor rolls, principals' lists and the like shows roughly a two-thirds female composition, and it does not vary much with the educational level—elementary school, secondary school, college, or university. A study done by Meyer and Thompson (9) in the elementary school classified the interactions between teachers and pupils into positive or negative categories. It was found that teachers attributed significantly more acts of disapproval to boys than to girls. If one examines this finding in relation to what goes into the making of one's self-image, it becomes apparent why boys are not doing as well as girls in school.

Two years ago we completed a study (10) in which we had separated boys from girls in the eighth grade for one hour per day in English instruction. If girls are markedly superior in language, we thought that if we removed the girls from the ball and chain effect of boys, then the achievement of each might go up. By the way, it did not. Curiously, we found when we sampled attitude that the boys enjoyed the segregated classes while the girls disliked them! As another dimension of this study, we used the Bales Interaction Analysis Recorder to determine whether teachers taught differently in all boy classes, all girl classes, or combined classes. Some of the categories of teacher behavior were the following: working with small groups, using audio-visual equipment, supporting behavior, disciplining behavior, and lecturing. We discovered that teachers of the all boy classes lectured two and a half times as much as they did to all girl classes or combined classes. What was distressing to us was that the teachers told us they didn't differentiate their instruction in any way. The point is, they *did* differentiate but were unaware of it.

A final point has to do with a factor which affects the progress of the sexes in school, and this is perception of self, perception of others (mainly teachers) and attitudes about the school. David Ausubel (2) used fifth and sixth graders to study children's perceptions of parental attitudes. His major finding was that girls perceive themselves as significantly more accepted and intrinsically valued than boys. If we consider what goes into the formation of one's self-image, there is cause to be concerned. Winker, studying the identifications of children, ages seven to sixteen years, found that girls identified more than boys with persons they knew, and in particular with mothers. On the other hand boys identified more with the general male societal role. Identification has a relation to language development for if a child identifies with someone close to him, like mother, it is much easier to learn vocabulary and voice inflection. On the other hand, if one identifies with the general societal role as males do, it is much more difficult to learn language. One has difficulty learning the role in general and the language in particular.

A study (1) published in the journal, *Psychology in the Schools,* reported elementary pupils' perception of the social-emotional environment of fourth, fifth, and sixth grade classrooms. One finding was that boys perceived teachers as more "directive," while girls perceived the teachers as "relatable." The girls' attitude toward school was significantly more positive than boys. What this adds up to in terms of the school experience for boys and girls is the following: that there are differences in skills and knowledges, but not in intellect; that there are differences in perception of self and the school experience, basically, being more negative for boys than for girls; and that teachers respond differently to boys than to girls. For instance, they tend to be more controlling of boys by virtue of lecturing, and they give higher grades to girls even though there is a comparable level of achievement.

It seems to me that counselors, particularly in the school, need to be concerned about this kind of individual difference that apparently is being overlooked. We cannot castigate teachers for the kinds of findings that have been reported, for we have done little to help teachers behave differently in the classroom.

The second major point to be discussed in this discourse has to do with motivation. This may be introduced best by citing a study completed in 1963 by Cutler and McNeil (6) at the University of Michigan. They had been carrying out research having to do with mental health consultation in the elementary schools. Teachers were provided with the services of a mental health consultant to help with any problem they perceived in the classroom. What happened to the *control groups* is of special interest. Cutler and McNeil state: "The global picture is one of the classroom in which the screws have gradually been tightened as the year passes, in which teachers concentrate increasingly on communication of content, but fail, meanwhile, to provide the appropriate climate in which this content may be learned. At the same time, pupils respond by losing motivation, cooperating less well, feeling less accepted by teachers and peers, becoming less adequate group members, and becoming anxious about school and standards of performance."

Two parts of that quote introduce the second topic of this paper. The teachers failed to provide the appropriate climate in which curriculum content may be learned, and the pupils responded by losing motivation. These two aspects highlight an apparent belief about classrooms that if the teacher can present the familiar, the known, and the predictable, these spur children to greater learning. Some teachers will even claim that the predictable environment provides "security" for pupils. Nothing could be further from the truth with respect to the development of motivation.

Two researchers (9) tried to find out the responses of first-grade children to novelty, seating them before a mock TV set. If they wanted the picture repeated that was already on the set, they were told to pull a lever. If they pushed a button, a new picture appeared. This was novelty. There were two figures presented on each picture. One of the figures was familiar, such as a bird, while the other figure was novel or incongruous, such as a creature having the front half of a bird and the back half of an automobile. The novel stimuli or unfamiliar stimuli elicited significantly more responses than did the familiar or the nonnovel stimuli, strongly suggesting that pupils preferred the different rather than the familiar stimuli in their environment.

The other study to be reported in this connection was done by Berlyne (3), who tried to determine the effect of pre-questioning upon learning of science concepts. An experimental group was given a questionnaire about invertebrate animals, which was not given to the control group. Later, both the control and experimental groups were given short paragraphs that described these invertebrates. This was information input. The pre-questionnaire did nothing more than "tune" the organism. A little bit later, both control and experimental subjects were given a 48-item test in which they were told to indicate whether they were *certain* of the answer from their previous knowledge or whether they were surprised by the question. A major finding was that the experimental subjects were significantly more certain of their responses and were correct more often than were those in the control group. What this adds up to is that the pre-questionnaire, in general, tended to predispose the learner toward information input. Instead of just *hearing* a teacher, the learner was *listening*. Instead of seeing, the learners were looking for something; they were curious.

In conclusion, I would suggest these things in terms of how the counselor, or the consultant, might function. I have implied that the elementary school counselor be extremely knowledgeable about learning and motivation in order to bring about the primary prevention of learning disabilities. If this counselor is engaged in primary prevention, he must work with teachers *before* youngsters have learning difficulties rather than work on a remedial basis. That is not to suggest that the counselor should not give direct service to individual children who have learning difficulties.

Counselors may help teachers to use individual differences constructively. Knowledge of individual differences is not enough, there must be some way for the teacher to translate them into action. That is why I dwelt upon sex differences in learning. For example, there are ways that tests can be constructed so that they perform better. It has been demonstrated that most teacher-made tests are tests of fact, and yet boys do better on tests of principle, that is, tests of concepts or generalizations.

The counselor might also work in the area of individual differences with teachers in helping them to establish experiences in the classroom in which analytical thinking skills of boys might come more into play. By working with teachers, the counselor could help to establish the proper amount of dissonance in a classroom so as to facilitate the development of motivation. The evidence is clear that learning and motivation occur best when the classroom situation is for the most part familiar and predictable, but there's always some dissonance, or lack of familiarity. The question for the teacher is: How do I know whether I have too much or not enough dissonance or consonance? Solutions to the problem may be worked out by the counselor and teacher together, each bringing his unique skills to the solution.

The counselor can help teachers to become better diagnosticians. I do not use this term in a clinical sense, but rather in the sense that in order to teach individuals and to use individual differences constructively, we must have some kind of diagnosis of the individuals to be taught. This diagnosis might occur along three different lines. First, data about intellectual factors should be collected. Notable examples of intellectual factors are intelligence test results and achievement test results. Second, the diagnosis or assessment must include nonintellectual factors, such as the youngster's test anxiety, his self-image as a learner, his attitudes about school, and other developmental factors. Third, counselors can help teachers to keep records that are useful to them. We don't have records now that are useful to teachers. It is far more useful for a teacher to have a running record of a pupil's skills, understandings, and knowledge, than it is to have on an accumulative record a grade that a youngster has received the previous year in reading or mathematics. It's much more helpful to teachers to know whether that youngster can divide three place numbers by two place numbers, whether he can identify words, whether he has or lacks certain kinds of skills, or has certain outstanding ones, than it is to know that he received a "B" in arithmetic.

The third suggestion as to ways in which the counselor can work with teachers is in terms of helping teachers with those youngsters who are experiencing difficulties in the classroom. It should be noted that the counselor works through the teacher to aid the youngster. Here, the counselor can assist the teacher to identify the problem that he is having with the youngster; to identify alternative solutions or courses of action; to select a course of action, try it out, and evaluate its effectiveness.

If he is to do the things suggested, the elementary school counselor should be characterized by certain personal traits. One of them is that he be nonevaluative in his work with teachers. He should be highly skilled in *not* evaluating teachers in minute-to-minute interaction with them. Should an administrator use a counselor to help evaluate the teacher, that counselor's effectiveness has immediately been lost. So, there are two dimensions of nonevaluative functioning: the way the counselor works with the teacher, and the way he works with the administrator who evaluates the teacher.

It's important that the counselor have the personal characteristic of an experimental attitude. This experimental attitude may be learned in part in the counselor education program by taking courses in research. But, the important point is that he learn or develop an *attitude* about problem-solving rather than that he become a skilled researcher in the classical sense of the term. This attitude coupled with a genuine concern for and liking of people is requisite to the success of the counselor.

References

1. Anderson, J., and DeVault, R. "The social-emotional climate of elementary school classrooms." *Psychology in the Schools,* Vol. 2, No. 1, 1965.
2. Ausubel, David. "Perceived parent attitudes as determinants of children's age structure." *Child Development,* 1954, 25:173–185.
3. Berlyne, Daniel. "An experimental study of human curiosity." *British Journal of Psychology,* 45:256–28. April 1952.
4. Carter, Robert. "How invalid are marks assigned by teachers?" *Journal of Educational Psychology,* 43:218–28, April 1952.
5. Clark, W. W. "Boys and girls—are there significant ability and achievement differences?" *Phi Delta Kappa,* 1959. 41:73–74.
6. Cutler, Richard, and McNeil, Elton. "Mental health consultation in the schools." Unpublished research report. Ann Arbor, University of Michigan. 1963.

7. Kostick, M. M. "A study of transfer: sex differences in the reasoning process." *Journal of Educational Psychology*, 45:449–58, December 1954.

8. Meyer, William J., and Thompson, G. G. "Sex differences in the distribution of teacher approval and disapproval among sixth grade children." *Journal of Educational Psychology*, 49:385–96, 1956.

9. Smock, C. D., and Holt, B. G. "Children's reactions to novelty: experimental study of curiosity motivation." *Child Development*, 33:631–42.

10. Waetjen, Walter, and Fisher, John K. "An investigation of the relationship between separation by sex of eighth grade boys and girls. English achievement and self-concept." *Journal of Educational Research*. June 1966.

A Creative School Mental Health Program

J. Clayton Lafferty, Donald Dennerll, and Peter Rettich

The image of himself that a child develops is a significant factor in determining his life's direction. While his first years at home are fundamental in determining later development, the experiences a child has in school become critical variations on a developing life theme. Perception, thought, and feeling systems become of the utmost importance in determining future behavior. Frequently, the seeds of later success and failure experiences are nurtured in the early elementary school years. The determination of many such experiences is, for the most part, within the control of the school.

The modern school often bases its efforts on a series of assumptions which are not valid for all children. It frequently perpetuates ways of thinking about behavior that may, in fact, complicate the disturbance of some children and prevent the full psychological development of others. If the school and the experiences that a child has there contribute to his sense of personal insignificance and inadequacy, he is very unlikely to derive much benefit from his educational experience. We must ask ourselves what kinds of things we can do for specific children and what kinds of activities will help most children develop as fully adequate human beings.

The project reported in this paper was designed to explore ways in which the school can more effectively help children to develop an adequate self-concept. It was prompted by a desire among the staff and administration of the Taylor Township (Michigan) School District to find better ways of working with children in order to prevent, as well as correct, problems of mental health.

Like most school systems, the Taylor Township School District has too few visiting teachers and psychologists to serve adequately the increasing number of children who are referred. It is highly unlikely that there will ever be a sufficient number of psychologists, social workers, and psychiatrists to treat properly all of the emotionally disturbed pupils in our schools. Therefore, what is apparently needed is a new approach— one that is preventive rather than rehabilitative in nature; one that can be carried out by the professional person who is at the very core of our educational process, the classroom teacher.[1]

Theoretical Background

The work of several psychologists—namely Ojemann, Prescott, Ellis, and McClelland and Atkinson—seemed especially meaningful for this project, and the major ideas of these theorists were combined to form the basis of our efforts. A common thread runs through these works. McClelland and Atkinson have described the life themes of the achieving personality. Ojemann has explored the effects of teaching children to think causally. From a different point of view, Prescott explored the process of teaching teachers how to think more causally about child behavior. Ellis has shown how persistent life themes can be modified through cognitive intervention—that a change in a person's beliefs or values results in a change of behavior.

The achievement-oriented personality, as described by McClelland and Atkinson, reveals a striking persistence in the completion of tasks.[2] This persistence in striving for accomplishment is based on independent action. The "achiever" is concerned more with self-imposed standards than with pleasing others. (Excessive concern with pleasing others is one of the self-defeating, negative attitudes described by Ellis.) The "achiever" chooses tasks or goals which are of moderate risk instead of tasks either very easy or very difficult. In other words, the level of aspiration is carefully realistic. Continued accomplishment gives him a feeling of confidence in his personal capabilities. The "achiever" is regarded as extremely ambitious, since accomplishment produces a change in the goal to one which is slightly more difficult than the goal just obtained. He is then motivated to achieve success rather than to avoid failure.

The significance of this factor rests on the fact that if an individual directs his attention to succeeding, rather than to avoiding failure, he is released from the anxiety associated with persistent fear of failure. Fear of failure activates the full range of defensive behavior, the purpose of which is self-protection, often at the expense of learning from experience. The person with an "achiever" personality is oriented generally toward the elimination of ineffectual behavior. The person oriented toward avoidance of failure is motivated to conceal ineffectual behavior, and thus ineffectual behavior continues uncorrected.

Ellis has theorized that negative emotional responses (guilt, fear, anger, anxiety, etc.) which people experience are not the direct consequence of external stimuli but stem from their interpretation of the significance of a particular stimulus.[3] From this point of view, a given emotion may be maintained only if it is supported by certain ideas, beliefs, or values. By identifying and understanding the way an individual interprets a situation, it can often be shown that his mechanisms are irrational. If they are irrational in nature, they can be replaced by more realistic and rational ideas. In other words, a reinterpretation of the significance of the person's thoughts can be effected. If successful, the resulting emotional response will be different.

To illustrate, many children feel that their personal worth is determined by the academic grades they receive in school.[4] They are apprehensive prior to each card marking, and they are depressed if the report card contains failing marks. Yet it is a well-known fact that feelings of personal inadequacy are frequently a prelude to failure. Thus a continuous reinforcement of the personal doubt and failure cycle is initiated. This cycle may be interrupted by reinterpreting the significance of the report card grades, i.e., by showing the child that the grades measure only certain aspects of his past achievement and indicate nothing about his personal worth. When the child can see that this is true, he will begin to feel more comfortable, become an acceptable person to himself, and thus perform in a less defeating manner. Children and adults frequently behave as though they believe that children who succeed in school are more worthwhile human beings than children who fail.

Surface Versus Causal Behavior

Ojemann has shown that children can be taught something about the causes of human behavior and that they can learn and apply these concepts.[5] Frequently, changing basic concepts about the causes of behavior alters behavior in a positive direction. As a child develops an approach to accounting for his life experiences by looking for the causes of behavior, he becomes more effective in coping with the reality that surrounds him.

The regular course of instruction in our public schools has the potential for developing an approach to human behavior that is causal in nature. Of course, successful implementation of such a program requires some preliminary teacher orientation. Frequently, it is necessary to help teachers readjust their own thinking. Changes will then occur in their classroom behavior. The general surface approach to children's behavior is contrasted in the chart on page 290 with the causal approach as viewed in terms of the teacher's behavior in the classroom.[6]

Prescott has created and described a program of child study wherein teachers, administrators, and supervisors organize themselves voluntarily to study individual children in their own classrooms and to gain deeper insight into the causes that underlie children's behavior and development.[7] Prescott believes that teachers progress toward this understanding through participating in a sequence of individual experiences in which each teacher selects a child in his classroom for study and then builds a case record of objective data.

Operational Mental Health

An adequate approach to a school mental health program must be based on the classroom and must necessarily encompass the style of classroom management, method of instruction, and instructional content. We believe that the work of the preceding men would provide a basic framework for reconsidering the potential impact of the school upon children and their development. Many school systems have provided special services programs which assist in correcting problems that handicap the child's ability to learn. The majority of these programs have been oriented toward a one-to-one clinical approach and have neglected the general problem of better group management in the educational setting.

In children's problems of social and emotional adjustment, there is need for some alteration of concepts about how behavior is changed. This new procedure must recognize the essential characteristic of the school as an institution which deals with groups. The critical shortage of special services personnel and the need for good mental health demand that more attention be given to programs which involve a larger number of children and to programs which help "normal" children become even more adequate human beings.

The concept of "mental health" has been conveyed to millions of people without benefit of an explicit operational technology. The difficulties are considerable in applying the mental health ideas which have been advocated by the fields of psychiatry, psychology, and social work. These three fields are frequently plagued with ambiguity and distortion of concepts.

One such distortion involves the concept that mental health is the abstract idea of simply loving children and accepting them. Such platitudes are extremely interesting, but they are often meaningless if they cannot be applied to face-to-face working relationships. Fostering mental health is not something that a person suddenly thinks he will do and then does. Children's mental health rests on the day-to-day human interaction in the classroom. The nature of this interaction depends upon the quality, content, and meaning of the specific verbal and non-verbal responses that teachers make to children. The kinds of decisions teachers make about behavior and their subsequent actions based on these decisions determine whether or not any program of fostering positive mental health exists. Teachers observe behavior, conclude something about it, and arrive at a decision which is colored by their previous experiences and beliefs. The

Surface Versus Causal Approaches to Children's Behavior

Surface	Causal
(1) The teacher responds to the "what" of the situation in an emotional way.	(1) The teacher responds to the "why" of the situation objectively.
(2) The teacher does not appear to think of the causes of behavior when he	(2) The teacher appears to be thinking of the causes of behavior when he
(a) responds to the action rather than to the reason for the action	(a) runs over in his mind possible reasons for the action
(b) labels behavior as "good," "bad," etc.	(b) seeks the meaning of the behavior and avoids snap judgments or hasty interpretations
(c) makes generalizations to apply to every situation, e.g., "all boys are like that"	(c) searches for specific and concrete clues derived from details of the behavior
(d) responds with a stock solution or rule of thumb procedure, e.g., lateness is punished by staying in after school.	(d) varies the method; uses a tentative approach, i.e., will try other ways of dealing with a situation if one does not work. In seeking a solution, takes into account motivating forces and particular method used.
	(3) The teacher thinks of alternative explanations for the behavior. The proposition that behavior has many causes may be elaborated as follows:
(3) The teacher does not take account of the multiplicity and complexity of causes.	(a) the same cause may result in a variety of behaviors;
	(b) a variety of causes may result in similar behavior.
(4) The teacher fails to take into account the later effects of the techniques employed and assumes the effects.	(4) The teacher checks for the effects of the method he employs and considers its effects before using it.
(5) The "surface" approach is characterized by a rigidity of techniques— essentially static.	(5) The "causal" approach is characterized by a flexibility, a tentativeness, a trying-out technique, which accommodates new information as it is accumulated—essentially dynamic.

function of the teacher in the classroom involves hundreds of critical decisions about children every day. These decisions constitute the essence of classroom management.

The questions we raised in our project were: 1) Do our school management procedures and philosophies perpetuate many of the learning and emotional problems that children have upon entering school? 2) Are these procedures conducive to a child's developing an appropriate concept of self? 3) Will application of the above ideas in the classroom significantly influence the mental health of children? 4) Do schools unwittingly perpetuate and reinforce ideas which are defeating to full human development?

Although teaching is essentially a group interpersonal process, the group process aspect does not generally receive much attention. The concept of individual differences is familiar to every teacher, but the implications for possible variation in content and methods conducive to mental health are not well understood. The concept of individual differences as they occur in a classroom group is often extremely difficult to apply. The zeal during past decades to use grouping techniques to solve the problem of wide ranges in individual abilities has been stifling and has caused a lack of attention to the real management-instruction problems in the classroom. An operational mental health program must take these management-instruction problems into account and help teachers to improve the quality of their interaction with children.

Significance of Teacher Behavior

Our program was directed toward increasing teacher competency as well as the satisfaction that can be derived from teaching. Previous studies have shown that consulting programs such as the one described in this paper tend to cause changes in teachers' self-concepts. Lafferty showed that a reduction in negative interpersonal responses occurred following a similar program.[8] The evidence indicating a positive relationship between negative self-concept and maladaptive behavior is overwhelming.

Ryans showed that teacher behavior which is characterized by certain crucial factors results in decreased anxiety and emotional readjustment.[9] These factors described by Ryans are: 1) acceptance of children; 2) a problem-solving orientation; 3) use of objective criteria in determining standards of behavior; and 4) techniques which are student-supportive in nature.

On the other hand, the following factors result in student behavior that is withdrawn, apathetic, aggressive, and emotionally disintegrating: 1) teacher behavior that is too demanding of children; 2) private criteria rather than objective or public rules for behavior; 3) techniques which are teacher-supportive in nature rather than student-supportive; and 4) an arbitrary judgmental attitude.

The significance of the teacher's role in mental health is well documented by research evidence. Bills has indicated that the concept of self held by a teacher has a direct effect on the child, specifically with respect to the child's self-feeling and thus his reaction to others.[10] He has also shown that teachers with negative feelings about self will produce negative feelings about self in a significantly large number of children in their classes.

Cutler and McNeil have presented additional evidence that children's behavior can be positively influenced by continuing mental health consultation with teachers: "Children from classrooms whose teachers were high participants [in a consulting program] showed generally a much more positive set of attitudes and reported behaviors than did children from 'control' classrooms."[11]

Emphasis on Working with Teachers

Our first step was to free ourselves of the narrow concept of special services by initiating a program of working with teachers. This program was designed to encourage teachers to share ideas about new approaches to curriculum content, to classroom management, and to individual communication with children. It was based upon the idea, presented by Lafferty, that special services is not a "tight little island" in the school system and that a better educational experience can be developed for children by facilitating cooperation between teachers and special services personnel. It is not easy for a school system to condone this kind of departure, for a number of reasons:

(1) With an already bursting number of referrals, it means that for at least several hours a week, no specific cases are seen. This results in a reduction of the traditional type of service.

(2) People responsible for curriculum may easily interpret this as an invasion of their territory.

(3) This kind of work is considerably more anxiety-provoking for the principal than simply attending to administrative detail.

(4) Traditionally, most special services consultants have worked with children on a one-to-one basis. Thus they deal with behavior quite different from classroom behavior and often do not recognize the management needs of teachers. Departures from tradition are never easy; thus changes in the concept of special services are difficult.

(5) This kind of consulting activity necessitates a change in established operational patterns, and the school is an institution not noted for welcoming changes readily.

(6) Some considerable resistance exists against the idea of giving teachers better clinical tools for understanding the children they teach. Our position is that teachers should be provided with more sophisticated ways of developing insight into the nature of children's learning.

A basic assumption in initiating this approach with a school staff was that the nature and scope of activities useful in developing a causal approach will be limited only by the ingenuity of the creative teacher. Activities were chosen that would stimulate a teacher's thinking about human behavior, provide a basic structure to build on, and suggest a broad range of techniques that would be useful as a starting point.

We recognized that teachers generally require some form of in-service training if they are to increase their effectiveness in dealing with human behavior. This was provided in bi-weekly group discussions in which volunteers from the teaching staff participated. The group discussions were organized around the major premise that *teacher behavior counts*. Our position was not that the teacher should take on an additional role but simply that he should appreciate more fully the psychological significance of teacher-pupil interaction.

Application to Classroom Setting

We asked the teachers to begin challenging some of their more conventional but often deadend notions and, in turn, to test the ideas of McClelland, Atkinson, Ojemann, and Ellis. It was our contention that need for approval and fear of failure are two of the main self-defeating ideas that prevent children from realizing their potential. Typically, "underachievers" are felt to be "lazy" or are described by some other surface phenomenon. Ellis lays the groundwork for looking at this behavior as an excessive concern with the overwhelming probability of failing at whatever the person may attempt.

The following example illustrates the application of Ellis' thinking to an actual classroom problem and shows how we worked with teachers in the program.*

In this instance, a teacher stated to us that he felt his class was not very responsive to open discussion and that, although he frequently provided ample opportunity for questions and discussion, the class did not respond.

This is a very frequent problem in our society. Most people are quite irrationally upset when they have to speak in front of a group. In fact, this is so common a response that it is seldom perceived as a neurotic expression of an irrational fear. The question to be considered about this class was, "Is it possible to teach these children something about the origins of these fears?" Further, as a direct source of help, how do they maintain the fear and continually reindoctrinate themselves with an idea that, if allowed to persist, will dramatically reduce their effectiveness as human beings?

In helping both the children and the teachers to understand this problem, a demonstration was held in the classroom. During a short presentation, the children were taught that thinking is an extremely important antecedent to acting, feeling, or emoting. In a number of simple examples, the following abstraction was demonstrated—that the stimulus is never directly related to the expression of emotion. In order to be upset about anything, a person first has to evaluate the event or experience. It was pointed out that this occurs very fast—so fast, in fact, that most people have to be retaught that this is what they do.

The instructor asked for a volunteer to try an experiment. One boy came forth. The task was simply to stand for thirty seconds in front of the class and let the class look at him. As you would expect, during the first ten seconds or so, the student laughed. After twenty seconds, he was feeling embarrassed. By the end of thirty seconds, he was quite upset.

The point of this situation was how the student became upset and what really happened. We turned first to a self-report from the student about what he thought happened. He said he was upset because all of his

* See Supplementary Instructional Materials at the end of this article, "The Mr. Swartz Episode."

classmates were looking at him. It was pointed out that this could not be the case since only being looked at is not upsetting. It is, rather, the thoughts one has about being looked at that are upsetting. The boy then said he felt stupid standing there. He thought that *they* thought there was something wrong with him. This statement was then used to demonstrate that it was what *he thought* that upset him, not the fact that the children were staring at him. It was pointed out that it is our thinking about how terrible it is to be wrong, to be looked at, or not to be liked that causes us our problems—not these facts in themselves.

Several other experiments were tried in which children were shown that they did not have to get upset about giving a speech if they thought differently about the situation. The discussion was immediately returned to the class's reluctance to discuss things. They quite readily agreed that the reason for this was that they were afraid of being wrong or making mistakes. As it happens, the teacher also shares this problem and has reinforced the idea in the children without meaning to do so. Currently, both the class and the teacher are working together to help reduce this fear that so often pervades the classroom. The teacher is helping the class and himself at the same time by recognizing a very basic principle in mental health: It is not so terrible to be wrong, since your personal worth as a human being is never at stake. It only hurts if you think it hurts.

Beginnings of a Technology of Mental Health

The concern of this project was to find ways in which already existing ideas in education and psychology can be applied to a program of mental health in a school setting. A summary of some of the basic concepts which formed a basis for the project and which grew out of our efforts to achieve the goals previously stated in this paper may help the reader to see possible application to different situations.

The authors are convinced that very little real communication occurs between teachers relative to their major concern—classroom management. It occurred to us that it is very difficult to obtain verbatim transcripts of what teachers actually do in the classroom. This is apparently a very well-guarded secret. It follows that any profession caught in the delicate position of having to operate day in and day out without a reasonably well-defined technology is in serious trouble. This is the current state of affairs in education. Generally, from any given educator's point of view, a teacher can be judged to be theoretically wrong on any single day. The teacher is then placed in a position of great technical insecurity. In addition, it is almost impossible for a teacher ever to evaluate fully the outcomes of his efforts.

If we had more specific ideas about teacher-pupil interaction, the teacher could more easily evaluate the effectiveness of teacher behavior on the child's thinking processes. Since research in education seems to show that very few programs affect achievement positively or negatively, the teacher must be helped to examine new dimensions for evidence of effective teaching. If the attorney wins a case, there is satisfaction; the physician has the advantage of seeing people get well. But the result of the teacher's efforts may not be observable for some years. Teachers, by and large, do not share ideas with each other in a free situation because they are very fearful that they will be judged to be wrong. Since the entire field of education relies very little on established research, these fears are exaggerated. The hope of this project was to create a comfortable enough atmosphere so teachers would lower the barriers and talk realistically about the actual teaching procedures used in the classroom.

If the process of education is concerned with the thought patterns of children (and we think that it should be), then this has been a project in basic education. If a child comes to the third grade spelling *cat* k-a-t, the alert teacher will in some way correct this idea and help the child to see that this is a distortion of reality and that in our society *cat* is spelled c-a-t. However, if that child has distorted ideas about his own worth as a human being, we do not generally question this. If he erroneously thinks that he is stupid, and because he believes this does not try, the school often inadvertently reinforces this nonsense instead of challenging it. We think that in a free society, it is the function of the school to help a student understand more realistically the nature of the ideas he holds about himself. One of the best places to start this process is to help teachers reassess the way in which they have learned to think about human behavior. All too often, teachers have learned about behavior in the same accidental way that children themselves learn about behavior.

We think that these concepts are important, that they are basic to education. We think they represent scientific thinking in the best sense of that term. It is, after all, human behavior that will either destroy us or enable us to rise to new plateaus of accomplishment.

Notes

1. Lafferty, J. Clayton. "Special Services—A Tight Little Island." *The School Administrator and School Mental Health Program: Proceedings of an Institute for School Administrators.* (Under a grant by the National Institute of Mental Health as a technical assistance program.) Ann Arbor: University of Michigan, 1962.
2. McClelland, David C., and others. *Action Motives and Phantasy.* New York: Appleton and Co., 1955.
3. Ellis, Albert, and Harper, Robert A. *Guide to Rational Living.* Englewood Cliffs, New Jersey: Prentice-Hall, 1961.
4. Lafferty, J. Clayton. *Values That Defeat Learning.* Proceedings of Inter-institutional Seminar on Child Growth and Development. Dearborn, Michigan: Edison Institute, 1963.
5. Ojemann, Ralph H. *The Preventive Psychiatry Research Program.* Iowa Child Research Program Welfare Research Station. Iowa City: University of Iowa.

6. Tasch, R. J. "Use of Causal Approach in Daily Relations with Children" in Ojemann, R. H., *Study of the Effect of a Teaching Program in Human Behavior and Emotional Development on Children of Different Age Levels and Backgrounds.* (Unpublished mimeographed paper, State University of Iowa, 1952.)

7. Prescott, Daniel A. *A Child Study Program.* Institute for Child Study, University of Maryland. (Contained in research evaluating a child study program—Monographs of the Society for Research in Child Development, Inc., Vol. XXI, Serial No. 62, No. 1, 1956. Brandt, R. M., and Perkins, H. Y.)

8. Lafferty, J. Clayton. "A Study of Changes in Self Concepts of Teachers Following Participation in a Consulting Mental Health Program." (Unpublished Ph.D. dissertation, University of Michigan, 1961.)

9. Ryans, David G. *Characteristics of Teachers.* Washington, D.C.: American Council on Education, 1960. 416 pp.

10. Bills, Robert E.; Vance, E. L.; and McLean, O. S. "An Index of Adjustment and Values." *Journal of Consulting Psychology* 15:257–61; 1951.

11. Cutler, R. L., and McNeil, E. B. *Mental Health Consultation in Schools; A Research Analysis.* National Institute of Mental Health, U.S.P.H.S. Grant M. H. 706. p. 161.

Supplementary Instructional Materials

It was our desire in this project to increase in a meaningful way the actual communication between teachers on what happens in the classroom. With this purpose in mind, the authors have included for distribution some of the actual tape recordings that were produced in the project. They are available for use by school and university personnel. *They may not be reproduced without written permission.*

The audio tape recordings of selected procedures and discussions emanating from this project may be purchased or rented from Dr. J. Clayton Lafferty, 3170 Penobscot Building, Detroit 26, Michigan.

Audio tape of T.V. show presented May 9, 1963—Part I. Time: 30 minutes. Lafferty. This was a spontaneous discussion with a group of sixth grade children relative to their perceptions about school. The tape presents interesting raw data for considering some basic issues confronting the teacher.

Audio tape of T.V. show. Time: 30 minutes. Lafferty. This tape is a spontaneous discussion with a group of sixth grade children on the subject of the nature of children's feelings about mistakes. It also involves the children's impressions of what factors seem to make for a "good" teacher.

A Group of Sixth Grade Students. Time: 20 minutes. Rettich and Lafferty. This tape has been selected as part of a teacher orientation program at Wayne State University, College of Education.

"The Mr. Swartz Episode." Time: 38 minutes. This tape presents an attempt to teach children something about the way in which embarrassment interferes with learning. It shows how children can control the degree to which they become disturbed and upset about things.

"Values That Defeat Learning." Time: 1 hour, 30 minutes. This is a presentation by Dr. Lafferty on the major ideas encompassed in this program. The ideas presented are an attempt to translate some principles of rational psychotherapy into an ongoing school program.

A Group of Fifth Grade "Underachievers." This tape is a recording of a group therapy session conducted by the project psychologist, Donald Dennerll. It is concerned with test-taking behavior and the fear of failure that children face.

Presentation for the Michigan Education Association Institute, sponsored by the Council for Exceptional Children. A panel discussion. The panel consists of the Taylor Township School District's Director of Special Services, Psychologist, Visiting Teacher, Principal of the Moody School, and a teacher from that school.

Index